PHILOSOPHY OF SPORT: KEY QUESTIONS

PHILOSOPHY OF SPORT: KEY QUESTIONS

EMILY RYALL

BLOOMSBURY

LONDON · OXFORD · NEW YORK · NEW DELHI · SYDNEY

To Jess.

Bloomsbury Sport
An imprint of Bloomsbury Publishing Plc

50 Bedford Square
London
WC1B 3DP
UK

1385 Broadway
New York
NY 10018
USA

www.bloomsbury.com

First published 2016

© Emily Ryall, 2016
Illustrations © Mark Silver, 2016

Emily Ryall has asserted her right under the Copyright, Designs and
Patents Act, 1988, to be identified as the Author of this work.

British Library Cataloguing-in-Publication Data
A catalogue record for this book is available from the British Library.

Library of Congress Cataloguing-in-Publication data has been applied for.

ISBN: PB: 978-1-4081-8139-3
ePDF: 978-1-4081-8858-3
ePub: 978-1-4081-8857-6

2 4 6 8 10 9 7 5 3 1

Typeset in Minion by Deanta Global Publishing Services, Chennai, India
Printed and bound in Great Britain by CPI Group (UK) Ltd, Croydon CR0 4YY

To find out more about our authors and books visit www.bloomsbury.com.
Here you will find extracts, author interviews, details of forthcoming
events and the option to sign up for our newsletters.

CONTENTS

Sport and the good life

Sport, art and aesthetics

Ethical questions in sport

INTRODUCTION

1 WHAT IS THE PHILOSOPHY OF SPORT?

A cursory glance at the daily sports news highlights perennial philosophical and ethical issues in sport: drug-taking, cheating, corruption, discrimination and violence, among many others. Indeed, the hot topics on the day of writing include: a criminal investigation into corruption within a high-profile sport governing body, concern over the effects of concussion in contact sport, a judicial challenge on whether a card game should be classified as a sport, officials banned for match fixing, further discussion about the introduction of goal-line technology, and ongoing lamentation by politicians about the low profile of women's sport. We are confronted with philosophical and ethical issues in sport on a daily basis and they are regularly the topic of heated arguments between aficionados everywhere. Sport is a large part of modern life. The issues that sport raises are even larger. And nearly everyone has an opinion.

Many of those interested in these types of issues and discussions have not been explicitly introduced to philosophic methods or to the philosophy of sport as a distinct academic subject. Yet, when these debates occur in the pub, on the terraces or in the media, those involved are engaging in a philosophical discussion about the meaning and value of sport and the concepts related to it.

This chapter aims to provide an overview to the uninitiated of the development and history of the philosophy of sport, the types of questions raised, and the methods used to answer them. It will demonstrate that what many people do naturally when they discuss sporting issues is essentially philosophise; but it will also highlight where and how philosophy is done badly and how philosophical arguments and skills can be improved.

HOW DID THE PHILOSOPHY OF SPORT ORIGINATE?

The philosophy of sport as an academic subject is a fairly recent notion. Although a few famous philosophers have mentioned sport in their writings (Plato, who was also an Olympic wrestler, is a primary example), it was only in the late 1960s and early 1970s when sport as a distinct subject worthy of philosophical investigation started to be taken seriously. The earliest publications in the area concentrated on the issue of play rather than sport, as given in Johan Huizinga's[1] *Homo Ludens: A Study of the Play-Element in Culture* and Roger Caillois's[2] *Man, Play and Games*. It wasn't until the late 1960s that academic interest in the philosophy of sport began to gain momentum, and this was primarily in North America. Howard Slusher's[3] *Man, Sport and Existence: A Critical Analysis*, and Paul Weiss'[4] *Sport; A Philosophic Inquiry*, were the first to focus on the nature of sport and its relation to human life, while Eleanor Metheny wrote two books that considered the aesthetic dimensions of sport and movement[5]. There was also a growing interest in the philosophy of physical education and sports pedagogy with publications such as Davis and Miller's[6] *The Philosophic Process in Physical Education*, Webster's[7] *Philosophy of Physical Education* and Zeigler's[8] *Problems in the History and Philosophy of Physical Education and Sport*. Scott Kretchmar[9] has since argued that many of the early publications in the philosophy of physical education and pedagogy provided little, if any, real philosophical insight into sport and were more concerned with using physical education and sport as a vehicle for teaching the established moral values of educational institutions. Such a focus arguably reduced the credibility of the philosophy of sport in more traditional philosophical circles and led to it being marginalised and isolated for much of the 1970s and 1980s.

Despite this slow start, interest in the subject has since grown considerably and has attracted commentary and publications from philosophers outside the traditional sports pedagogy and physical education backgrounds. This can be seen in the extensive bibliographic resources that are now available, the creation of many national and international associations, and two journals whose sole remit is the philosophy of sport. The area's broadening appeal and respectability in wider philosophic circles is also increasingly apparent. There are now sessions dedicated to the philosophy of sport in the American Philosophical Association conferences, and in 2012 the Royal Institute of Philosophy (established by Bertrand Russell in 1925) held a series of public lectures and published a collection of essays on the subject.

WHAT KINDS OF PHILOSOPHICAL QUESTIONS ARE FOUND IN SPORT?

In traditional philosophical circles the study of sport has been largely overlooked or dismissed as uninteresting and unworthy of investigation. Even some scholars who have produced considerable work in the field, such as Graham McFee[10], have argued that apart from a few specific ethical issues, there isn't really such a thing called 'the philosophy of sport'. Similarly, David Best criticised the academic study of sports by claiming, 'the very notion of a *subject* of sport makes no sense.'[11] In some ways, Best was right: one cannot study sport as such; rather students of sport look at a set of aspects or disciplines that relate to sport in some way, such as biomechanics, physiology, psychology, sociology, history or pedagogy. Students apply disciplinary theory to sport-specific examples; so one might learn about the workings of the heart and circulatory system, memory function, the way in which sport was used as a tool in facilitating the expansion of the British Empire, or effective teaching strategies. Sport is simply used as the peg on which to hang knowledge or ideas about other subject areas. This is arguably the case for the philosophy of sport too. Students taking philosophy courses in sports programmes might learn about particular ethical theories, major philosophical figures, or key debates that form the core curriculum of traditional philosophy departments. But (and this is a direct counter to McFee's claim) they will also study philosophical issues that have a special and particular application to sport, or are questions about which sport is able to provide a greater clarity. These, might be questions about the nature of sport and its relation to the concepts of play, games and leisure. It might be about the way in which sport provides us with understanding of abstract ethical concepts, such as fairness and respect; as can be seen in our use of popular sporting metaphors such as 'level playing-field', 'it's just not cricket' and 'pulling together'. It might be about the value that sport has in human life or what part it plays in a good life. There are also ethical issues that seem unique to sport, such as doping, fair play and gamesmanship. And sport might also help us come to new understandings and perspectives about concepts such as 'equality' and 'fairness' in relation to issues such as sex, sexuality, race and disability. These types of issues suggest that sport is a worthy topic for philosophical investigation and that McFee's and Best's scepticism is misplaced.

WHAT IS PHILOSOPHY?

In order to understand the philosophy of sport, some knowledge is needed about what it is to study philosophy. In the same way that studying sports physiology, sports biomechanics or sports psychology requires knowledge about physiology, biomechanics or psychology, studying the philosophy of sport requires knowledge about the content and methods of philosophy. Obviously there is little space available here to provide a detailed account of the history of philosophy and philosophical methods but what I will try to do is provide a general indication of its subject and methods.

Philosophy provides the foundation for all other subject disciplines. Prior to the period of the Enlightenment in the 17th to 19th centuries, the separate subject areas that we distinguish today did not exist. Those who were fortunate enough to be educated or had free time to study the world were few in number and were not able to depend upon the wealth of scientific and empirical knowledge that enables scholars and academics to specialise (in ever increasing ways) today. Anyone who was interested in issues that now fall under the umbrella of 'science' was simply called a 'natural philosopher'. Additionally, the power of the church and organised religion meant that free, open and critical investigation was stifled or even punished. As such, sound scientific processes and research were non-existent, and knowledge about the world was often dictated by those in authority and religious doctrine. Those who challenged received opinion were generally labelled as heretics, witches and alchemists.

Despite this, there have been times of great philosophic thought that have provided rigorous and critical insight into the world and our life within it. The most notable records of this have come from Mediterranean Europe, particularly ancient Greece around 6 BCE, and provide us with the familiar names of Socrates, Plato and Aristotle, among others.

These philosophers asked questions about the nature of the world and how to live a 'good' life. They ask difficult questions that others often take for granted. Fundamental philosophical questions are therefore often framed as: 'What things exist in the world?', 'How do we know they exist?', 'How should I live?' and 'How should I treat others?' Philosophical questions are questions about reality, knowledge, truth, value, meaning and ethics, and lie at the heart of all other disciplines. This is why reaching a deep understanding of other disciplines requires grappling with difficult philosophical questions as well. Therefore, any serious study of sport requires engagement with philosophical questions such as: 'What is the value of sport?', 'How do we ensure sporting competition is fair?', 'What does good sport look like?' and 'Is sporting knowledge different from other types of knowledge?'

WHAT IS THE POINT OF STUDYING THE PHILOSOPHY OF SPORT?

As has been indicated, philosophy can be considered the oldest discipline in the world: this is why most people can name ancient philosophers rather than ancient scientists, historians, psychologists or political theorists. Philosophy at its core is concerned with understanding the world and our relation to it. Its etymology comes from the Greek meaning 'love of wisdom', thus indicating that philosophers (or at least genuine philosophers) are seeking convincing and sound answers to problems. They are not content to accept popular opinion or the beliefs of others but rather probe further to discover whether these beliefs can be justified and ask deeper questions about the assumptions on which these beliefs rest. Many of the early philosophers can be seen as polymaths in that they were interested in a range of subjects and questions. Over the centuries, as our knowledge about the world has developed, and the methods through which we find answers to those questions has matured and become more systematic and rigorous, individuals have increasingly specialised their forms of enquiry to narrower areas. Today, individuals tend to concentrate on ever-more discrete disciplines, such as biochemistry, social psychology, medieval history and quantum physics. The advantage in such specialisation is that a researcher is able to involve herself in understanding complex problems and issues in far greater depth. The disadvantage however, is that often a novel approach or consideration from an alternative perspective might yield a better insight into the problem at hand. Therefore, a lack of breadth of knowledge across a range of subjects can mean these opportunities are missed. One of the benefits of having a general understanding and interest in a variety of areas and disciplines is that it enables the researcher to apply methods and knowledge from one area to others. This is arguably one of the strengths of studying sports-related subjects; far from being the 'easy' or 'non-serious' academic subject that it is often portrayed as, it demands a lot from its students. Its multi-disciplinary nature requires students to have knowledge about a wide range of subject areas. Most students studying a degree in sport and exercise are introduced to a range of different disciplines and methods of research. This can be challenging to a student who has to master a variety of expectations in each area of study but it also can provide for fruitful and novel research and produces a well-rounded scholar with an array of skills.

Although philosophy often has a reputation for pointless navel-gazing or asking irrelevant questions, when it is done well it can be useful for clarifying problems and producing good, well-reasoned and logical arguments. It is important to recognise that philosophy is an activity that requires commitment and practice, in addition to an honest desire to get things right; it is not simply learning about the ideas and theories of other people. This is why it is useful for everyone to be familiar with philosophic methods whatever their area of interest or study.

WHAT METHODS DO PHILOSOPHERS USE?

Philosophers essentially ask questions. They can be questions about the justification for a particular belief, for instance, the belief that 'it is right to ban the use of particular substances in sport', or they can be questions about the meaning of particular words, for instance, 'does sport by definition involve competition?'

Perhaps one of the best ways of thinking about the work of a philosopher is to compare it to that of a gardener. When faced with a patch of land that is overgrown and full of rubbish, a gardener has to work out which plants are worth keeping and which are harmful weeds, and then needs to decide how to structure and organise the garden to make best use of what is left. Similarly, when faced with a difficult issue, a philosopher has to decide which arguments and points have some merit and which are baseless and harmful. She then has to put the useful aspects into a coherent and rational order so that they help us understand the nature of the problem and how to best solve it. As such, philosophers rarely come to definitive answers to problems; rather they enable us to see a problem more clearly.

Philosophy is often divided into two schools of thought: Analytic and Continental. This distinction is fairly simplistic as many theorists will often use ideas and methods from both schools, but dividing the methods of philosophy this way provides an indication of how philosophy can be carried out. Essentially, Analytical philosophy is concerned with logical and linguistic analysis, such as whether a conclusion logically and explicitly follows from its premises, or whether the meaning of a word can be formulated through necessary and sufficient conditions. In contrast, Continental philosophy is focused much more on understanding issues by appealing to human sense and experience rather than an abstract logical form. Critics of the Continental approach argue that it is vague, non-specific and without clear rationality. Defenders argue that they are able to elucidate answers to real and deep philosophical questions in a much more meaningful way than can be provided through a logical or linguistic analysis. An example of how they differ in response to the same philosophical question can be seen in the definition of sport in Chapter 2.

Three analytical methods that are useful in philosophy are: the Socratic method; conceptual analysis; and logical deduction. These are used to good effect in Bernard Suits' book, *The Grasshopper: Games, Life and Utopia*.[12] The first two methods will be outlined below and in Chapter 2, while the third will be discussed in more detail in Chapters 3 and 5.

WHAT IS THE SOCRATIC METHOD?

Socrates is one of the more famous ancient Greek philosophers. He is renowned for defending his right to ask (often difficult and uncomfortable) philosophical questions to the death. His habit of questioning accepted beliefs and the authority of those in power frequently got him into trouble. Eventually, the city authorities were so annoyed about his subordination and the influence he had upon others that he was forced to choose exile or death. He chose to drink a cup of poisonous hemlock over rescinding his right to question and criticise. The legacy he left still influences Western society and education today.

One of the methods that Socrates used to highlight flawed thinking or bad arguments was to ask questions until his opponent ended up at a dead end or contradiction. This is the method that is most often used by those in the legal profession as a way of extracting the truth from defendants or witnesses. Socrates rarely stated his own opinion on issues: indeed, he is attributed as saying, 'The only thing I know is that I know nothing'.[13] Yet Socrates' modesty belies his sharp and incisive mind that quickly seized upon logical inconsistencies in the arguments given by others.

Suits' *Grasshopper* uses Socratic dialogue in an attempt to formulate a definition of games and game playing. The parallels between the life (and death) of Socrates and of Suits' 'Grasshopper' are deliberate. In this extract below, two of his protagonists, Skepticus and Prudence, try to make sense of Grasshopper's claim that a perfect life is one that is devoted to playing games:

Skepticus [S]: ... I had put it to [Grasshopper] that while all work and no play undoubtedly makes Jack a dull ant, all play and no work makes Jack a dead grasshopper.

Prudence [P]: Yes, you were challenging him to justify his existence.

S: Quite so. And he made three replies to that challenge. The first he called the theological answer and the second he called the logical answer.

P: That's right.

S: And what about the third answer, Prudence?

P: The third answer was the dream.

S: Yes, a dream about people playing games. That is what is so strange.

…

S: … His first two answers – the theological answer and the logical answer – really amounted to the same thing, did they not? Each was a way of expressing the grasshopper's determination to remain true to himself, even at the cost of his life.

P: Yes, that's right.

S. And his remaining true to himself, Prudence, what did that consist in?

P: Why, in refusing to work and insisting upon devoting himself exclusively to play.

S: And what did the words 'work' and 'play' mean in that context?

P: Pretty much what most people usually mean by those words, I should think. Working is doing things you have to do and playing is doing things for the fun of it.

S: So that for 'play' we could substitute the expression 'doing things we value for their own sake,' and for 'work' we could substitute the expression 'doing things we value for the sake of something else.'

P: Yes. Work is a kind of necessary evil which we accept because it makes it possible for us to do things we think of as being good in themselves.

S: So that under the heading 'play' we could include any number of quite different things: vacationing in Florida, collecting stamps, reading a novel, playing chess, or playing the trombone?

P: Yes, all of those things would count as 'play' as we are using the word. We are using 'play' as equivalent to 'leisure activities.'

S: Then it is clear, is it not, that 'playing,' in this usage, cannot be the same as 'playing games,' since there are many leisure activities, as we have just noted, that are not games.

P: No, they are not the same; playing games is just one kind of leisure activity.

S: Therefore, when the Grasshopper was extolling the life of play he meant by that life, presumably, not doing any specific thing, but doing any of a number of quite different things… So the Grasshopper surely was not arguing that the life he was seeking to justify – the life of the Grasshopper – was identical with just one of these leisure activities. He was not contending, for example, that the life of the Grasshopper is identical with playing the trombone.

P: Of course not, Skepiticus, how absurd!

S: Yes, that would be absurd. And that is precisely why I find the Grasshopper's third answer so strange. For in that answer he seemed to be taking the view not that the life of the Grasshopper ought not to consist in leisure activities, but that it ought to consist in playing games. For he began his answer, you will recall, by telling us that he sometimes fancied that everyone alive was really a grasshopper in disguise.

…

P: Well, tell me, Skepticus. What did the Grasshopper say about games?

S: First he presented a definition of games or, to be more precise, a definition of game playing. Then he invited me to subject that definition to a series of tests. I was to advance against the definition the most compelling objections I could devise, and he was to answer those objections.

P: And did the definition withstand your attacks?

S: He was able, or so it seemed to me, to defend the definition against all of my challenges. Furthermore, in the course of meeting those challenges a number of features of game playing not contained in the definition itself were brought to light, so that at the end we had developed a rather elaborated outline, at least, of a general theory of games.

As is indicated in this dialogue, through a series of conjecture and refutation, example and counter-example, Suits presents a robust definition of game playing.[14] The use of the Socratic method enables an interrogation of the logic underlying the various arguments.

WHAT IS CONCEPTUAL ANALYSIS?

Suits' work is also an excellent example of the philosophic method of conceptual analysis. Disagreements on subjects generally come down to either a difference in fundamental value (for instance, in valuing autonomy over equality) or a confusion or difference over the meaning and use of particular terms. In the dialogue above, Skepticus asks Prudence to clarify what he means by 'work' and 'play'. Although Prudence responds that the words mean what most people generally take them to mean, being forced to clearly define them helps to ensure that they are starting from the same point. Suits' *Grasshopper* is essentially a conceptual analysis of the term 'game' and was written in direct response to another philosopher, Wittgenstein, who argued that the word was impossible to define. Even if people ultimately disagree about what a term 'really' means, the method of conceptual analysis is important for clearly laying out the ground and ensuring that subsequent confusion in discussions is reduced. That said, there are often disagreements about the meaning of particular words, as can be seen from the fact that there are already more papers in the philosophy of sport on this very subject than most people would ever wish to read. There was also a disappointing period of history in the early 20th century when much of academic philosophy was dominated by interminable discussion about the meaning of words rather than real philosophical and ethical issues that were affecting the rest of the world. Despite this, conceptual analysis is a vital part of the philosopher's toolkit and helps to ensure the clarity of any resulting discussion.

The rest of this book will cover some of the key questions found in the philosophy of sport and provide some indication as to how various philosophers have attempted to answer them.

INDEPENDENT STUDY QUESTIONS:

- *How is philosophy related to other disciplines?*
- *What kinds of issues did scholars consider in the early years of the philosophy of sport?*
- *What kinds of questions can be found in the philosophy of sport?*
- *What methods are used in philosophy and how did Suits employ them in his book?*

INTERVIEW WITH A PHILOSOPHER

WARREN FRALEIGH

Warren Fraleigh is considered one of the founding
fathers of the philosophy of sport. While a Professor
in Physical Education at State University of New York,
Brockport College, he was instrumental in setting up
the initial group that later became the International
Association for the Philosophy of Sport (IAPS). The
IAPS 'Warren Fraleigh Distinguished Scholar' award was
named in his honour. At university he played American
football and basketball and later he coached basketball
and baseball.

- *Can you give me a little bit on your background and what got you interested in the philosophy of sport?*
  - Since I am a long-time sport participant and a former coach I have long been interested in the nature of sport, its ethics and aesthetics. I came to more philosophic concerns in the study of educational philosophy, curriculum study and theology. When I arrived at State University of New York, College at Brockport, the college had a large population of students in Physical Education. They all had a required course in philosophy of sport. This made it necessary to hire professors who had background and interest in the subject. So, we hired, early on, Francis Keenan, Scott Kretchmar, Klaus Meier, Bob Osterhoudt, Ken Ravizza, Carol Susswein, Ginny Studer and Caroline Thomas. This group met together to define the content of the philosophy courses and to discuss philosophy of sport. Also, the group decided to host conferences at the college. The college hosted two conferences including one sponsored by the State University of New York Center for Philosophic Exchange. Paul Weiss spoke at one conference and we had a conversation on developing an organisation. Out of this, I chaired a Steering Committee, which laid the groundwork for a meeting scheduled by Paul Weiss at the Eastern District of The American Philosophic Association in 1972. Then, the first official meeting was held at Brockport in 1973.
- *What do you think is the most interesting problem in the philosophy of sport?*
  - At present, I think the most interesting problem is expanding the study of sport, internationalising it, which is now happening through IAPS, getting instruction into sports organisations and into the preparation of coaches so that the practice of sport becomes more influenced by sport philosophy.

○ I also think that the development of sport philosophy may follow the route of becoming philosophies of sports as proposed by Gunnar Breivik in his paper presented at the IAPS conference in Porto in 2012.

• *What book or paper has influenced you the most and why?*

○ There are lots! For insight into humans: Reinhold Neibuhr's *The Nature and Destiny of Man*, John A.T. Robinson's *The Body: A Study in Pauline Theology*, Macintyre's *After Virtue: A Study in Moral Theory*, and Kurt Baier's *The Moral Point of View*. For philosophy of sport: Bernard Suits' *The Grasshopper, Games, Life, and Utopia*, Robert Simon's *Fair Play*, Kretchmar's 'From Test to Contest: An Analysis of Two Kinds of Counterpoint in Sport'. For relating philosophy and sociology: Bill Morgan's *Why Sports Matter Morally*. And for relating philosophy and psychology: Jonathan Haidt's *The Happiness Hypothesis*.

Key Readings

Fraleigh, W.P., *Right Actions in Sport: Ethics for Contestants* (Leeds: Human Kinetics, 1984).

Fraleigh, W.P., 'Intentional Rules Violations—One More Time', *Journal of the Philosophy of Sport*, 30(2) (2003), pp. 166–176.

DEFINING SPORT

2 WHAT IS SPORT?

Sport at its very least is a human practice that involves the body to a greater or lesser extent, and is related to practices such as games, play and leisure. How it is defined and delineated from other human activities that are not sport, however, is a difficult philosophical task. This chapter will attempt to show how the concept of sport can be characterised and it will outline differing approaches in doing so.

As illustrated in Chapter 1, the method of conceptual analysis is one that is often used by philosophers. It is a way of clearly defining terms that are used in statements we make about the world and enables us to reach sound conclusions. So for instance, statements such as 'Sport is good for you', or adverts claiming 'This product has been proven to make you perform better', would lead a philosopher to ask the questions: 'What do you mean by 'sport' and 'good'?' 'Is this all sports or just particular sports, or just particular elements of sport?', 'What constitutes 'proof'?' or 'What do you mean by 'better'?' Asking these types of questions about the definition of words helps to ensure that people are not talking at cross purposes (that is, they are not talking about different things), which is often the cause of disagreements. It also helps reach a better understanding of problems and find more effective ways of solving them.

How philosophers go about understanding particular terms or words, however, is a matter for disagreement in itself. As outlined in Chapter 1, philosophy is often broken into two different schools of thought and these have developed from particular philosophers doing philosophy in a particular way, in a particular place and time. The Analytic approach is generally associated with Anglo-American philosophy, such as Bertrand Russell, W.V.O. Quine and A.L. Austin (although paradoxically it has roots in Continental Europe), whereas the Continental approach is often associated with philosophers from mainland Europe, such as Friedrich Nietzsche, Jean-Paul Sartre and Martin Heidegger.[1]

Analytic philosophy holds that words can be defined according to necessary and sufficient conditions; whereas the Continental method maintains that the meaning of words is much more flexible and open to change. When considering the definition of sport, these two perspectives can also be categorised as the *Analytic-Definitional-Formal* approach, and the *Contextual-Contested-Contingent* approach.

This difference in approaches can be seen when it comes to understanding concepts such as 'sport', 'games' and 'play'. Analytic philosophers wish to pin down these terms to necessary and sufficient conditions, whereas those with more of a Continental perspective argue that it is impossible to define sport in this way and that understanding sport depends on the situation, person and context.

WHAT IS MEANT BY NECESSARY AND SUFFICIENT CONDITIONS? (THE ANALYTIC APPROACH TO SPORT)

Imagine a school is conducting an audit of their PE equipment and this task falls upon someone who isn't particularly sporty or has much experience with modern PE. The problem is that the PE store also doubles up as the grounds-store and so contains gardening equipment too. To help this naïve individual (you may wonder why they have been given this job but let us imagine that they have), the PE staff need to draw up a list of criteria to indicate whether an object belongs to the PE department. The criteria need to be broad enough to contain all the PE equipment but also narrow enough to ensure that gardening equipment isn't also

Figure 2.1 – Illustration of necessary and sufficient conditions

included. They might start off with the necessary criterion: 'Do not include any item that requires an electrical power source', which would correctly rule out the lawn-mower, strimmer and hedge trimmer. However, this isn't sufficiently narrow as it wouldn't cover shears, trowels and forks. Equally, if the set of criteria is too narrow, for instance, 'Do not include anything that requires an electrical power source and anything that has pointy or sharp ends', then although it would now preclude shears, trowels and forks, it wouldn't include javelins. The criteria need to be broad enough to contain all the (necessary) PE equipment, but (sufficiently) narrow enough so that it doesn't include anything else (Figure 2.1).

WHAT IS A GAME? (SUITS' ANSWER)

The most famous example of this type of analytical philosophy in the area of sport was undertaken by the Canadian philosopher Bernard Suits. In the late 1960s, Suits attempted to define game playing[2], which he later developed into his definition of sport. In order to understand Suits' position on sports, his definition of games first needs consideration.

Suits' analysis of game playing in his book *The Grasshopper: Games, Life and Utopia* is an excellent example of analytical philosophy, as he begins with a tentative and provisional definition before considering possible objections and counter-examples. This is an attempt to ensure his definition is both sufficiently narrow yet necessarily broad enough to contain everything and only those things that are games. Suits concluded that a game must have four elements: *the goal, the means, the rules* and the *lusory attitude* (Figure 2.2).

The goal

The goal is the purpose of the activity. Obviously the purpose or motivation that one has for playing a game can be many things, for instance, to spend time with friends, to get fitter, to acquire money, etc. Yet for any particular game there is always a particular aim that defines that game. This distinct goal – part of the game itself rather than the motivations a person might have for playing it – is the pre-lusory[3] goal. It is the goal that determines how to win the game. So the pre-lusory goal for golf is to get the ball in the cup, the pre-lusory goal in cribbage is to get your peg to the end of the cribbage board, and if you're the chaser in stuck-in-the-mud, then it's to tag everyone before they can be released by another player.

The means

While the goal of a game specifies the aim of the game, not all ways of fulfilling that aim are permitted. Suits distinguishes between two different means, a means of achieving the pre-lusory goal and a means of winning the game. If the goal of the game is to put a golf ball in the cup, this can be easily achieved by walking to the hole and dropping it in. However, this is not a means to win the game of golf, since at the very least a golf club is required. Suits categorises these as *lusory means* since they are permitted ways of achieving the goal.

The rules

The ways in which the permitted means are proscribed are the *rules*. So in golf, a rule stipulates that the golf ball must be hit in a particular way, and that the ball must not be interfered with during play. Equally, a rule in cribbage stipulates that two points are awarded for holding cards that add up to 15 (a seven and an eight for example). These types of rules Suits calls *constitutive rules*. Suits also recognised that there are other types of rules in game playing, for instance, *rules of skill*, which give guidance about how best to carry out the constitutive rules. So a rule of skill in golf is to keep your head still when you strike the ball. Constitutive rules determine how the game can be played; whilst rules of skill determine how to play the game well.[4]

The lusory attitude

Suits' final element of game playing is the *lusory attitude*. This is the conscious awareness that one is involved in playing a game and the tacit acceptance of its rules. Suits' inclusion of the lusory attitude has generated discussion as to whether a player who deliberately breaks the rules can still be said to be playing the game. This question is considered in more detail in Chapter 3. Suits maintained it is impossible for a player to win a game if they have broken the

Element of Game Playing:	Definition:	Example:
(Pre-lusory) Goal:	The attempt to bring about a specific state of affairs	Getting a golf ball into a cup
(Lusory) Means:	Permitted (legal) ways to attempt to achieve the goal	Hitting the ball only with the use of a golf-club
(Constitutive) Rules:	Proscribed ways of reaching a pre-lusory goal that prohibit the use of the most efficient means	'The ball must be fairly struck at with the head of the club and must not be pushed, scraped or spooned' (Rule 14-1)
Lusory Attitude:	The acceptance of the constitutive rules in order to allow the game to exist	'I am involved in this activity in an attempt to try to win whilst abiding by the rules of the game'

Figure 2.2 – Suits' elements of game playing

rules.[5] This is because the ends (the pre-lusory goal) and (constitutive) rules are inseparable: the end only makes sense in the context of the rules. By breaking a rule you cannot attain the end that the rules entail. By breaking a constitutive rule, either the game breaks down completely and becomes unplayable, or participants accept that a new game with new rules has been created; as in the case of William Webb Ellis who was reported to have broken a constitutive rule of football by picking up the ball and running with it – thereby creating a new game of rugby football. Each game has its own set of constitutive rules, and it is the acceptance of all the rules inherent in the game that encapsulates the lusory attitude.

To summarise, Suits provides two analytic definitions of game playing (a long one and a short one):

'To play a game is to attempt to achieve a specific state of affairs (pre-lusory goal), *using only means permitted by rules* (lusory means), *where the rules prohibit more efficient in favour of less efficient means* (constitutive rules), *and where such rules are accepted just because they make possible such activity* (lusory attitude).

Playing a game is the voluntary attempt to overcome unnecessary obstacles.'[6]

WHAT IS SPORT?

So far, we have just considered the concept of a game, for this is where the discussion on the definition of sport emerged. That there seems to be a close relation between games and sport seems fairly uncontroversial, as many (though not all) sports are also games[7]. Roberts[8] lists four criteria for defining sport:

1. it is outside or apart from the rest of life, in terms of its location, duration and rules;
2. it is based on physical skill that can be improved through practice and preparation;
3. it requires a degree of stamina and exertion; and
4. it is competitive and directed towards the goal of winning.

This is similar to a definition provided by Coakley:

'Sports are institutionalised competitive activities that involve rigorous physical exertion or the use of relatively complex physical skills by participants motivated by internal and external rewards.'[9]

These definitions share similarities with the one that Suits provided. Suits argued that sports can be defined a sub-set of games but with added conditions: that the game must involve *physical skill*, have a degree of *stability*, and a *wide following*. Stipulating skill as a necessary condition eliminates games of chance or luck such as roulette. That the skill needs to be physical also seems reasonable as most sports seem to require a physical element (and conforms to our stereotypical image of a sportsperson as someone who is physically fit). However, this criterion causes disagreement over whether some activities, such as snooker, lawn bowls and chess, are really sports. One way of overcoming these difficult cases is to require the physical skill to be necessary to the game. So in snooker, a degree of physical skill is required to manoeuvre the cue in such a way to hit the desired ball. In contrast, the game of chess only requires the mental skill to choose which pieces to move and in which way. Consequently, in snooker, a person wouldn't be playing snooker if they were telling someone else which ball to hit and at what angle, whereas a person could be playing chess if they directed someone else to move the pieces (as in chess played on a computer). If physical skill is a necessary condition of sport, then it follows that snooker is a sport whilst chess is not.

Nevertheless, this resolution still doesn't satisfy everyone as we shall shortly see. Suits included two other conditions, stability and wide-following, in an attempt to exclude crazes and parochial activities such as 'hula-hoop' and 'welly throwing', which he believed were not sports but which might have fulfilled the criterion of physical skill. However, there are those who take the contextual approach and argue that these types of activities should be considered sports.

WHAT IS THE CONTEXTUAL APPROACH TO SPORT?

One of the criticisms of analytic definitions is that they are too restrictive and do not allow for a pluralism of views: they will necessarily fail in accounting for all instances of sport. Such a view was articulated by Frank McBride who argued that philosophers 'ought not waste their time attempting to define 'sport''[10] since the word is used in so many different ways in so many different contexts (McBride points to the *Oxford English Dictionary*, which stipulates 127 different uses of the term). Graham McFee also points out that as we all agree that there is such a thing as sport – though we might disagree as to what particular activities count as sport – it is neither necessary nor helpful to formally define it.[11]

Those who advocate a contextual approach argue that sport is defined not through formulating a set of necessary and sufficient conditions but through recognising shared meanings that are subject to flexibility and change according to context, culture and historical period.

What one person or group of people might categorise as sport might differ depending on location or time. So whereas chess is not classified as a sport in the United Kingdom and US, in many European countries it is. To argue that these people are incorrectly applying the term 'sport' seems perverse. This in some respects seems reasonable. As Steven Connor[12] comprehensively outlines, the applications of the word 'sport' have changed throughout English history. The etymology comes from the French word 'disport' which means 'to show' or 'to display' and was associated with aristocratic leisure pursuits, which is why we also use the word to refer to hunting and shooting activities. Equally, the German word 'spiel' is used to mean both 'game' and 'sport' and indicates how a direct translation can be problematic. One only needs to look to the wide variety of activities referred to as sports across the world, including 'ear pulling', 'bog snorkelling', 'sheep shearing' and the ethically dubious 'wife grabbing' to illustrate how broadly the term is used.

A final problem with the analytical method favoured by Suits is that one must already start with an understanding of what activities are games or sports before one formulates necessary and sufficient criteria; since it is from an analysis of similarities and differences between games and non-games, or sports and non-sports that a definition emerges. That one must already be able to recognise what is a game or sport in order to define it seems to undermine the very point of constructing a definition in the first place.

WHICH APPROACH SHOULD BE USED IN UNDERSTANDING SPORT?

The more flexible approach to language as suggested by the contextual approach seems congruent with the way in which language is used and understood in the real world. That there are frequent debates on whether a particular activity is a sport or merely a game or leisure pursuit indicates that there is discrepancy in how a term is applied. This approach, therefore, is culturally and historically sensitive and does not merely define sport from one particular (e.g. affluent, white, Western, male) perspective. However, the contextual approach is criticised for being relativistic and descriptive in that it seems to suggest that sport can be anything that anyone wants it to be, and since this clearly isn't the case then the contextual approach isn't particularly helpful. It is also limited in its usefulness when it comes to arbitration and policy making. The strength of the Analytic approach is it provides a clear benchmark for decision-making, which is necessary in relation to policy and funding issues. Governing bodies such as the International Olympic Committee (IOC), the World Anti-Doping Agency (WADA) or UK Sport require an analytic definition with a set of clearly defined criteria by which to judge applications and proposals.

Both ways of understanding sport have their merits and their drawbacks. The normative benefits of the Analytic approach are arguably more useful in reaching practical decisions yet proponents also need to accept that analytic definitions of sport are not absolute and may need to be adjusted depending on purpose and context.

INDEPENDENT STUDY QUESTIONS:

- *One way of formulating definitions is by identifying similarities and differences between other terms: what is the relationship between sport, play and games? How do they differ?*
- *Can you think of any examples of sport that don't fit with Coakley's definition? If so, to what extent is his definition too narrow?*
- *Is Suits correct in saying that sports are a subset of games? Can you think of any sports that aren't games?*
- *Which approach for understanding sport do you favour and why?*

3 CAN CHEATERS EVER WIN?

In 2012, Lance Armstrong, the formerly revered US cyclist, was stripped of his Tour de France titles for doping offences. For the 13 years after his first victory in 1999, Lance Armstrong was classified as a winner, and then, due to the fact he was found to have cheated, it was judged that he was not. In fact, the prevalence of doping in the late 1990s and early 2000s means there is now no official winner of the competition between 1999 and 2005. Similarly, in 1988 Ben Johnson won the Seoul Olympic men's 100m but due to doping offences he too was stripped of his medal, which was then awarded to Carl Lewis. Yet in the years that followed, Lewis and four of the six other athletes who were in that final were also implicated in doping. If six out of the eight participants in that race were cheating, it means, strictly speaking, only two athletes actually took part. The same logic proposes that for those seven years of the Tour de France, so many cyclists were found to be cheating it is possible the races did not take place at all. While such a conclusion may seem absurd, the philosophical question these examples raise is this: if everyone involved in a game breaks the rules of that game, does the game still exist? Or alternatively, as Craig Lehman put it, can cheaters play the game?[1] This is the question that will be explored in this chapter.

ARE YOU STILL PLAYING IF YOU ARE CHEATING?

Suits' definition of game playing has generated discussion as to whether, due to the necessity of the lusory attitude (the acceptance of the rules in order to play the game), a player who deliberately breaks the rules is actually playing that game. Suits himself argued that it is impossible for a player to win a game if they have broken the rules. This position is known as the *logical incompatibility* thesis and can be expressed in the following syllogism:[2]

P1: To play a game is an attempt to reach a specified end by accepting the rules that define that game.

P2: To cheat is to not accept the rules of the game.

C1: Therefore, to cheat is to not play the game.

P3: One can only win a game by playing it.

C2: Therefore, one cannot win by cheating.

For example, the game of darts requires that players stand 2.37m away from the dartboard. If a player decides to walk up to the board and stick their darts in a chosen area, then they are not playing the game of darts. Equally, if they attach a homing device to the dart so that it always lands on the desired score regardless of skill, then again, they are not playing the game of darts. Winning and cheating are, according to this argument, logically incompatible. This account is also known as the *formalist position* as it maintains that a game is defined by its formal (constitutive) rules. It is summarised by William Morgan:

> 'According to formalism, the various derivative notions of a game are
> to be defined exclusively in terms of its formal rules. What it means to
> engage in a game, to count as a legitimate instance of a game, to qualify
> as a bona fide action of a game, and to win a game is to act in accordance
> with the appropriate rules of the game. All instances and actions that
> fall outside the rules of the game, therefore, do not count as legitimate
> instances or actions of a game.'[3]

However, critics of this position have argued that this argument is only reasonable if you already accept Suits' conception of game playing. If you accept that the means dictated by the rules are the only way that a goal is to be attained, then the formalist position logically follows. However, this seems to abstract the definition of a game out of its usual context; i.e. the part of human culture and society in which it is situated. Whereas the formalist approach follows Suits' line, non-formalists, or conventionalists, maintain that a game is much more than merely the tacit or explicit acceptance of the constitutive rules.

Critics point to three problems with formalism. One, as authors such as Craig Lehman have noted[4], is that in real life players are always committing infractions of rules (often unintentionally) yet are still considered to be part of the game. Indeed, the very existence of rules to restart games when infractions occur (regulative rules) acknowledges this. For instance, if a player accidentally steps inside a prohibited area in netball, they are penalised by having the ball awarded to the opposing team. The regulative and restorative rules enable the game to continue despite the infraction of a constitutive rule.

A second criticism, argued by D'Agostino[5] and Kreider[6], is that rather than being logically incompatible, cheating logically entails the playing of the game. The concept of cheating only makes sense if the person who is cheating is considered part of the game. They may not be playing the game fairly or with due respect but they are still playing the game.

The third criticism is provided by authors such as Graham McFee[7] who note that we frequently modify the (official) rules of a game in order to make the game more equal, more challenging or easier, and yet doing so is still to play the game. McFee uses the example of providing a queen advantage in chess, but we could easily use countless other examples of modified games, for instance, agreeing to uncontested scrums in rugby, or playing on a slightly smaller than (officially) allowed pitch in football. The point that McFee makes is that a formalist approach to defining sport will always leave ambiguous cases, since many real-life instances of game playing do not abide by all the official constitutive rules. We adapt and modify games according to the context yet are still playing the game that is defined by its more formal, constitutive rules.

ARE THERE DIFFERENT TYPES OF RULES IN SPORT?

The central point of dispute between the formalist and the non-formalist account is the part that the rules play within sport.

Cesar Torres[8] points to three types of rules that are present in sport: *constitutive*, *regulative* and *auxiliary*. The constitutive rules are the ones that the formalist relies upon and are generally considered the ones that define a game. They are the rules that enable the game to exist in the first place; such as the rule that you must hit the white ball with the cue in snooker, or that players must release the ball within three seconds in handball. They are the rules that direct the permitted (and prohibited) means to achieve the end. A violation of the constitutive rules (such as the ball being kicked out of the play area) will temporarily end the game until it is restarted by a regulative rule. Regulative rules come into effect when the constitutive rules have been broken and provide a way of restoring play through a penalty or compensation to the opposition. Lastly, auxiliary rules are additional rules that are not concerned with the sport itself and therefore are generally rules concerned with player safety or tradition, e.g. weight classifications, banned substances or clothing restrictions.

In response to the first criticism, a formalist would argue that for the duration of time between a rule infraction and the restorative penalty, the game is no longer being played. The game has effectively broken down and needs to be restarted. It is only through the employment of a regulative rule that this can happen. The regulative rules in effect ensure that the constitutive rules are preserved. It also allows for the fact that the perfect game, where no constitutive rules are broken, is practically impossible. The accusation against formalism, however, is that often the distinction between regulative, constitutive and auxiliary rules is unclear. Did Lance Armstrong break a constitutive rule of cycling the Tour de France? Arguably not. He was the fastest person to cycle the required distance along the designated route using the means of a bicycle. Taking a performance-enhancing substance seems to be outside what makes a bicycle race a bicycle race. The rule that Armstrong broke was an auxiliary one that exists due to social norms and conventions about the morality of doping. It could perhaps be argued that Armstrong broke a regulative rule that stipulates the consequences of doping:

> 'For violations under article 21.7 (Trafficking or Attempted Trafficking) or article 21.8 (Administration or Attempted Administration of a Prohibited Substance or Prohibited Method), the period of Ineligibility imposed shall be a minimum of 4 (four) years up to lifetime Ineligibility...'[9]

Yet such a rule does not allow for the game to continue or simply be restarted; it demands that participants are ejected from the game completely. This rule therefore seems to differ substantially from the 'normal' regulative rules that enable the game to be restored, such as:

> *'If the ball is kicked off by the wrong type of kick, or from the incorrect place, the opposing team has two choices: to have the ball kicked off again, or to have a scrum at the centre of the half way line and they throw in the ball.'*[10]

As such, Armstrong's violation of the formal rules of cycling meant that he was no longer deemed to be able to play the game at all. While one of the reasons for this severe penalty is related to social norms and fears about doping and the harm it causes, an additional reason is concerned with the nature of doping as a form of cheating. The regulative rules allow for infractions by providing restorative penalties to allow justice to be served. Most infractions within a game are thus transparent, and are either accidental or poor attempts at deceit. Successful cheating, however, and particularly cheating through the methods of doping, is an attempt to obscure the fact that a rule has been broken. It arguably undermines the game completely since it doesn't allow for a regulative rule to be enforced and justice to be served. The deceptive nature of cheating means that while other participants hold the lusory attitude, the cheater merely pretends to everyone else that they do. Cheating, on this account, relies on the fact that everyone else is playing the game and everyone else believes that the cheater is also playing the game. The formalist maintains that the cheater merely achieves the goal of convincing others that they have been playing the game, when in reality, they have not.

The non-formalist would respond by maintaining that this type of analysis and argument is unnecessary since it is the ethos of the sport that provides a better explanation as to why some rules are more strictly enforced (such as using the feet to play the ball in football, or the anti-doping rules) while others are more flexible (such as the number of players on a team or whether an accidental handball is awarded). As Craig Lehman argues, formalists mistake conceptual confusion with a moral concern.[11] When we are dismayed at a player's deliberate attempt to break rules (either through a professional foul or an attempt to deceive officials), it is not because we believe that they are conceptually confused (i.e. that they don't understand what it is to play a game), but rather because we think they are morally mistaken. This view can be described as *broad internalism*. Broad internalism refutes the formalist position and maintains that the internal values and moral rules attached to sport ultimately define it, not the formal, constitutive rules.[12] Cheating on this account, is primarily a moral matter not a conceptual one.

This concept of ethos, as described by broad internalists, is explored further in later chapters on the issues of fair play, gamesmanship, sport as an educational tool, and the nature of competition.

INDEPENDENT STUDY QUESTIONS:

- *What is the logical incompatibility thesis and how does it relate to formalism?*
- *What are the criticisms of the formalist position?*
- *What are the different types of rules in sport? Give an example for each.*
- *Does breaking a rule mean that the game is no longer being played?*

INTERVIEW WITH A PHILOSOPHER

JIM PARRY

Jim Parry is former Head of the Philosophy Department
at the University of Leeds, UK, and University Life
Fellow, and also Visiting Professor at Charles University
in Prague, Czech Republic. He is a former Chair of the
British Philosophy of Sport Association and one of most
prominent British philosophers of sport, having written
and collaborated on a variety of issues in the area since
the early 1980s. He was a semi-professional footballer
and P.E. teacher.

- *Can you give me a little bit on your background and what got you interested in the philosophy of sport?*

  o I was a footballer with Derby County for four years before I began a Philosophy degree in Wales. While studying, I played for Bangor City and the British Universities and then after that for many years as a semi-professional. I went on to study for a teaching qualification in P.E. and English at Aberystwyth before teaching for three years in Cheshire. During that time, I saw an Easter school advertised by the North West Counties P.E. Association, which included a course on the philosophy of physical education run by David Aspin, who was one of the early authors in the field. It introduced me to the idea that there was a philosophy of physical education! Following this I applied to the University of Manchester to do a Masters in Philosophy and Education under David's supervision. (Incidentally, David later organised the first British philosophy of sport conference in 1983 at King's College London.) After that I got a job at Lady Mabel College, a specialist Physical Education teacher training college, teaching philosophy of education, before moving to Leeds University, where I remained for 30 years. I am proud to say that for many years I ran the only philosophy of sport course to be offered by a philosophy department in the UK.

- *What do you think is the most interesting problem in the philosophy of sport?*

  o I think it's the logic of sport rules and their relation to morality – questions about the ways in which the rules of sport are conceived and work. My thoughts around this initially stemmed from my interest in jurisprudence, and the literature regarding the nature of legal rules, without thinking about its application to sport. Later, one of my former students, Leo Hsu, took up this theme for his PhD thesis, 'The Role of the Rule in Sport'.

- *What book or paper has influenced you the most and why?*
  - Wittgenstein's *Philosophical Investigations* because it demonstrates philosophical methodology. It wears its conception of the philosophical enterprise on its sleeve.

Key Readings

Parry, S.J., 'The power of sport in peacemaking and peacekeeping', *Sport in Society: Cultures, Commerce, Media, Politics*, 15(6) (2012), pp. 775–787.

Martínková I. and Parry S.J., 'An Introduction to the Phenomenological Study of Sport', *Sport, Ethics and Philosophy*, 5(3) (2011), pp. 185–201.

McNamee, M.J. and Parry, S.J. (Eds.) *Ethics and Sport* (London: E & FN Spon, 1998).

SPORT, KNOWLEDGE AND TRUTH

4 ARE THERE DIFFERENT TYPES OF SPORTING KNOWLEDGE?

We have all come across exceptionally skilful athletes who can kick or throw a ball to pinpoint accuracy but who are unable to teach a novice the basics of the movement. Equally, we have met excellent coaches who can develop the skills of the complete beginner as well as the elite performer but who are unable to demonstrate the action themselves.

These examples suggest that being able to do something and understanding the processes involved in doing it are two different things. As such we might call the first 'practical knowledge' and the second 'theoretical knowledge'. However, this begs the question, what is knowledge and what is the relationship between these two different types? This chapter will outline the various ways in which knowledge can be defined and categorised and demonstrate how it relates to sporting excellence.

WHAT IS KNOWLEDGE?

Knowledge is one of those elusive terms that we all use daily in our lives and yet is difficult to pin down into a formal definition. One of the simplest definitions is: 'justified true belief'. This can be expressed in the following form:

A knows that P Iff;[1]

1. P;

2. A believes that P;

3. A's belief that P is justified.[2]

Knowledge must be dependent on belief (it would seem contradictory otherwise) but this is not sufficient as beliefs can turn out to be false. Therefore, it seems that truth is also a requirement. Yet believing something that is true might just be a lucky guess or is based on other mistaken beliefs: I might believe that Andy Murray won the Wimbledon men's singles title in 2013, and although this might be true, if my belief stemmed from a mis-recollection that I watched the men's finals that year when actually I was remembering the semi-final between Murray and Janowicz, it wouldn't be sufficient for it to be called knowledge. True belief must also be appropriately justified. In other words, my belief that Murray won the Wimbledon men's singles in 2013 cannot be justified by a mistaken memory.

There are problems with this definition however, as it results in an infinite regress for justifying justification. So I might say I know that Murray won the Wimbledon men's singles title in 2013 and I am justified in this belief because I read a match report in the paper. But a sceptic might then ask how I can know that the match report was an accurate picture of reality; to which I might respond by explaining that the reporter is well known and respected or by giving evidence of the score from other sources. Yet this would not satisfy the sceptic who would want further justification for justifying this evidence, and so on. All justification is based upon the belief in the truth of other evidence and this can go on ad infinitum.

One way of breaking down knowledge into different types is to say that there is a difference between facts that are true by definition (*analytic* statements) and facts that are true by experience (*synthetic* statements). They are also referred to as *a priori* and *a posteriori*. A priori knowledge is based upon maths, logic and language, and requires no external verification, such as: the square root of 16 is four, or all swimmers can propel themselves unaided through water. A posteriori knowledge is based upon our direct experience of the world and is the type of knowledge that we associate with direct observation or scientific investigation: such as, humans require oxygen to survive, or Natalia Molchanova is a record-breaking free diver. These two types of knowledge also relate to the deductive and inductive reasoning covered in Chapter 5.

There have been attempts to distinguish further between different types of knowledge above and beyond the analytic/synthetic distinction. Bonjour provides eleven different forms: [3]

1. Facts about my present subjective experiences or states of consciousness: e.g. that I am currently thinking about how to explain epistemology to you.

2. Facts about my presently perceived physical environment: e.g. that I am looking at a computer screen in front of me.

3. Facts about the larger perceptible and social world beyond my present experience: e.g. that there is a racecourse in Cheltenham.

4. Facts about my personal past that I experienced: e.g. that I took part in a yacht race to France.

5. Facts about the historical past that I did not experience: e.g. that Jesse Owens won the 100m in the 1936 Berlin Olympics.

6. Facts about the experiences and mental states of other people (and some animals): e.g. that the crowd watching the match are enjoying it; that the injured dog is in pain.

7. Facts about the dispositional and character traits of people (and some animals): e.g. that John has a superstition about wearing particular socks on the day of a match; that Elle is a determined person.

8. General and causal facts concerning observable objects and processes: e.g. that a ball will always fall to the ground.

9. Facts about future events: e.g. that I am coaching rugby this evening; that all humans will eventually die.

10. Facts outside the range of anyone's direct observation or that could not in principle be observed: e.g. that it is very hot at the centre of the sun; that human evolution has occurred.

11. Facts that do not seem to depend on sensory experience at all: e.g. that $2 + 2 = 4$.

This long list of different types of knowledge demonstrates that what constitutes knowledge is much more varied and complex than we might at first anticipate.

WHAT IS THE DIFFERENCE BETWEEN THEORETICAL KNOWLEDGE AND PRACTICAL KNOWLEDGE?

Most of the definitions and examples of knowledge that have been covered so far are examples of theoretical knowledge; of 'knowing that'. Generally, this type of knowledge has been the focus of philosophical discussions in the past. Yet as was illustrated at the beginning of this chapter, there are other forms of knowledge, such as the practical knowledge required for 'doing' sport. The focus upon theoretical knowledge makes sense in (Western analytical) philosophy, which traditionally has been concerned with abstract ideas and concepts. In contrast and by its nature, practical knowledge is something that is experienced through and by the body. So one might be able to read and understand a whole book on the biomechanics of bowling a ball but that wouldn't mean that one is able to bowl. Indeed, knowledge about the biomechanics of bowling is only possible after detailed testing and measuring of human subjects who have actually bowled, i.e. who know *how* to do it. The ability to do something must necessarily come before the theoretical knowledge about how it is done. As Gilbert Ryle said, 'efficient practice precedes the theory of it'.[4]

The translation of practical knowledge into theoretical knowledge has become the focus for sports scientists and coaches because it is this theoretical knowledge that can then be used as a template from which to assess and alter practical skill. A good coach is able to observe an athlete and identify aspects of performance that affect how well a person is able to carry out a particular skill. They will notice the player's foot position is leading to instability, or that their grip on the racquet means they are not able to hit the ball cleanly. One of the criticisms of this model of coaching, however, is that it can be quite inflexible if the theoretical template used is considered the only way to carry out that action. Once habits are formed they are very difficult to break and athletes will often struggle to learn a new 'biomechanically efficient' way of performing a skill, especially if the way they have performed it so far has been relatively successful. If a bowler is able to bowl successfully for seven out of eight occasions and has been doing so for the past nine years, but is then told that they need to completely change their bowling technique for it to be more successful, it is unlikely they will be able to do so. A good coach will be able to use their theoretical knowledge , including those about human dispositions and character traits, to adapt and compensate for errors and inefficiencies rather than use the template as an exact procedure to be followed.

WHAT IS PHENOMENOLOGICAL KNOWLEDGE?

Practical knowledge can also be understood in relation to phenomenology. Phenomenology describes the 'raw sense' experience of being in the world: what it feels like to carry out an action or experience an event. Michael Polanyi highlighted that by virtue of being human in the world we necessarily have a relation to it.[5] So while I am playing hockey, my focal awareness may be on the ball coming towards me, but equally I have a subsidiary awareness of holding the hockey stick in my hand and manipulating it in a way that will stop the ball cleanly. In this sense, the stick becomes an extension of my body and I experience it as part of my body. Polanyi's ideas are supported by evidence from experiments in psychology; most famously by the 'Rubber Hand Illusion' whereby participants experience (evidenced by self-reporting, behaviour and physiological reactions) a fake arm as if it were their own.[6] The 'raw-sense' experience of the world can be categorised as *phenomenological* or *phenomenal knowledge*.[7] It refers to the way that we, as humans, are inexorably part of the world and that our knowledge and understanding of it is dependent on the way in which we directly experience it. Merleau-Ponty referred to this as the *body-subject* which enables us to react to the world in an intentional way. Gunnar Breivik explains it as a type of sporting knowledge:

> 'For instance, the movements and positions of football players on the field are defined and solicited by the movements of the ball and the other players. It is the situation that defines the body, its movements and positions. And more than that, good football players are able to read the situation before the ball is played. Therefore, the best players tend to be at the right place at the right time. And even more than that, they are ready for the action that the situation demands.'[8]

Phenomenological knowledge is subconscious. It is also often referred to in the psychological literature as 'flow'. It is the ability to execute and complete actions without being consciously aware of the intention behind the movement. The way in which the body is able to react and respond to the world appropriately is also a key aspect of Eastern conceptions of the body and is explored further in Chapter 8.

WHAT KNOWLEDGE IS REQUIRED FOR SPORTING EXCELLENCE?

This chapter has highlighted the fact that knowledge is a complex term that covers many different instances of the relationship that we have with the world. While theoretical knowledge (knowledge of facts about the world) has traditionally dominated philosophical discussion, the practical knowledge of being able to successfully carry out actions is essential for sport. While athletes may depend on the expertise and analysis of sports scientists and coaches, ultimately they are the ones who have to be able to control their body and react to their environment in order to put this skill into action. Generally in sport, it is this practical and phenomenological knowledge that comes first. Indeed, that most of the knowledge we first acquire, as children, is the practical knowledge of being able to do things suggests that the historical tendency to emphasise and promote theoretical knowledge above other types of knowledge is misguided.

INDEPENDENT STUDY QUESTIONS

- *What is the difference between theoretical knowledge and practical knowledge?*
- *How can knowledge be categorised into different types and how do they relate to one another?*
- *What types of knowledge are required for sporting excellence?*

HOW CAN PHILOSOPHY UNDERPIN RESEARCH IN SPORT?

Studying sport is inherently multi-disciplinary and students are expected to have a knowledge (often deep) of a broad range of disciplines. That expectation has both advantages and drawbacks. One of the advantages is that a greater knowledge of a broader range of disciplines and their common methods allows for a wider framework of connections and relationships. Becoming acquainted with research methods across a spectrum of disciplines as well as their value and limitations prevents students from being drawn into disciplinary silos where one particular method (and its underpinning axioms) is seen as *the* method for doing research. One of the dangers of familiarity with a range of methods, however, is to fall into relativism: the belief that any method of investigation is as good as any other, and that choice of method depends simply on whether one prefers to collect numerical (quantitative) or linguistic (qualitative) data. This is where the philosopher has a role to play: that of deciphering the underlying assumptions behind different methods and highlighting their limitations and advantages. As has been demonstrated in Chapter 1, philosophy forces assumptions to be questioned and arguments to be defended. This is also the case when evaluating the methods behind research in sport.

The methods associated with empirical research[1] in sport are often divided into the sciences and the social sciences. Social science has its roots in science but its focus is upon human rather than non-human phenomena.[2] As such, it is useful to consider the concept of science first before reflecting upon how the social sciences differ.

WHAT IS SCIENCE?

Science currently holds a place in Western society as the best way of understanding how the world works: it is generally understood as a way to discover truths or facts. As such, the mark of an advanced civilisation is whether it uses scientific methods over 'primitive' approaches such as religious superstition, witchcraft or New Age mysticism.

Science as we understand it today is a relatively recent invention that was formalised during the period of the Enlightenment in the mid-17th to

18th century. Before this, there were individuals doing what we might call science but it wasn't recognised by those in power (often religious authorities) as a genuine way to learn about the world. The term 'natural philosopher' was given to those individuals who were interested in finding out about the world and its workings. As philosophy can be translated as 'love of wisdom' this connection makes sense; for a 'natural philosopher' is interested in discovering facts about the natural world. Similarly, the word 'science' comes from the Latin 'scientia' which translates as 'knowledge'.

The way in which science distinguishes itself from other methods of investigation is through being systematic: that is, it is a logical, ordered and transparent process that can be replicated. This differs from religious or supernatural approaches whereby truths are ethereally bestowed and generally restricted to 'chosen' or special individuals to propagate outwards. Science is considered to be useful in its ability to predict future events and explain past occurrences, as Hempel explains:

> 'Science is widely conceived as seeking to formulate an increasingly comprehensive, systematically organised, world view that is explanatory and predictive.'[3]

That science should both be able to explain and predict highlights two fundamental aspects of scientific enquiry. The methods that are used in order to do this are *deduction* and *induction* (Figure 5.1). The deductive method is the one that was highlighted in Chapter 3, as demonstrated through Aristotle's syllogisms and the deductive example of cheating in sport. Deduction enables us to use knowledge that we already have in order to ascertain new information. For instance, if I already know that all people reading this are highly intelligent, and I know that Sarah is reading this, then I can deduce that Sarah is highly intelligent. Deduction works from the general to the specific and is founded in logic. An objection to the deductive method is that it doesn't really give us any new knowledge; it just clarifies and makes explicit what is already known. The question then, is where does our knowledge of these general statements

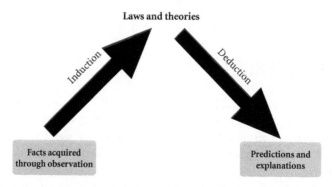

Figure 5.1 – Induction and Deduction (adapted from Chalmers, 1980)

(i.e. that all people reading this are highly intelligent) come from? The answer lies in the inductive method. It can also be called the experimental method or empirical research. The inductive method works by conducting tests on individual phenomena and extrapolating the results outwards. As such, it works from the specific to the general. It is a generalisation based on a set of (experimental) observations.

The traditional method of induction is known as 'positivism', which holds that it is possible to conduct experiments in order to discover proven truths about the world. It works by formulating hypotheses generated from initial observations, which then can be tested and verified. In order for observations to become scientific laws, it must pass three requirements: (1) the number of observations forming the basis of a generalisation must be large; (2) the observations must be repeated under a wide variety of conditions; (3) no accepted observation statement should conflict with the derived law.[4] For instance, if we were testing the hypothesis that elite male marathon runners have a VO_2 max greater than 50, then we would use observations of a large number of marathon runners to verify this. If, after substantial tests and observations, we can find no example of an elite male marathon runner that contradicts this hypothesis, we can be confident that our hypothesis is proven true.

However, the Scottish philosopher David Hume identified a problem with the method of induction. This issue was later reframed by Bertrand Russell in his story of the inductivist turkey:[5]

> 'There once was a turkey who was incredibly intelligent and observed that he was fed at 9 a.m. every morning. Being a good inductivist (positivist), he formed his observation into a hypothesis, which he tested under a variety of conditions (weather, weekday, ground conditions) and concluded after hundreds of tests that there was a natural law that dictated he would get fed every day at 9 a.m. That was of course, until Christmas Eve, when instead of getting fed at 9 a.m., the farmer came to wring his neck.'

The problem highlighted by this story is that no matter how many times an experiment is carried out, it does not prove that the results will always hold true for the future. It works on the assumption that the future will continue in the same way as the past. Hume provides a convincing argument that this assumption was unjustified and unjustifiable. It seems to suggest that the foundations upon which the scientific method of induction rests is shaky at the very least.

One of the solutions to this problem was provided by Karl Popper[6], who argued that the method of induction is unnecessary. Popper noted that a single contradictory observation is sufficient to disprove a theory (as in the case of the single instance where the turkey was not fed at 9 a.m.). Therefore, instead of trying to prove their theories to be true, scientists should be trying to prove them to be false. This is his theory of falsification. Popper believed that although scientific investigation allows us to head in the right direction of searching for truth, it is an unending endeavour. Knowledge is necessarily provisional rather than absolute as there is always a possibility that it will be shown to be false. All we are able to do, through repeated testing, is to eliminate weaker theories in favour of stronger ones, while being open to the possibility that even our strongest theories will not survive.

In response to Popper, Thomas Kuhn[7] argued that this view of science is an idealised one. Scientists do not simply discard their theories (or hypotheses) on the basis of a single contrary instance; instead they are rightly much more dogmatic and will often hold on to theories in spite of contradictory evidence. Instead, what often happens in science is that particular theories tend to dominate even if there are small pieces of evidence that seem to falsify them. It is only once this falsifying evidence has built to such an extent that the scientific community is forced to re-evaluate the accepted theory and put a new theory in its place, which takes into account the new evidence.

What these discussions and disagreements suggest then is that the method(s) of science is much more difficult to ascertain and justify than we might be led to believe. The picture of the scientist as a detached, objective researcher who proves hypotheses may be naïve and unrealistic. Kuhn appears to be correct in pointing out that science is ultimately a human and cultural activity and the history of scientific belief supports this view. Nevertheless, there does seem to be something special about a way of investigating the world that has given us incredible technology and insight in the arenas of sport, human capability and athletic performance.

Most of the methods above refer to the natural sciences (biology, chemistry, physics, etc.), yet the majority of research in sport is carried out on humans. While this may contain elements of the natural sciences (e.g. biomechanical or biochemical analysis), it also includes research that focuses upon human action, perception and belief. This type of research, which takes the human as a whole (rather than at a cellular level for example), and focuses upon human behaviour and interaction, is labelled as social science. The types of methods that are used in the social sciences, and their limitations, are the next point of enquiry.

WHAT ARE THE SOCIAL (HUMAN) SCIENCES?

The social sciences emerged in the 19th century but gained prominence as a set of discrete disciplines with a particular set of methods in the 20th century. As with the development of the natural sciences, scholars interested in studying human and social environments were also often influenced by philosophical ideas and theory. The social sciences cover a range of disciplines from the more familiar and broader disciplines of sociology (the study of human society) and psychology (the study of mind and behaviour), to anthropology, history, linguistics and communication theory, economics, criminology and law. In many respects, the study of sport is a social science as 'sport' is a social construct: it only exists as a human practice.

The concept of a social science has always been controversial due to the problems it has in controlling variables. While the natural sciences aim to produce a closed environment whereby variables can be tightly controlled and measured, the study of 'open' environments is inherently much more complex. The consequence of not being able to isolate individual variables in the study of human behaviour and interaction means that the conclusions that can be logically drawn from studies are weaker (since it is much more difficult to determine cause and effect) but also the types of research that can be carried out are restricted due to ethical considerations.[8]

Respondents to this critique of the validity of the social sciences argue that as there is no single and clearly defined scientific method, the idea of a social science can be justified. Indeed, the argument provided by Kuhn against Positivism is often used by social scientists to defend their practice.[9] Despite this, there are those who contest the notion of a social science. Nicholas Taleb, for instance, criticises those who wish to emulate the natural sciences in discovering human laws, and particularly the way researchers attach the label 'science' on to their work in order to increase its credibility. He argues that rather than accept the study of humans as a valuable and intellectual but non-scientific discipline, there is often an attempt to market it as an 'exact science':

> 'By 'exact science' I mean a second-rate engineering problem for those who want to pretend that they are in the physics department – so-called physics envy. In other words, an intellectual fraud.'[10]

Taleb's criticism highlights a key problem when studying humans: the extent to which humans are governed by causal laws.

As was illustrated previously, the natural sciences work on the assumption that the future is predictable and repeatable. A key tenet of good science is the notion of reliability in that the results will be the same every time the same experiment is repeated. It works on the assumption that there are causal laws that remain consistent.

This view represents the philosophical theory of reductive materialism. It takes a Newtonian view that everything follows a pre-determined path that is directed by the laws of nature. Everything in the world works in a causal way similar to the workings of a clock. It is simply up to us to discover what the laws governing nature are, and then we will be able to predict the future with accuracy.[11] According to this theory, humans, being part of the world, are governed by causal laws in the same way that billiard balls are governed. It supposes that if we can predict the trajectory of a ball by knowing the force and angles that are applied to it, we can also predict the action of a human if we have similar knowledge about the precise determinants of human behaviour (e.g. environment, genetics, hormones, neural electro-chemical reactions in the brain, etc.). According to this view, humans are merely very complex machines. Yet our experience of actually being human seems very different to this. At the very least, we feel as if we have free will and can decide to choose how we act. Although there are researchers who argue our feeling of free will is just an illusion (and that we are indeed just complex machines), it nevertheless poses a problem for the issue of reliability. The fact that humans feel autonomous, are self-aware and are able to reflect upon their position as research subjects means that they are very different from other objects such as balls. Studying humans is very different from studying inanimate objects. Humans, and their actions, are influenced in a way that other objects are not: they question, assume, draw conclusions and ultimately try to make sense of what is going on around them. This highlights the problem of ensuring validity in human research: for instance, if a human participant is second-guessing what the researcher wants them to do (participant bias), then the study is not going to be able to research what it intends. This type of problem is not an issue when studying inanimate objects or animals, which do not possess this self-conscious, reflective ability that is common to most humans.

These difficulties in studying human behaviour and interaction led the philosopher, Peter Winch, to argue that social scientists misunderstand their practice.[12] They cannot replicate the methods of the natural sciences in studying humans; if they do, they will simply produce bad philosophy. Both Winch's and Taleb's view reiterates that of the philosopher Wittgenstein, who saw that the apparent and impressive progress made by the natural sciences, and the subsequent authority it is given, leads others to try to emulate it:

> '[They] constantly see the method of science before their eyes, and are irresistibly tempted to ask and answer questions in the way science does.'[13]

Winch argues that the fundamental mistake social scientists make is in believing that humans are the same type of thing as other (non-human) objects. He argues that instead of being governed by causal laws, humans are guided by rules: and as the popular idiom states, rules can be broken; laws cannot. These rules are primarily determined by how language is understood. Much of the research conducted in sports is dependent on participants understanding commands and turning their own raw-sense experiences into meaningful language that can be then reported back to the researcher. So, for instance, a sports psychologist who is researching the use of imagery in athletic performance might ask their participants whether they imagine themselves kicking a ball in the first-person (as if they were actually doing it) or in the second person (as if they were a spectator or video camera watching them). Such research is based on the assumption that the participant fully understands what the researcher is trying to get at in their questioning and has the same understanding and experience of the concepts as the researcher, is able to reflect upon their own phenomenological experiences and formulate this experience – that is outside the bounds of language – into words. They then have to translate this experience into a meaningful sentence to report back to the researcher, who then has to translate it into something that is meaningful for their research. As the researcher has no way of actually experiencing what the participant is experiencing, they have to rely on inference and assumption, which has significant bearing on the scientific notions of objectivity, validity and reliability.

There are two ways of responding to these criticisms aimed at the social sciences. The first is to argue that science is a broad enough term to be able to accommodate the methods used in understanding human interaction and behaviour. In other words, as long as the conclusions are meaningful, reasonable and enable a greater understanding of a phenomenon, it doesn't matter if they do not adhere to the strict criteria required by positivists. The second approach is for social scientists to argue that their methods can be scientifically validated once we have a greater understanding of the underlying mechanisms of human behaviour. For instance, researchers working in areas such as neuro-psychology and genetics often hold to the materialist view that human action can be predicted once these underlying mechanisms are discovered.

This chapter has indicated why an understanding of philosophy can help those studying and researching sport. Being aware of the conceptual and epistemological problems behind attempts to understand sport and athletic performance enables researchers to fully understand their methods of investigation and ensure that they reach sound conclusions about the strength of their claims.

INDEPENDENT STUDY QUESTIONS:

- *Explain the difference between deduction and induction and give examples of your own.*
- *What is positivism in science?*
- *What was Hume's problem of induction and how does Popper attempt to overcome it? Do you agree with Popper?*
- *Can you think of any issue in sports science that is contested or where you have heard conflicting evidence? How do you decide which is the best theory?*
- *What are the key problems associated with carrying out research in sports sciences?*

6 IS THE REFEREE ALWAYS RIGHT?

The above question may at first seem a bit odd as there have been many instances whereby referees and officials have made wrong decisions in sport. An umpire may call a batsman out through wrongly judging that the ball clipped the bat before being caught behind; a referee may mistakenly allow play to continue when a foul has been committed; or a time-keeper may allow far more time to be added on to the clock than was taken up by injury. Nevertheless, common phrases such as 'play to the whistle' and 'it's for the referee to decide', in addition to laws such as the one stipulated by rugby union which unequivocally states, 'The referee is the sole judge of fact and of Law during a match'[1], indicates this question is more complicated than it initially seems.

This type of epistemological question is of interest to philosophers of sport because it considers the nature of knowledge and truth in a sports setting. It highlights the contested nature of these concepts and demonstrates the relationship between the way in which we understand and answer these types of questions and the values we attach to sport. In addition to this epistemological question there is an ethical question about how sport ought to be officiated and the role that technology should play within it.

WHAT IS THE PURPOSE OF OFFICIALS IN SPORT?

While there are many examples of officials in sport, the ones who are the focus of this discussion are those who are central to the game being played; that is, they determine the start and end of the game and ensure the rules are being followed. Often the powers given to this type of official have been determined by the history and evolution of the sport in question and frequently replicated the social class differences of those who played them. So sports that evolved from the organised leisure time allocated by factory owners, such as football, tended to be enforced by officials drawn from the management, while the gentlemanly pursuit of cricket was overseen by the members of the household's staff. This resulted in different sports awarding their officials differing degrees of authority. While cricket umpires were originally members of the household staff who safeguarded coats and hats and counted the number of balls in an over, football referees were given much more authority in determining how the game was to be played. This historical and cultural context also partly explains the attitude towards officials from players from different sports, and the amount of respect or deference they are generally given: the contrasting examples of the way in which rugby and football referees are treated by players being a case in point.

Despite the differing roles and respect afforded to officials in sport, at the very least, they ought to be fair, impartial and ultimately just. That is, they do not favour one competitor over the other and they attempt to apply the rules consistently. However, justice is not the same as accuracy: an official may be unbiased or unpartisan but still make errors of accuracy.

WHAT GIVES AUTHORITY TO AN OFFICIAL?

Collins[2] outlines two necessary aspects that categorise an official:

1. *Ontological authority*: considers that the judgement that an official makes determines reality. So if an official judges that a goal is scored, history will record that fact. This type of authority mirrors the earlier quoted rule in rugby, that the referee is sole judge of fact, despite what players, coaches or video replays may suggest.

2. *Epistemological privilege*: refers to the belief that the official is the best person, in the best position, to determine facts about the game. This is based upon assumptions regarding the following; officials possess:

   a. A *superior view* – that the actual physical position taken by the official affords the most accurate view, i.e. the umpire's chair above the centre of the court, or the referee who is close to the ball.

   b. *Specialist skills* – that they have been trained in the rules of the sport and have experience in applying those rules.

Until recently, epistemological privilege and ontological authority was generally taken for granted. However, the introduction and advancement of technology in sport means that an official's epistemological privilege has been eroded. The clearest illustration of this is the use of multi-angle cameras and video replay, which has resulted in the epistemological privilege of 'superior view' being transferred to the armchair viewer sitting at home with the live-pause facility on his remote control. As such, officials and referees are no longer in the best physical position to judge facts of the matter. Such a discontinuity between the official's ontological authority and their epistemological privilege affects both the credibility of the match official and the sport itself.

This was the case in the 2010 football World Cup when the referee awarded Argentina a goal against Mexico. A replay of the incident immediately after the initial decision to award the goal was shown inside the stadium to spectators, players and officials alike, indicating an offside infringement. There was a clear disparity between the referee's ontological authority and his epistemological privilege, since, through the video replay, the spectator was able to make a more accurate judgement about what occurred on the field of play. Collins clarifies this disparity further by distinguishing between two types of justice: presumptive justice and transparent justice. Presumptive justice can be defined as the justice that is assumed to have been meted from the position of the official who exercises ontological authority, and transparent justice can be understood as justice that is seen to have been dispensed from all other perspectives. Prior to the television replay, presumptive justice was sufficient in matters of adjudication in sport, since everyone had to accept the official's decision because the official *qua* official was always right. But now replays of incidents are available to all, both inside and outside the stadium, presumptive justice has become increasingly inadequate; the epistemological privilege, in the sense of a superior view, now rests with others rather than the official.

Such a disparity causes problems for sport. As Tijs Tummers, secretary of FIFPro's (the professional football players' union) technical committee said of the Argentina incident:

> '[The referee] would undoubtedly have heard that Tevez was offside, the whole stadium had already seen it by then via images on the scoreboard. Yet, because the referee was not allowed to rely on video images, he had to award the goal, which he knew should have been disallowed. You could see the doubt in his eyes.'[3]

TO WHAT EXTENT SHOULD TECHNOLOGY BE USED IN OFFICIATING?

The question then is what should be done about this technological undermining of an official's authority. Two contrasting responses can be provided; from football and rugby union. The football governing body's (FIFA's) response was to reduce the amount of replayed action that could be shown in the stadium, to lessen the likelihood of spectator unrest. Yet, this does not prevent the authority of officials being discredited by television pundits, managers and the media following the game. In contrast, rugby union seems to have embraced television technology with enthusiasm. While the fourth official in rugby union, who had access to all camera angles, was originally called upon to make decisions that the referee was uncertain about, the use of large screens within stadiums now means that the referee is able to watch replays of events before making a judgement. Allowing officials to use technology in this way arguably restores their epistemological privilege as they also have the superior skills to be able to make a good judgment.

One common criticism of referees turning to video replays is that it is time-consuming and reduces the flow of the game. This criticism is directed more towards invasion games such as rugby, football and hockey, rather than sports in which there are frequent breaks in play, such as tennis and cricket. It was one of the key arguments given by FIFA in their rejection of goal-line technology[4], since football relies on the possibility of a team turning a defensive situation (such as a goal-line clearance) into a counter-attack. If a referee stopped play because he was unsure whether a goal had been scored in order to watch a replay, it would disrupt this aspect of the game. Furthermore, one of the reasons for the advantage rule in many sports is to ensure the continuity and flow of a game. If games were stopped every time an infringement was committed it would become fragmented and less enjoyable for players and spectators alike.

Rugby too has been criticised for relying too much on video replays and disrupting the continuity of the game.[5] Referees have been censured for no longer using video replays solely to determine whether the ball has been touched down in the try area but instead for asking for replays of events leading up to the try, which may go back several plays or phases. The fourth official, sitting in front of a bank of screens, seems with greater frequency to be stepping into the jurisdiction of the on-the-pitch referee. For instance, the fourth official in England's 2015 Six Nations match against France asked the referee to stop the game to return to an infringement he had seen but which the referee had not. One may well ask whether in future, due to the epistemological privilege video technology affords, the primary role of officiating will reside with video referees rather than an official who is on the field of play.

Using technology to ensure correct decisions are made in sport is an argument that appears to be persuasive. Seth Bordner summarises it as follows:

'1. The normative atmosphere of sports requires that we reliably and correctly determine what happens in sporting contests; if we choose to devote our time and attention to sport (as participants or spectators), we ought to do what we can to get the calls right.

2. (In many cases) we can reliably and correctly determine what happens in sporting contests only with the use of technological aids.

3. So, if we choose to devote our time and attention to sport, we ought to use technological aids to get the calls right (in many cases).'[6]

The first premise upon which this syllogism rests appears sound. The rules of sport determine how the game is played and therefore we should ensure that correct decisions are made when a rule is broken.[7] The second premise, however, needs further interrogation.

IS TECHNOLOGY ALWAYS RIGHT?

Bordner takes his second premise as given and argues it is both 'obvious and uncontroversial'[8]. However, technology is not infallible. One of the reasons that FIFA rejected goal-line technology was due to its unreliability. The initial tests FIFA conducted prior to introducing goal-line technology specified a 100 per cent accuracy rate. All candidates failed.[9] Arguably technology can never be 100 per cent accurate, not least because there is an almost infinite number of variables to take into account when assessing a ball in flight. All sports that utilise officiating technology have seen instances where the technology has failed or has produced results that are incongruent with later analysis and the judgement of experts. Additionally, despite the manufacturers of Hawk-Eye insisting that their product is 100 per cent reliable[10], all technologies tolerate a degree of statistical error, which means that incorrect decisions will undoubtedly be made at some point. Bordner's response to the fallibility of technology is to argue that technology is still more accurate and reliable than human perception. However, such a view does not take into account the difference between making a judgement and determining matters of fact.

To illustrate, let us imagine that technology is being used to determine a leg-before-wicket (lbw) decision in cricket. This rule specifies that the striker is called out if the ball would have knocked the bails off the stumps had the striker's leg (or other body part) not stopped it. First, any margin of error within the technology could result in an incorrect call. The technology could predict that the ball would have hit the stumps when in fact it would have gone past them, or vice versa. Second, even if the path of a ball could be accurately plotted, it would not determine whether the bails would fall. If the ball skimmed the top of the bails, it would be impossible to determine whether the force generated by the ball would be greater than the force keeping the bails on the stumps.[11] The only way to know this would be if the ball actually hit the stumps, but since it did not, we can never be certain. The call of lbw in cricket is a matter of judgement rather than a matter of fact. If we return to our initial concept of an official, while umpires have the ontological authority to make judgements in sport, technology does not.

Collins' categorisation of officials in sport demonstrates that it involves more than simply making accurate decisions in sport. It also requires the human characteristic of good judgement. Good judgement rests on the ability to make accurate decisions, through ensuring a position of epistemological privilege in having the skills to know what the correct decision is but also being in a good position to observe the game. This may in part be aided by technology. Yet good judgement also requires an understanding of the meaning and context of sport, in ensuring that the game can be played and other intrinsic values, such as enjoyment, community and play are upheld. This can only be achieved if authority ultimately rests with a human official.

INDEPENDENT STUDY QUESTIONS:

- *What role does an official play in sport?*
- *What is the difference between ontological authority and epistemological privilege?*
- *In what ways has technology undermined the authority of an official?*
- *What are the problems with using technology to make officiating decisions?*
- *How should technology be used in officiating sport?*

7 HOW MUCH IS TOO MUCH TECHNOLOGY IN SPORT?

Technology is arguably a prerequisite of sport. Although it might be possible to imagine informal play or games without it, it is far more difficult to conceive of technology-free sport as it is constructed today. While many think of sports technology as the latest cutting-edge equipment, such as goal-line technology, altitude chambers and biometric tracking devices, most of the technology in sport is much older and simpler, such as balls, racquets, footwear, goalposts and netting. This chapter will attempt to outline how technology can be defined, how it affects the nature of sporting competition, and whether limits should be placed on its use.

WHAT IS THE ROLE OF TECHNOLOGY IN SPORT?

Definitions of technology are contested and range from narrow ones that focus upon the human use of material objects, through to 'the application of scientific knowledge for practical purposes'[1], to a broader conception that encompasses:

> *'The whole range of means by which humans act on their environments or seek to transcend the limits of their natural capacities.'*[2]

Its etymological roots stem from the Greek concept 'technē' which meant 'craft' or 'art', thus suggesting an expertise in producing a tool or artefact.[3] Essentially, technology is the outcome of an explicit attempt to provide solutions to identified problems. There have been a handful of attempts to give a typology of sporting technology but a reasonable place to start is Butryn,[4] who distinguished five categories (set out below). I have included an additional one, which I think that Butryn neglects and that is technology that aids decision-making on rule-breaking, such as, 'Was the ball in or out?' 'Would it have hit the wicket?' or 'Was it over the line?'

1. *landscape* technologies, i.e. playing surfaces and arena;
2. *implement* technologies, i.e. tools and equipment, such as balls and racquets;
3. medical and *rehabilitative* technologies, e.g. cortisone injections, altitude chambers;

4. *movement* and biomechanical skill analysis, e.g. 2D and 3D analysis and movement-tracking;
5. *self* technologies that are directly designed to affect the human body and mind, e.g. genetic modifications and psychological interventions;
6. *adjudication* technologies, e.g. Hawk-Eye, video replays.

While some of these categories may overlap (for instance, the rehabilitative technologies and self-technologies), they all indicate the way in which we attempt to gain mastery over our performance in sport, to reduce the part that luck and chance play in the outcome, and to quantify results to an exact measurement.

One of the contradictions found in elite sport is the fact that sport by its nature is inefficient since it involves the overcoming of unnecessary obstacles (see Suits' definition in Chapter 2) and yet there is a perfectionist desire to make performance as efficient as possible. This contradiction is exemplified in the attempt to test the limits of the 'natural' human while at the same time constantly striving (through scientific and technological knowledge and innovation) to surpass these 'natural' limits. At the elite level, increases in sporting performance are undoubtedly led by technology, whether that is a diagnostic analysis of a sporting skill to improve efficiency, the development of material technology to reduce friction and wind-resistance, the use of nutritional supplements, or the support of a sports psychologist. All of this demonstrates that the concept of the 'natural' athlete is more of an illusion than we would like to admit.

WHAT ARE THE PROBLEMS WITH TECHNOLOGY IN SPORT?

Technology, as we have seen, is the outcome of an explicit attempt to provide solutions to identified problems. However, as Tenner[5] notes, the implementation of technology often yields ironic, unintended consequences – *revenge effects*. This is where the application of technological solutions creates additional problems that are worse than the one that the technology originally intended to solve. Pam Sailors[6] discusses these effects in the context of running; a sport that is generally considered to be one where technology is least required and employed. The development of running shoes in terms of cushioning and stability, for instance, has been argued to increase the chance of injury as it masks biomechanical problems and fools the brain into believing that the wearer's technique is safe and efficient. It allows wearers to run for far longer than they would be able to do otherwise, thus storing up longer-term problems in the future.

Tenner also suggests that rather than solve problems, technology may complicate them further. Sailors points to the example of the GPS watch to illustrate this. She argues that the data provided by GPS watches has the effect of dictating the length, quality and emotional effect of a run. Sailors cites the runner who came home early because his GPS batteries were dead, the son who feels compelled to always beat his last time, the chat-room arguments about whether a certified marathon course is actually the 'right' distance, and her own experience of running around cul-de-sac in order to finish her run on a round number.

Technology may also have the effect of regenerating problems by amplifying them rather than solving them. The example Sailors provides is the computer chip that is now attached to a runner's shoe in races in order to provide them with a more accurate race time. This technology was introduced as a solution to the problem that in large races it often took runners at the back of the field a significant amount of time to actually cross the start line, meaning the time that was displayed as they crossed the finish line wasn't an accurate reflection of the time it took them to run the distance. The chip was designed to overcome this problem; it records the exact time that each individual runner crosses the start line and the exact time that they cross the finish line, thus eliminating the 'wasted' time that runners experience getting to the start line once the race has begun. Yet it led to disagreements over results. For instance, a runner who was towards the back of the field when the race started could record a faster time than one who crossed the finish line before her. This technology regenerated problems because it raised new questions about how the winner was determined: the first over the finish line or the fastest time?

WHEN IS TECHNOLOGY UNACCEPTABLE IN SPORT?

Most of the technology given in the above examples is accepted in sport if it doesn't contravene the concept of fairness. If the impact of the technology on overall performance appears to be minimal, then it is often tolerated. Indeed, the notion of performance enhancement is one of the main criteria used by the World Anti-Doping Agency (WADA) to assess whether a particular technology is accepted.[7] WADA do not ban a method or substance purely because it enhances performance (otherwise any way in which performance was enhanced would be banned – and that would include practising and training) but use this criterion in conjunction with another two: whether it is harmful to health, and whether it contravenes the 'spirit of sport'. Technology is prohibited when it is judged to provide an unfair advantage.

The line between a fair advantage and an unfair one is often quite blurred. Sometimes judgements are based on how accessible and available the technology is; sometimes it is dependent on the perceptions of the public and media commentators. This was seen most recently in the sport of swimming, which had initially accepted the use of polyurethane costumes until 43 world records were broken at a single meet in Rome in 2009.[8] The degree of margin was so great between those who wore the costumes and those who didn't that it led to the sport being seen as a farce. Swimming no longer appeared to be about who swam the fastest but rather who had the best technology. This led the sport's governing body FINA to re-evaluate their permitted technical specifications and tighten their regulations.

Another related criterion that is used to determine the acceptability of technology is whether it will change the nature of the sport. For instance, if an athlete attempted to take part in the 100m sprint wearing jet-powered roller skates, it would be argued that the athlete is not sprinting. They might be competing in a different sport – jet-powered roller-racing – but not 100m sprinting. This formed part of the debate that surrounded Oscar Pistorius, aka 'The Blade Runner', when he wished to compete in able-bodied athletic competitions. The question that the authorities had to answer was whether the use of prosthetic lower limbs could be classified as sprinting or whether it was a different activity (such as the ability to use prosthetic devices as a means of transport without the use of 'normal' lower limbs). In order to resolve this issue, various biomechanical and physiological tests were carried out to ascertain whether it was essentially the same action with the same energy requirements. That the results were inconclusive demonstrates how difficult, and arbitrary, these judgements often are. The first set of tests concluded that the prosthetic limbs constituted an unfair advantage due to reduced drag and weight, while the second concluded that this was offset by increased energy expenditure to gain initial momentum. After appeal, Pistorius was cleared to run but as prosthetics develop further this issue is likely to be considered by the authorities again.

There is a range of other factors that influence decisions about whether technology is used in sport. One of the ongoing sagas in football is whether goal-line technology (GLT) should be implemented. In 2010, FIFA president Sepp Blatter outlined eight reasons why GLT should not be used in football. The reasons given by FIFA can be broadly separated into three categories: those dealing with the nature and value of the game of football; those related to issues of justice; and those concerned with the practical implementation of goal-line technology. While some of the reasons given were reasonable concerns about the accuracy and reliability of the technology, the other, less convincing, reasons were due to issues of history and convention. Blatter argued that one of the values of football was its simplicity and the fact that it is the same game throughout the world and at all levels. He also suggested that fans enjoyed debating controversial decisions and that this was an important element in its popularity. There was a further fear that implementing goal-line technology would lead to a 'slippery slope' whereby there would be calls to introduce other officiating technologies in order to regulate aspects such as fouls and off-sides. I have argued elsewhere[9] that these eight reasons are not sufficient to prohibit the introduction of goal-line technology but the scope of the reasons given by FIFA demonstrate the way in which decisions about technology are made.

WHAT MIGHT BE THE FUTURE OF TECHNOLOGY IN SPORT?

In one sense it is the governing bodies that determine the constitutive rules of their sport and ultimately decide whether a technology is accepted or not. Yet it needs to be remembered that sport is merely part of a wider society, which might hold differing attitudes towards particular technological innovations. Some commentators have argued that Pistorius was able to compete in the Olympics because he was seen to pose no threat to the nature of the sport. In other words, he was accepted as long as he didn't win. However, problems may arise if the technological development of prosthetic limbs reaches a point whereby athletes using them are outperforming 'able-bodied' athletes. However, enforcing a ban on their use in sport might not be as simple as changing the rules over polyurethane suits. Butryn's category of 'self technologies' represents the most problematic area for sport as human enhancement in other areas of life becomes the norm. It is already not unusual for people to undergo surgical operations to repair damaged tendons and ligaments or to undergo laser eye surgery to improve their vision. Further developments in prosthetic technology have connected biological tissue and nerve endings to prosthetic limbs to make them more controllable and to be used more 'naturally'. Arguably there could come a time when individuals replace limbs with 'cyborgnetic' upgrades and this will pose a real problem for the authorities when it comes to deciding what is fair and unfair competition. This is equally the case for advancements in genetic technologies, which will be used to both eliminate illness and disease and enhance human abilities outside of the sphere of sport. Currently, genetic technology is classified as a form of doping by WADA, but this ban might be impossible to enforce if athletes have undergone genetic therapy at a pre-embryonic state or whilst as a child, years before their interest in elite sport developed. These types of technology are the ones that will pose the most difficult problems for elite sport and for the notion of testing the 'natural' abilities of the human athlete.

The question of how future technology will affect the concept of elite sport then remains. There have been some compelling arguments that suggest that for sport to make sense in a new world of biotechnologies we will need to move away from the linear performance-based assessment of sport (exemplified by events such as running, throwing, jumping and swimming), towards a more aesthetic and experiential appreciation of sport. This shift in value represents what Sigmund Loland[10] defines as a 'thick theory' of sport, whereby our concern with the quantified sports record (such as the fastest time for the 100m sprint or the highest vertical jump) will diminish. The value of sport could instead be found in the creative freedom and possibilities that new technologies allow. This has arguably already been seen in the popularity of events such as snowboarding, wingsuit-flying and other 'extreme' sports in which new technologies have widened the possibilities for human achievement. That is not to say that our previous interest in traditional sports will necessarily wane; rather we may be forced to confront questions about the value of sport and what it is that sport is designed to test.

INDEPENDENT STUDY QUESTIONS:

- *What are the six types of technologies that are identified? Give an example for each.*
- *What are the criteria for determining whether technology should be accepted or prohibited in sport?*
- *To what extent can the concept of testing the 'natural' athlete still make sense in the light of technology?*
- *What does Loland mean by 'thick' and 'thin' theory of sport?*
- *To what extent do you agree with the idea that the value of the sports record will diminish with advances in technology?*

INTERVIEW WITH A PHILOSOPHER

R. SCOTT KRETCHMAR

Scott Kretchmar is one of the key figures credited with developing the philosophy of sport, particularly in North America, and has influenced many of his students to stay working in the field. A 'Graduate Essay Prize' is named in his honour and awarded annually at the International Association for the Philosophy of Sport conference. A tournament-level table-tennis player in his younger days, he still plays matches against his students but also has gravitated towards 'non-competitive' sports such as running and cycling. As a fan of Cleveland sports teams, he says he always roots for hapless underdogs. He is Professor of Exercise and Sport Science at Pennsylvania State University.

- *Can you give me a little bit on your background and what got you interested in the philosophy of sport?*

  - As an undergraduate at Oberlin College, I was originally studying religion. So questions about 'ultimate meanings' were always of interest to me. I also remember taking a class that emphasised a dualistic interpretation of human beings and recall being convinced intuitively that this was not right. Of course, I didn't have the vocabulary or the background to provide an alternative theory but it was a turning point in my undergraduate education. I wanted to study with people who would help me answer the mind–body question. I changed from religion to physical education and studied with Ruth Brunner at Oberlin. She was a disciple of Eleanor Metheny, then a professor at the University of Southern California. Not surprisingly, when I graduated a year later, I matriculated directly into the doctoral programme at USC to study with Metheny and Howard Slusher.

- *What do you think is the most interesting problem in the philosophy of sport?*

  - The role of play and games in the evolution of human intelligence. I've always been impressed with the kind of thinking required to negotiate the requirements imposed by sport and other forms of play. The fact that this intellection is predominantly non-verbal only adds to the mystery of the problem. My gut feeling is that verbalisation and other forms of 'high' intellectual activity have been overemphasised in coming to understand who we are and how we came to be this way. Of course, this also has important implications for axiology and the surprising hold that 'mere' games have on many people. But I think it all begins with an appreciation of the sophistication required for participation in games and an understanding of our evolutionary journey *vis-a-vis* play and games.

- *What book or paper has influenced you the most and why?*
  - The most important book is probably Suits' *Grasshopper*. I've used it in my graduate courses for years, and I always find something new in it. I think that's one of the characteristics of a classic. It is complex, rich, and open to a variety of interpretations. Interestingly, I've come to believe more and more that Suits missed the boat on a number of major issues, but that has not reduced my indebtedness to the book.

Key Readings

Kretchmar, R.S., 'From test to contest: An analysis of two kinds of counterpoint in sport', *Journal of the Philosophy of Sport*, 2(1) (1975), pp. 23–30.

Kretchmar, R.S., 'Pluralistic internalism', *Journal of the Philosophy of Sport*, 42(1) (2015), pp. 83–100.

Kretchmar, R.S., *Practical Philosophy of Sport and Physical Activity* (2nd ed.) (Leeds: Human Kinetics, 2005).

INTERVIEW WITH A PHILOSOPHER
MIKE McNAMEE

Mike McNamee is one of the most prolific authors in the philosophy of sport with over 20 edited collections and anthologies across a broad range of issues in sport, in addition to an extensive number of journal articles, book chapters, and sole or co-authored books. He was the Founding Chair of the British Association for the Philosophy of Sport and its official publication, *Sport, Ethics and Philosophy*, of which he is Editor-in-chief. He is currently Professor of Applied Ethics at Swansea University, UK.

- *Can you give me a little bit on your background and what got you interested in the philosophy of sport?*

  ○ My first degree was in Human Movement Studies and part of the course was philosophy and aesthetics, which I really enjoyed. I was also able to take courses in the Philosophy of Human Movement and Physical Education, which included visiting lectures by David Best, Graham McFee and Jim Parry and this cemented my interest. I later took postgraduate degrees in the Philosophy of Education, working with Jim Parry at Leeds for my MA and PhD, after which I took another MA, this time in Wittgensteinian Studies at Swansea. After my PhD in the early 1990s I was fortunate enough to get the first job in the UK that was specifically in the philosophy of sport, which was at what is now Cardiff Metropolitan University. By this time, degrees in Human Movement Studies were being replaced by Sports Science and Sports Studies degrees, of which philosophy of sport was seen as a foundational discipline in most, though not all, UK higher education institutions.

- *What do you think is the most interesting problem in the philosophy of sport?*

  ○ I think from an academic perspective there has been a recent tendency for the philosophy of sport to be more narrowly defined as only being about ethics. In some ways you might say that ethics has increased the exposure of the philosophy of sport but at the same time I fear this has limited its influence and scope. There seems to be a real need for philosophy, analytic philosophy in particular, to have more of an influence upon policy-making and this is much wider than ethical problems. We need to make sure that work done in the philosophy of sport makes the transition from academic publications to policy implementation and impacts on sports practices themselves.

- *What book or paper has influenced you the most and why?*
  - Mary Midgley's *Beast and Man: Roots of Human Nature.* I first read it while I was studying for my MA and I thought it was a beautiful work. It was philosophically sharp and clear and bit on to the analytical weaknesses of scientists such as Dawkins. It showed why philosophy mattered and why scientists needed philosophical underpinnings, and it included ideas of humans – by nature – as playing animals. Several years later I had a copy of the book in my bag while I was waiting for a train to leave at Oxford Station and I happened to see Mary Midgley walk past. I jumped off the train and ran to catch up with her to tell her how inspiring I had found her book. I later wrote to her to ask for some clarification about her interpretation of the Aristotelian concepts of *form* and *matter* in the book and asked whether she remembered me. 'Of course I remember you, Mike', she replied. 'It's not often one is accosted by one's philosophical fans!' We have corresponded ever since.

Key Readings

McNamee, M.J., *Sports, Virtues and Vices: Morality Plays* (Abingdon: Routledge, 2008).

McNamee, M.J., *Sports, Medicine, Ethics* (Abingdon: Routledge, 2014).

McNamee, M.J. and Morgan, W.J., *Handbook of the Philosophy of Sport* (Abingdon: Routledge, 2015).

SPORT, BODY AND MIND

8 IS THE BODY JUST ANOTHER TOOL IN SPORT?

Traditionally, and certainly in academia, the body is reduced to a secondary consideration. It is the mind or soul that is of primary importance and of greater worth; the body is often considered as an imperfect vehicle that contains these elements. Indeed, those who spend time perfecting their bodily appearance, whether through cosmetic surgery, steroids or pumping weights are often denigrated and chastised by the learned elite. Spending time on your body is considered vain and shallow, spending time developing your mind by contrast is not. Athletes, however, are caught between these two views. The picture of the 'dumb jock' is widely known, yet we also celebrate and worship our athletic heroes rather than our scientists or politicians. Physical excellence through athletic enterprise is considered praiseworthy because it requires the cultivation and discipline of both body and mind. Nevertheless, critics of modern elite and professional sport also point to the manner in which the body is instrumentalised, and the way in which athletes are treated as mere objects to be used in the quest to reach ever-increasing performance targets.

This chapter will consider how the human body is conceived, how this relates to sport and athletics, and the moral implications that follow. A brief outline of the ancient Greek conception of the body will be provided before considering the way Western culture separates body from mind as exemplified by Descartes' dualism, and how this leads to a technological attitude in sport. Finally, some Eastern approaches will be considered in order to provide a different perspective on the way in which the human body can be understood.

SHOULD WE SEPARATE BODY FROM MIND?

The common-sense notion that the body is substantially different to the soul (or mind) is an old idea. The phenomenological experience of being human seems to reinforce this duality; the body just *feels* separate to our thoughts and emotions. While there were varying conceptions of the body and its relation to the soul in ancient Greece, a common view was that the body and soul were inter-dependent and inseparable. While the body was the physical manifestation of a person, the soul was required in order to give it life. A body without a soul was simply a corpse. As such, physical education was a much more holistic practice; training the body was also considered to be training the soul. One of the functions of the ancient Greek gymnasiums was to cultivate *aretē* or excellence and it was through careful training of the body that the soul was able to develop. It is notable that Plato, one of the most renowned ancient Greek philosophers, and the first person to establish a higher-education academy, was also a competitive wrestler. The fact that the ancient Greeks viewed their Olympic athletes as gods shows that physical health and sporting prowess was as revered as intellectual ability.

It is from the writings of the French philosopher, René Descartes, that the divide between body and mind became most established. While the ancient Greeks believed that the soul could be perfected through the body, it was arguably Descartes' conception of a separate body and mind that led to the denigration of the body and its reduction in value. This dualistic view was reinforced and amplified by the later Christian and Catholic Church, which saw the body as an impure vessel that transported disease and was created by God to punish man for their sins.[1] This perception of the body has dominated in Western society for the past millennia and has influenced the way in which it has subsequently been treated.

Descartes' view stems from a starting position of extreme scepticism about knowledge. He began with the question, 'What can we be sure to know?', and noted it is theoretically possible to doubt the existence of the external world, including our body, since we could later find out that we were dreaming, hallucinating, or being manipulated by an evil demon to think that we exist in the world.[2] As such, if it is possible to doubt the existence of our body and the external world, is there anything we can't doubt? Descartes concluded that the only thing we could not doubt the existence of was the very thing that was doing the doubting, that is, the mind. This argument formulates part of Descartes' famous phrase 'cogito ergo sum': 'I think therefore I am'.

Descartes argument for the existence of both mind and body (dualism) can be articulated as follows:

P1: I can doubt the existence of all physical matter including the body.

P2: I cannot doubt the existence of a 'thing' (the 'I' or mind or soul) that is able to do this doubting.

C1: Therefore this thing that is doing the doubting cannot be physical.

C2: Therefore, there must be two separate types of things, the physical (body) and the immaterial mind/soul.

Although this argument may seem logically sound, there are problems with Descartes' reasoning; most notably, that just because it is possible to doubt the existence of one thing doesn't mean that it's not identical to another thing that you can't doubt. For instance, I could doubt the existence of a philosophy lecturer who is writing a book on the philosophy of sport and enjoys surfing and rugby. I can't, however, doubt the existence of myself. By Descartes' reasoning, these two things cannot therefore be the same thing, yet they are; they are just different ways of expressing it. Gilbert Ryle called Descartes' dualism 'the ghost in the machine'[3]: the mind is something that is immaterial and intangible and yet supposedly interacts and controls our body. How something that is non-physical interacts with something that is physical is a detail that Descartes was a little vague about. He speculates (without evidence) that it occurs in the pineal gland in the brain, which we now understand plays a role in hormone regulation. Nevertheless, Descartes' dualism has prevailed in much of Western thought and is still common today, and it is this perspective that influences many of our views on ethical issues, such as the use of drugs and genetic technology, as well as our attitude towards sport in general. While the 'Naturalistic' ancient Greek attitude towards the body was tempered by a more holistic and interrelated conception of the person that aimed for a balance between body and soul, the 'Anti-naturalistic' view, in contrast, sees the body as a means to an end, and a slave to the desires and ambitions of the mind.

IS THE BODY A MACHINE?

One reaction to the problem of mind/body interaction faced by Descartes was to take a different approach, and to view the body as a complex and purely physical machine. This view is called *reductive materialism* and can be associated with the growth, development and dominance of modern science from the Industrial Revolution of the late 18th century onwards. It can be seen most recently with developments in neuroscience in particular, whereby the human is reduced to a collection of neural networks and electro-chemical reactions in the brain. One of the criticisms of reductive materialism is that it leads to a 'technological attitude' whereby the human is viewed and treated as a machine to be honed and perfected through scientific intervention.

Ken Saltman suggests that bodybuilding – the sport (if it can be called such a thing) in which the product of labour is the body itself – is the essence of this attitude. Saltman argues that bodybuilders treat their bodies as an object to be manipulated and reworked to such an extent that they become 'more human than human so as to be unhuman'.[4] This is arguably also seen, although perhaps not to the same extent, in the treatment of the elite athlete whereby teams of biomechanists, physiologists, physiotherapists, nutritionists and psychologists measure and quantify every element of athletic performance in an attempt to improve its functioning. As Saltman notes, such practices highlight the fiction of 'natural' ideals in a contemporary culture that is dominated and driven by science and technology.

WHAT'S WRONG WITH THE TECHNOLOGICAL ATTITUDE?

The question that this raises is why such a conception of the body is necessarily a bad thing. After all, if the body is being perfected and athletic performances are getting better, is it not an example of the striving for excellence that the ancient Greeks so admired? One of the problems with such an attitude is that it falls foul of the deficient logic of ever-increasing progress criticised by Sigmund Loland[5] which was covered in Chapter 7. The other problem is that such an attitude is liable to leave the athlete, the person whose body is being perfected, out of the frame. Such a conception implicitly treats the athlete (by the sport scientists, the coaches, the management, the media, the public) as an object to be tested, consumed and disregarded at will. Often the athlete herself is complicit in this attitude and is guilty of bad faith in viewing herself as an object to be used in the attainment of sporting goals.[6] To use a Kantian analysis, treating a person in this way is to not give them the respect that they deserve by virtue of the fact that they are human subjects and not non-human objects.[7] Treating the body as a machine and using the metaphors 'break-down', 'repair' and 'enhance' neglects to acknowledge and develop the whole person that they are. The negative consequences can be seen in the ruthless way in which professional contracts are terminated or athletes are dropped from teams when they fail to perform or recover from injury, as well as the difficulties that athletes face upon retirement when their whole identity has been built upon their physical abilities and performances. Although scientific understandings of the body may produce knowledge about the make-up and functioning of the human, it cannot deal with the raw-sense experience of being human. Reducing our experience of watching sport (for instance) to 'merely' the firing of hundreds of thousands of neurons in our brain is not, and never can be, the *actual* experience of watching sport.

WHAT IS AN ALTERNATIVE CONCEPTION OF THE SPORTING BODY?

While the ancient Greeks viewed the body and mind in a more inter-dependent way to Descartes and his progenies, it is in the Eastern traditions where this distinction between body and mind completely dissolves. This can be seen most markedly in the disciplined and focused training found in martial arts, which aim to cultivate the unity and wisdom of the body/mind as a whole. Chinese and East Asian conceptions of the body are often so at odds with the dominant Cartesian Western model that it is difficult, if not impossible, to translate many of the ideas across. These understandings tend to focus upon the concepts of energy (*qi*) and blood flow (*xue*) rather than describe human functioning in biomechanical or physiological terms.[8] Eastern conceptions of knowledge are also more akin to that of wisdom in recognising correct movement to produce harmony with one's environment, rather than the Western understanding that is based upon logic, rationality and empiricism. Similarly, phenomenology is an (Western) approach that rejects a materialist and objective conception of the body and argues that a true understanding of the human can only come about through a rich, necessarily subjective and individualistic description of human experience itself.

The value of Eastern and phenomenological approaches to the body can be seen in the way in which they recognise and view the person as a whole that is also connected to the world around them. The discipline and commitment that is required to cultivate wisdom in Eastern philosophies is similar to the ancient Greek ideal of *aretē* and avoids the commodification of the body that is seen in much of Westernised professional and elite sport. Arguably, it is these conceptions of the body that provide a much more healthy and proper way to develop athletic potential than the technological approach that dominates much of modern sport today.

INDEPENDENT STUDY QUESTIONS:

- *To what extent is it useful to divide the human into body and mind, and what are its limitations?*
- *Is the metaphor 'body as machine' a helpful one in sport? What are its benefits and drawbacks?*
- *Which approach informs the way that most athletes are currently treated in sport and should this change? If so, how?*

9 IS SPORTING SUCCESS 'MIND OVER MATTER'?[1]

A generally accepted belief in sport (and perhaps also in life) is that winning is not merely about having skill, technique and fitness; it is about having the 'right mentality'. Success, so the cliché goes, is 10 per cent physical and 90 per cent mental. Naturally, this is an absurd exaggeration and succumbs to the dualistic fallacy outlined in the previous chapter. Nevertheless, it does raise some important questions about how we view success and the way in which we ascribe particular values in leading to it.

This chapter will consider the way success in sport is seen to be determined by mental ability. In particular, it will concentrate on the commonly used term in sport, 'mental toughness' and will highlight the assumptions inherent in this concept and the criticisms associated with it. Finally, it will argue that sporting success is not the same as sporting excellence and as such suggests that there are attributes other than 'mental toughness' that should be prioritised.

WHAT IS 'MENTAL TOUGHNESS'?

It is generally accepted that to compete in sport at the highest level, physical excellence is not enough. Athletes also require a set of mental attributes that enable the performance of complex physical skills under intense pressure and with a high degree of proficiency. As a result, these mental attributes are often valued above physical skill as the most fundamental contributor to elite sporting success. The mental characteristics associated with successful performances include attributes such as: self-confidence; concentration and focus; stress/anxiety-management; motivation and desire; resilience; and control. More recently, these characteristics have been replaced with the more general term 'mental toughness'. As the associated sporting literature is replete with promising young but ultimately failed athletes, it is mental toughness that is seen to hold the key to elite sporting success.

The problem however is that 'mental toughness' is difficult to define and, therefore, even more difficult to measure. It is an ambiguous term that is often articulated in a way that is self-referential and circular. This can be seen in many commonly used definitions of the term, such as this one:

> 'Mental toughness is having the natural or developed psychological edge
> that enables you to: generally, cope better than your opponents with

the many demands (competition, training, lifestyle) that sport places upon the performer; specifically, be more consistent and better than your opponents in remaining determined, focused, confident, and in control under pressure.'[2]

The issue with such definitions is that mental toughness is often defined by success. In effect, such definitions say, 'to be a successful athlete, you need to be mentally tough, and this can be measured by being successful'. The problem with this argument is it would be logically contradictory to find a successful athlete who was not mentally tough. Successful athletes are by definition 'more consistent and better than opponents' as Jones's definition stipulates. Equally, athletes who are not successful or who decide to give up on their goals will be labelled as 'mentally weak'. The issue with Jones' definition, as with many others, is that it has to turn to successful sporting performance as a measurement of 'mental toughness' when at the same time it suggests that success is determined by it. This also raises an epistemological problem, since the attributes of mental toughness are only applied after success has been achieved. The narrative of sporting success and failure means an athlete who demonstrates, for instance, 'unshakeable self-belief' but who ultimately fails in her sporting goal is considered self-deluded or arrogant, while an athlete who seems unconvinced about her own ability is seen as possessing an inner confidence and determination of which they were consciously unaware.

CAN MENTAL TOUGHNESS BE MEASURED?

One of the problems with psychological phenomena is it is immaterial; that is, it is not something that has a physical quality that can be touched, weighed or manipulated like other objects. As such, inferences and assumptions have to be made as to what it is and whether it is present. One way that psychologists do this is to create psychometric questionnaires that attempt to measure the consistency of responses to questions that are judged to be relevant to the phenomena they are testing. So questionnaires about mental toughness will ask about ambition to succeed, responses to failure, control over the future, and confidence in one's abilities; questions that psychologists believe to be indicators of mental toughness. Yet as in all questionnaires that rely upon self-reporting, there is an assumption that answers to these questions will measure this psychological property and that the responses that are given are accurate and truthful. The latter problem can be mitigated to a degree by using a variety of similar questions, as the more consistent a person is in their responses, the more it is judged their results can be trusted. Yet the assumption about what questions will demonstrate mental toughness is dependent upon a consensus about the concept itself; a problem that even those at the centre of the field recognise:

'Confusion over how to conceptualise and operationalise mental toughness has discouraged a common language among researchers, thereby the construct has a different meaning to different people. Consequently, the conceptual and practical implications differ as a function of the operationalisation used.'[3]

The range of characteristics and attributes that are cited as evidence of 'mental toughness' are so broad that they are arguably of little worth, especially when it comes to measuring or quantifying it. As such, what this thing called 'mental toughness' actually is, and whether there is any point in attempting to measure it, still remains unresolved.

IS MENTAL TOUGHNESS AN ELITIST IDEAL?

One of the main criticisms of 'mental toughness' is that it is a pseudo-scientific construction – that is, it appears to be a scientific and measurable concept when it is not. It is characterised by romantic notions of sporting idealism, elitist values, and metaphorical images of triumph and victory. One of the common elements of mental toughness is an 'unshakeable self-belief' that enables the overcoming of obstacles. Yet, sport is set up in such a way that only a small number of people are able to overcome obstacles (usually in the form of other competitors) and succeed to the elite level since it is winning that epitomises success. As such, mental toughness is an elitist quality, unattainable to the majority.

The metaphor of mental toughness as an 'unshakeable object' that cannot be moved or displaced, alongside the phenomenal and almost mystical nature of these qualities as 'unbelievable' or 'insatiable', work to create a very specific image of the ideal sporting hero. This romanticised and idealised portrait of the doggedly determined individual who is able to rise up and overcome anything that is thrown at her is perhaps best captured by the Hollywood-style fantasy that can be called the 'Hollywood hero athlete'. An example is boxer Rocky Balboa in the popular *Rocky* series of films. After being initially defeated by his rival, Rocky undergoes hours of intense, arduous training during which his trainer pushes him to his physical, mental, and emotional limits. During a gruelling and intense rematch, Rocky calls upon all the strength he can muster to defeat his rival in the final round and achieve ultimate success. The Hollywood saga of the gritty underdog whose perseverance leads to eventual glory connects with a number of sporting values that are shared in the conceptualisation of mental toughness. In the process, an ideal is created to which all potential athletes can aspire. The values underpinning this ideal include complete dedication, unwavering commitment to the goal, and a work ethic unmatched by any of one's competitors. In addition, the ability to rise up and overcome adversity features prominently in both the Hollywood hero narrative, and the mental toughness ideal. Descriptions of mental toughness provided in the sports psychology literature serve to reinforce the power and value of the Hollywood hero athlete as the ideal image for all athletes to aspire to. Yet it also feeds into a wider neo-liberal, elitist narrative. As Seán Crosson notes in his analysis of the Hollywood sports film, placing the emphasis of sporting success onto an individual's mental characteristics and virtue removes the responsibility for wider social mobility and success from others:

> 'It is a tiny minority of individuals in American society – and indeed in societies around the world – who ever manage to enjoy professional success through sport. There are even fewer who manage to overcome underprivileged and challenging circumstances to do so. However, in sports film after sports film, we encounter individuals who manage to achieve both these goals... sports films suggest that through sport and individual effort the American Dream of upward social mobility and success can be achieved. It is a double lie.'[4]

The concept of mental toughness therefore demands complicity with particular elitist values and sporting ideals. In the current climate of elite 'do-or-die' sport, athletes are expected to demonstrate their mental strength as total commitment to absolute success and those who do not achieve success are labelled as weak. Equally, those who are perceived to be weak or lacking in mental toughness may also be considered as not worthy of success. 'Mentally weak' athletes are derided and viewed with contempt or a lack of respect. Compare, for example, the case of US gymnast Kerri Strug with that of NBA basketball star Tracy McGrady. At the 1996 Atlanta Olympics under Romanian coach Béla Károlyi, Strug needed to perform one final vault routine after badly injuring her ankle on a previous attempt if she was to defeat the Russians and secure team gold for the United States. Her coach, Károlyi, persuaded her to do so: she landed her final vault before collapsing on to her knees. Strug was applauded by the media and commentators for her mental toughness and courage and was celebrated by the American public. In contrast, Tracy McGrady was heavily criticised by the American media who labelled him 'soft' after struggling to come back from a knee injury.[5] McGrady's character and mental toughness were called into question, supposedly because he was unwilling to 'play through the pain'. The notion that one should 'give everything' to succeed in sport dominates. The judgement made by McGrady that he simply did not want to risk re-injury and wished to prioritise other aspects of his life over sport was overlooked. Equally, a different interpretation of Strug is that she was mentally weak and allowed herself to be bullied by her coach. The belief that mentally tough athletes should be 'pushing back the boundaries of physical and emotional pain, while still maintaining technique and effort under distress'[6] ignores wider questions about what is ultimately of value and important in life and how sport fits into this.

HOW CAN THE QUALITIES ASSOCIATED WITH MENTAL TOUGHNESS BE BETTER DESCRIBED?

While an analytic definition of mental toughness is almost impossible to achieve, there are qualities, characteristics and virtues to which it alludes, such as tenacity, resilience and determination. Such qualities are commended in Aristotle's pentathlete for example. Heather Reid argues that Aristotle's pentathlete represents three ethical values: aspiring to excellence by cultivating a habit of training for physical fitness and skill, possessing a sense of balance and moderation, and appreciating friendship and acknowledging service to one's community.[7] Many of the qualities associated with mental toughness (for instance, a strong sense of self-belief, resilience, focused concentration, courage and persistence in the face of adversity, and powerful intrinsic motivation) represent those advocated by Aristotle's pentathlete and can be seen to contribute to human excellence. The problem arises when such qualities are regarded as avenues to ultimate success and formulated into a pseudo-scientific and measurable concept that can be used by sports psychologists and coaches. It is this association with success that transforms mental toughness from an expression of human excellence into an elitist ideal; a product of a society that demands winners and adulates successful heroes. The concept of mental toughness has been criticised for its overemphasis upon winning and focus upon measurable success.[8] Yet the qualities often associated with the concept of mental toughness are of value in and of themselves, independent of their association with winning. The mental excellences that are said to constitute mental toughness should be seen as ends in themselves, rather than means to an end. Unfortunately, when it comes to elite-level sport, sports psychology seems to have forgotten the notion of a 'mastery-oriented motivational climate', in which athletes are praised for effort and determination and for the mastery of various sporting skills rather than for achieving objective success and superiority.[9] Arguably, it is the experience of excellence that counts, not whether the experience will lead to ultimate sporting victory. Focusing upon the qualities associated with mental toughness rather than the elusive concept itself returns the value of sport to the experience of competing rather than on success that is measurable by victory over others.

When the concept of mental toughness, and its associated features, is seen as the key to ultimate success in sport and in wider life, it risks valuing success itself rather than the qualities and virtues that may (or may not) lead to it. Shifting the focus back on to the development of a virtuous soul and the internal goods associated with sport is a way of valuing sporting excellence without idolising elitism and those external goods that are available to a limited few. As Aristotle's pentathlete demonstrates, excellence is not merely possessing physical skill and ability, nor is it about having a particular 'mental attitude'; rather it is a combination of a variety of physical, mental and 'spiritual' factors that work together as a whole.[10]

INDEPENDENT STUDY QUESTIONS:

- What are the problems with attempting to define and measure 'mental toughness'?
- How do Hollywood films in particular represent mental toughness and how accurate is this depiction?
- What is meant by the 'Hollywood Hero' athlete and how does the narrative of sporting success affect the way in which mental toughness is ascribed?
- What mental qualities should sports psychologists and coaches focus upon and how do these relate to success and excellence in sport?

10 IS IT RIGHT TO SEPARATE SPORT ACCORDING TO SEX?

WHAT IS 'THE OTHER' IN SPORT? (PRELIMINARIES)

The next three chapters are focused upon sex, gender and disability in sport and all of these can be included under the umbrella term 'the Other'. 'The Other' refers to a concept that arose predominantly from Existential and Continental philosophy and refers to those that are outside the boundaries of what is considered 'the norm' or the 'prevailing' or 'dominant' view. The 'normal' conception of sport is one that is carried out by able-bodied, heterosexual males, and so 'the Other' refers to conceptions that differ from this. In general conversation 'the Other' is distinguished from 'the norm' by using additional descriptive labels; so while the England men's team is just referred to as 'the England football team', and the men's world cup is just 'the World Cup', all women's sport is given the prefix 'women' or 'ladies' such as 'England *Ladies* football team' or '*Women's* World Cup'.

The evolution of sport in many ways mirrors that of society. That is, sport was created by men for men, whether that was at the ancient Olympiad or Gladiatorial Games which demonstrated the power, strength and speed of the strongest and fittest; the hunts organised by rich male aristocrats who had the liberty and resources to go out shooting for fun; or the formation of sports teams from the factory floor brought about by the Industrial Revolution. Throughout history 'the Other' (i.e. those who are not able-bodied, white, heterosexual men) have been excluded from sport as they have from wider society in general.

In some respects, it is understandable how sport has developed in this way, as it was generally men who were able to carry out the greatest physical performances, and who wielded the most power in society. The few people who had disabilities or who were women that could carry out impressive athletic feats were reduced to appearing as acts in circus freak shows: they really were 'the Other' in this respect. Yet as society has become increasingly democratised, and good arguments have been made for the inclusion of all in all areas of public life, the sporting world has struggled to keep up. As the standard conception of elite sport is an able-bodied and male one, problems are caused when those who do not fit this mould challenge it. The speculation and resistance faced by athletes such as Oscar Pistorius and Caster Semenya for their incredible sporting performances suggest that there is a limit to how good female or disabled athletes can be. If they surpass this, then they are considered to be cheating: either by using unfair prosthetic blades, or by not being a 'true' woman. In contrast, elite male athletes, such as Usain Bolt and Michael Phelps do not face the same scrutiny over similar spectacular performances; instead, they are celebrated and held up as 'super-men' for pushing the boundaries of human ability and achievement.[1]

The problem for sport is in ensuring fairness but also in providing opportunities for all. If sporting competitions were not separated into different sex or ability categories, then arguably there would be very few, if any, elite female or disabled athletes, as the statistics point to the average abled-bodied male being faster and stronger than the average person with a disability or the average female. This is often an argument that is used in favour of separating sport according to sex and (dis)ability. Nevertheless, advances in technology and greater opportunities for women and those with disabilities challenge the dominant model of elite men's able-bodied sport. The result of this is that sporting authorities are forced to reassess the concept of fair competition in sport in order to justify the ways in which sport is segregated on the basis of sex and (dis)ability.

While this chapter will consider philosophical questions about the way in which sport is segregated according to sex, the following chapter will address some of the consequences of this in relation to transgender participation in sport. Chapter 12 will consider philosophical and ethical issues related to the concept of elite disability sport.

WHY IS SPORT SEPARATED ON THE BASIS OF SEX?

As Tännsjö argues in his paper 'Against Sexual Discrimination in Sports'[2], while sexual discrimination is generally objectionable in most areas of Western life, within sport it is accepted and rarely, if ever, questioned. The opportunities for women to participate in sport are intrinsically linked with the opportunities and perception of women in history generally. Women were given the right to vote later than men, were provided with far fewer opportunities for education than men, and until recently were considered property of their husbands; which meant that rape and domestic violence against women were an accepted part of marital relationships. While many would argue that women still face violence and disadvantage today, the London Olympic Games in 2012 was the first Games in which every participating country brought at least one female athlete. In this context, it is unsurprising that women in sport have been marginalised. The history of women's participation in sport is relatively sparse. In the ancient Greek Olympics, women were barred from even spectating, let alone participating, due to the nakedness of the male competitors. When the Olympics were revived in 1896, women again were denied a place on the grounds that it was inappropriate for them to participate in demanding physical activity for their fragile bodies – despite the fact that most women carried out extremely physically demanding tasks in their daily household life. It was the Great War of 1914–1918 that gave some women their first opportunity to participate in sport and allowed them to start to develop their potential. With the absence of men, who were fighting and dying, women's sport filled the gap for sporting entertainment. Indeed, women's football was reportedly attracting tens of thousands of spectators per game. This growth and acceptance of women's sport didn't last, however, as the Football Association (FA) banned women playing on their grounds (which included many public parks) from 1922 until 1972. These practical and psychological barriers, which were replicated in the majority of sports (with perhaps the exception of tennis and equestrian events that were generally the preserve of the rich, who had far greater leisure opportunities) meant that women's sporting progress was stunted, while men continued to develop and professionalise. All of this provides some evidence for why women's technical proficiency in sport lags behind that of men; they simply haven't had the same opportunities to grow and develop and thus expectations about what they are able to achieve have been so much lower.

There are, however, a few contrasting differences between women's sport during the 20th century in the UK and USA, and sport at the same time in the Communist USSR and East Germany. Under the Communist regime, women were given far greater opportunities to participate in sport as Communist ideology presented all citizens as being equal (even if this was not the case in reality). As such, Soviet and East German women dominated sport in many Olympic events between the post-war period of 1945 and the fall of Communism in the late 1980s. Although it was subsequently discovered that there were many questionable and illegal ethical practices going on in these countries (such as the use of doping methods and extreme training regimes), it is important to note that many of these stories, and the over-arching anti-Communist narrative, were magnified and used as political tools in the Cold War rhetoric by the USA and their allies in order to demonise these women, many of whom did not conform to Western notions of 'femininity'.

Nevertheless, despite Communist ideology providing greater opportunities for women's sport, segregation on the grounds of sex was still assumed and unquestioned in the same way it is in the rest of the world. As sexual discrimination has been gradually eradicated in other areas of life, such as education, business, politics and the military, it begs the question: why is it so widely accepted in sport?

WHAT ARE THE ARGUMENTS FOR SEX DISCRIMINATION IN SPORT?

Tännsjö's essay outlines the four main arguments used in defence of segregated sports:

1. Sex categories in sport have the same function as weight categories in that they are a practical way to ensure good and fair competition.
2. Sex categories in sport protect women (and men) from violent outbursts as men find it difficult to control their emotions if their pride is dented by a superior woman.

3. Female sports showcase different (feminine) values and if these sports were to become obsolete, so would the values they represent.

4. Sex categories in sport allow women a chance of winning as unsegregated sport would be dominated by men; women would consequently become disillusioned and give up participating.

Tännsjö responds to these arguments by taking each one in turn. On the first, he agrees that although it might generally be the case that most men are bigger/ stronger/faster than most women, this is not always the case. It is therefore unfair to those women who are able to compete with men on grounds of power/strength/ speed to be prohibited from doing so simply because they are classified as female. Tännsjö asks whether categorising someone according to their sex is really the same as categorising according to weight. Weight categories are used in some sports, particularly combat sports and martial arts in order to try to ensure the sport is fair and the competition is good. Weight in these sports, therefore, is a *relevant* category in determining the outcome. Sex, according to Tännsjö, is not. Despite the statistical generalisations which suggest that *on average* men will outperform women in sport, there will be some women who will be stronger, fitter, faster or more talented than most men and therefore they should not be prevented from participating at the level which enables them to reach their potential.

One response to Tännsjö's argument is to maintain that sex *is* a relevant category since statistically most men outperform most women in the same way that most heavyweight boxers would beat most lightweight boxers. As most men have a higher proportion of muscle mass compared to most women, and most women have a higher proportion of body fat compared to most men, discrimination on weight or height alone is insufficient, rather it is the body composition that is important, and this can generally be determined by sex.

Tännsjö's second argument is a rather bizarre one. It suggests that sex segregation should occur for reasons of mutual safety. Nevertheless, perhaps there is a degree of merit in the claim that men are threatened by talented women. As has already been noted, the FA banned women's football in the UK following its popularity in the early 20th century, and Coggon *et al.* note the sudden sex segregation of Olympic skeet shooting after a women won gold.[3] Tännsjö himself also admits to the anger and humiliation he feels if he is beaten by a woman in sport. His solution is to suggest that men should be heavily penalised if they are over-aggressive as a consequence. He suggests that perpetrators are issued with 'red cards' and ejected from the competition. But this seems no different to the way that sport is currently policed. If a rugby player retaliates after a strong (but legal) tackle by punching his opponent, he will be appropriately sanctioned. All that Tännsjö seems to be saying is that men need to learn to control their tempers when they are fairly beaten by a woman. Managing one's emotions in sport is necessary for all competitors (male or female) and is already covered by the rules of the sport through regulations and penalties.

Tännsjö later suggests that perhaps sports should be modified to reduce the opportunities men have to be aggressive, so they test 'feminine' rather than 'masculine' qualities. This is similar to the points he makes when dealing with the third argument; that 'female' sports represent particular 'feminine' qualities.

This argument presupposes that there are 'feminine' sports that naturally suit women, and 'masculine' sports that naturally suit men. Although Tännsjö agrees that such a description is far too simplistic and degrading to both men and women, he does accept there may be a grain of truth in it. The 'genuine' and 'unique' female qualities he points to are 'inventiveness, sensibility, cooperation, strategy, playfulness, [and] wit'[4] and he recommends changing sport to ensure these qualities are a more relevant factor in determining outcome. Tännsjö suggests that sports should reflect a pluralism of values and qualities. The problem, however, is that the notion of 'masculinity' and 'femininity' is bound up in other wider sociological and cultural issues. Changing sports so that they focus less on pure physical qualities such as strength, speed and endurance, and more on Tännsjö's 'feminine' qualities may be an ideological step too far, as those 'masculine' qualities are exactly the qualities that sport has evolved to test. Nevertheless, as some spectators of sport are pointing out, in the same way that some prefer watching lower-weight boxers to heavyweights, women's sport has the potential to be a better example of technical expertise, agility and balance and therefore be of aesthetic merit, as they compensate for the overall lack of speed, power and strength with other qualities.

The final argument in favour of sexual discrimination in sport seems to be the most forceful. Since statistically most men will beat most women it therefore follows that most winners of sporting competitions, if mixed, would be men. The assumption that is therefore made is that as a consequence many women will give up participating at all. There is evidence to suggest that girls are put off sport at school when it is a mixed-sex activity and dominated by boys, but there are also wider cultural factors and expectations that affect female participation. Tännsjö points to other areas of life that are dominated by men (such as business, science and politics) and notes there are no calls to create women-only Parliaments or academic departments. Instead, the processes and governance of institutions are changed in order to allow women to succeed in these positions. The same, Tännsjö argues, should be done in sport:

> 'If such obstacles are eliminated, if new weight and length classes are introduced in many sports, if the rules are changed so as to render it impossible for aggressive athletes to punish their competitors, and if severe punishments are introduced for violations of the rules, then women can actually compete successfully and safely with men in many sports.'[5]

There are sports in which women are competing on a par with men, such as equestrian events, sailing and some ultra-endurance races, and this seems to support Tännsjö's argument that sex segregation in sport is not a necessity. However, if all sports became mixed-sex competitions it is likely that those who would dissent most would be elite female athletes. The sports in which women would be least successful when competing with men are those ones that rely on strength and speed and so their (already small) public platform and profile would disappear completely as they slipped down the performance rankings. Consider the 100m sprint for example. The current men's world record is 9.58 seconds while the women's is 10.49 seconds.[6] A woman running at the female world record-speed would only just get past the preliminary stages of most men's events and would be unlikely to reach any final competition. Analysis across a range of running and swimming races suggests that the record speeds for women's events are currently about 10 per cent slower than those of men, which indicates that there is a significant number of men whose performances are better than those of the best women. This would similarly be the case for most other sports that rely on strength and speed, such as football, hockey and rugby; very few, if any, women would be able to compete at the elite level. If sports were non-segregated then arguably women at the elite level would be even more invisible than they are today. Nevertheless, just because this is a reason for segregation, it does not automatically follow that segregation should occur. It would be akin to arguing that because sprinting is dominated by those of Afro-Caribbean descent, competitions should be segregated on race and skin colour; an argument that few would be willing to make. Perhaps the most relevant parallel in this discussion is the fact that many countries are now adjusting their policies regarding women fighting on the front line. Similar reasons were given for preventing women taking up these military positions, yet policies were changed on the basis that if (exceptional) women were able to reach the necessary standards required to perform these roles, then they should be given the opportunity to do so. Generalisations based upon the average woman are not sufficient to exclude exceptional ones.

This chapter has highlighted some of the problems associated with separating sport according to sex. There are various reasons given supporting the segregation of sport, with the most prominent relating to generalisations about the differences in the abilities of men and women. Similar generalisations were made about the ability of women in other fields, such as science, business and, more recently, the military, and yet there are women who, given the opportunity, have succeeded alongside men. Arguably, the greatest factors in the perceptions of women's abilities are ones that are cultural and historical. Sport is one of the most conservative spheres of human activity and perhaps that is why it is one of the last areas of society where sexual discrimination is generally accepted without question.

INDEPENDENT STUDY QUESTIONS

- To what extent does the term 'the Other' help in understanding the history and development of sport?
- Which of Tännsjö's reasons for sex segregation seems to be most and/or least persuasive and why?
- To what extent is it reasonable to compare the changes to front-line military duty with sex segregation in sport?
- Do you think it is likely that sport in the future will see a reduction in sex segregation? Explain your answer.

11 DOES SPORT DISCRIMINATE AGAINST TRANS*¹ ATHLETES?

The previous chapter considered the arguments in support of segregating sport according to sex; however, this was based on the assumption that everyone can be classified according to two binary categories: 'male' or 'female'. This consequence of such an assumption means that those who do not 'fit' this binary distinction, or who do not or ascribe themselves to one of these categories are either given little opportunity to participate in sport, or are subject to discrimination and abuse. This chapter will consider the concepts of sex and gender in more detail and discuss the ways in which sport restricts opportunities for those who do not fall into binary norms.

WHAT IS MEANT BY 'MALE' AND 'FEMALE'?

This might seem to be an obvious and trivial question as the classification of sex is the first description given to a newborn baby; as evidenced by the customary question, 'Is it a boy or a girl?' For the majority of cases, sex is determined by an examination of the external sex organs, yet this method isn't always sufficient. Other methods of determining sex are: internal genitalia (e.g. womb, ovaries), chromosomes (e.g. XX or XY), and hormone levels. This illustrates that sex is more complex than a simple distinction between 'male' and 'female'. There are cases whereby someone might have female sex organs and male hormone levels, or XXY chromosomes, or undeveloped testes. As such, although the term 'sex' usually refers to 'male' or 'female', this binary biological classification isn't always straightforward. As a more helpful and flexible alternative, the term 'gender' refers to the sex that an individual most identifies with. So while an individual may be born with particular male sex organs, they may wish to identify themselves as female as they feel more comfortable with the 'feminine' qualities and characteristics associated with females. Equally, an individual may identify themselves as having no gender, a mix of both genders, or a gender that changes over time. A person's gender may be expressed in different ways, so they may look male but act in ways that aren't considered to be 'masculine' and vice-versa (sexuality is something different again and refers to sexual attraction). All of this creates problems for sport, which has been defined along very traditional and distinct lines: it is designed to demonstrate and test the 'masculine' qualities of men. So men with 'feminine' interests and characteristics have no place in sport whilst women are often expected to compensate for their 'masculine' interest in sport by emphasising their femininity in other ways (through hair, make-up or glamorous photo shoots) or risk being labelled a 'lesbian' or a 'gender-freak'.

One sport that challenges the traditional conception of sport and allows individuals to play with their gender expression is Roller Derby. Roller Derby is effectively a team sport on roller skates, whereby competitors race each other round a track and an element of contact and physical aggression is allowed. It is a sport that was created by women for women (or rather, 'by the skaters for the skaters') and has been argued to reshape ideas about women, femininity, and sport.[2] One of the values of Roller Derby is the theatrical construction of names and personas. Pam Sailors argues that this allows competitors to play with the traditional binary conception of gender by portraying a mixture of hyper-femininity and hyper-masculinity at the same time. Critics of this interpretation have suggested that participants may be subject to a false consciousness; in that they falsely believe that they are empowered while they are still under the power of (typically male) others. This is an accusation that Sailors believes is true for members of the Lingerie Football League (a female American Football league in which players accentuate their 'femininity' by, as the title suggests, wearing minimal clothing for the benefit of predominantly male spectators) but one that is not applicable to Roller Derby whose audience and *raison-d'être* is different. Sailors warns however, that Roller Derby's value lies precisely with the fact that it is *not* the same as other sex-delineated sports and states, 'If roller derby becomes a sport with leagues for men and women, comparable to existing sports, it will lose one of its unique aspects that empowers women.'[3]

With the exception of a few sports such as Roller Derby, women tied to the concept of 'femininity' have had to fight long battles to be able to participate, and be accepted, into the masculine world of sport. One of the consequences of the binary categorisation of 'male' and 'female' is that sport has also been segregated along these lines.

WHAT'S WRONG WITH SEX TESTING IN SPORT?

One of the consequences of separating sport along lines of sex is that it causes problems for any individual who is perceived to fall outside the clear binary categories of 'male' and 'female'. As highlighted at the beginning of Chapter 10, this is primarily a problem for successful female athletes as they challenge the traditional norms of sporting competition and notions of 'femininity'. As such, women in sport have generally had to prove their femininity in one way or another, either through ensuring their achievements do not surpass expectations or through emphasising other aspects, such as their looks or demeanour. Women who do neither of these often find themselves and their sex challenged. In essence, exceptional performances by women in sport are often seen as being 'too good for a woman'.

Sex (often wrongly called 'gender') testing was first officially made mandatory in 1950 before the European Athletic Championships, following years of ongoing speculation and accusations that men were entering women's athletic events. Sex testing continued until the IAAF stopped testing in 1991 and the IOC ended it in 2000. However, since this time there have been ongoing tests for suspected individuals and the IAAF announced in 2012 that they would like to bring back wider sex testing.

Early testing generally involved external examination of genitalia but later tests were conducted in other ways, such as examining chromosomes, genes and testosterone levels. However, as was noted at the beginning of this chapter, sex testing is conceptually problematic because a clear distinction between male and female cannot always be made. The reason that the methods of sex testing have had to evolve is that there are always ambiguous cases and, due to the way sex is defined and constructed, there is never going to be one test that will provide a definitive answer in all cases. Sex testing is also ethically concerning. That sex and gender are core components of an individual's identity means that any questions raised about this will undoubtedly be of a sensitive nature. The IAAF's treatment of Caster Semenya in the 2009 World Athletics Championships demonstrated a clear lack of respect for the individual and an insensitivity to the issue. Without Semenya's awareness or consent, the IAAF publicly announced they were going to verify her sex. The point to make here is the inequity between the treatment of men and the treatment of women. Sex testing always happens to women. It was solely women who were subject to the humiliating and degrading process of the 'nude parades' in the 1960s and 1970s (though a notable exception was made for HRH Princess Anne who competed for Great Britain in the 1976 Olympics) and it is only women who have had their sex questioned. That there have been relatively few, if any, clear-cut cases of a man pretending to be a woman in order to win an athletic competition suggests that the conceptual, practical and ethical problems of conducting sex tests far outweigh any benefits.

HOW DOES SPORT ACCOMMODATE TRANSSEXUAL ATHLETES?

That sport is generally segregated on grounds of sex is also problematic for those who are intersex, transsexual or transgender. While intersex individuals may not fall biologically into a 'male' or 'female' category, trans* individuals may have a particular biological makeup but wish to live as the opposite gender. Additionally, they may or may not want to undergo sex reassignment to change their biology. In 2004, government legislation was passed to prohibit discrimination against transsexuals and or transgender persons. This created difficulties for sporting bodies, however, who were often unsure how to ensure that transsexuals were not subject to discrimination and were provided opportunities to participate in sport. In response, the Department for Culture, Media and Sport (DCMS) issued guidelines addressing this matter and noted the concerns expressed by sporting bodies.[4] The DCMS agreed with sports bodies that people who had undertaken gender reassignment did not always have the automatic right to participate in sport for the gender that they had acquired. They provided three conditions under which discrimination against trans* athletes would be acceptable:

1. that decisions on these issues are made by the relevant governing body responsible for regulating the participation of persons as competitors, and;
2. that the sport concerned is one where the physical strength, stamina or physique of average persons of one gender would put them at a disadvantage to average persons of the other gender; and
3. that the prohibition or restriction is necessary to secure fair competition or the safety of competitors (including the safety of transsexual competitors).

Ultimately, decisions about whether individuals are eligible to compete is left up to the individual governing body but the DCMS guidelines make it clear that no discrimination should take place unless there is a clear need as set out by the conditions, and that it must only apply to competitors and not those involved in another capacity, e.g. officiating, managing or coaching. The DCMS recognise that this is a sensitive area and should be approached as such by taking into account the views of the trans* community and individuals affected. The DCMS document also notes that there may be issues with sex testing at the elite level in some sports. If sex tests are deemed necessary by the governing body, then the DCMS argues that this should be determined by the sex assigned at birth rather than by other means, such as physical examination.

Nevertheless, as noted out by Coggon, Hammond and Holm[5], problems may occur when there is a disparity between the guidance and the law set out by governments or the policy of sporting authorities. For instance, there was a conflict between the guidelines given by the DCMS and the IOC[6] that could have caused potential problems at the London Olympics. The IOC guidance for pre-pubescent and post-pubescent reassignment differed. It stated that any person undergoing gender reassignment before puberty should be allowed to compete in sport as that gender without further barriers or investigation. Those undergoing reassignment after puberty were only eligible to compete in a different gender to that assigned at birth provided that:

- surgical anatomical changes have been completed, including external genitalia changes and gonadectomy (the surgical removal of the testes or ovaries);
- legal recognition of the acquired gender has been conferred by the appropriate official authorities;

- hormonal therapy appropriate to the acquired gender has been administered in a verifiable manner and for a sufficient length of time to minimise gender-related advantages in sport competitions;
- eligibility occurs no less than two years after gonadectomy;
- a confidential case-by-case evaluation is provided.

As Coggon, Hammond and Holm note, the IOC guidelines provided an additional criterion absent from the DCMS document, which states that surgery (gonadectomy) must have been undertaken at least two years previously. British law, however, does not require such surgery before an individual is able to be legally recognised as being their acquired gender. The DCMS guidelines state that all sporting bodies must abide by the legal requirements of the UK Gender Recognition Act, but as the IOC requirements for competition were stricter than those required by UK law, an appeal could have been made to the European Court of Human Rights in order to contest the IOC ruling.

Coggon, Hammond and Holm conclude that the UK guidelines are appropriate for sports for which it is deemed sex does not provide an advantage (e.g. sailing, shooting, equestrian events, lawn bowls, etc.) and in these cases the sporting authorities should accept whatever sex is given by the individual participants. However, for sports that are affected by sex-related differences (e.g. contact sports, weightlifting, athletics, etc.), Coggon et al. argue that the IOC is correct in its attempt to balance the rights of the individual with wider considerations of fairness. Nevertheless, they note that the IOC's criterion relating to surgery was too strict. Although there is evidence to suggest that differences in athletic performance are related to variations in hormone levels (which are affected by gonadectomy) this does not extend to other sex-assignment surgery, which may make no difference to athletic performance. The criterion should instead be based on the best scientific evidence available for sex differences in performance; which, as noted, is immensely difficult due to the range of individual differences within the sexes. In 2015, the IOC significantly changed its guidelines for the eligibility of trans* athletes in competition. 'Female' to 'male' athletes would face no restriction on competition in any sport whilst 'male' to 'female' athletes must demonstrate a specified testosterone level for 12 months prior to competition. The IOC's change in guidelines was in part a recognition that "surgical anatomical changes as a pre-condition to particpation [in sport] is not necessary to preserve fair copetition and may be inconsistent with developing legislation and notions of human rights." The most important conclusion is that individuals ought to be treated with sensitivity and respect and the barriers and prejudices they face in all aspects of their lives should be recognised. While sport needs to be constructed fairly it also needs to respond progressively to the limitations and idiosyncrasies that are a result of history and culture rather than being rationally determined.

The question about sex segregation in sports is a complex one that needs to be understood in the context of wider issues about the way we construct and conceive of sex and gender differences in society. Ultimately, Tännsjö may have been right when he concluded that sports will have to evolve and adapt in order to ensure a greater level of fairness and inclusivity, and to overcome the conceptual and ethical problems of gender verification and sex testing.[7] It may be that this change will occur naturally and will be related to developments in technology and the ways in which it will be further integrated with the human body. Nonetheless, the issue of sex discrimination and the implications it has upon individual athletes is one that the sporting authorities need to understand and consider much more carefully.

INDEPENDENT STUDY QUESTIONS

- *What are the various ways in which sex can be determined and what are the implications of this on the binary categories of 'male' and 'female'?*
- *Are there any good arguments for sex testing in sport?*
- *What problems arise when different institutions (such as government and sporting bodies) hold conflicting positions on determining a person's sex?*
- *How can we ensure that trans* individuals have opportunities to participate in sport at all levels of competition?*

12 IS ELITE DISABILITY SPORT AN OXYMORON?

Disability sports have gained increasing prominence in the wider sports and broadcast media over the last twenty years as general attitudes towards disability have changed and events such as the Paralympics have become further embedded into the wider Olympic movement. Since 2001, cities bidding to host the Olympic Games are also required to host the Paralympic Games immediately afterwards. However, disability sports, particularly at the elite competitive end, highlight contentious issues around the concepts of disability/ability, fairness and equity, and the effect that technological innovations and advancements have on these. This chapter will consider some of these questions and concepts.

WHAT IS DISABILITY IN SPORT?

Similar to the way in which women have historically been marginalised in sport, disabled athletes have also faced discrimination and barriers to participation. Equally, as women have challenged perceptions of their physical capabilities, so too, disabled athletes have contested the dominant model of the elite athlete.

The notion of an elite disability sport can be quite conceptually difficult to defend. If sport, at the elite, linear end (i.e. those quantifiable sports such as running, jumping, throwing and swimming) is designed to rank athletic performance then the terms 'disabled' and 'elite' appear oppositional. The problem here is in defining disability and in distinguishing relevant categories of ability and disability. This is an issue that those involved in administrating disability sport have had to wrestle with and is discussed by Jones and Howe[1], who point to the myriad competing factors involved in creating fair and worthy competition, entertaining and marketable sport, and ensuring inclusive and integrative opportunities for the wider disabled communities.

Although the Paralympic Games have been held alongside the Olympics since 1988, it wasn't until 2001 that a mutual agreement between the IOC and the IPC (International Paralympic Committee) formally gave the responsibility to the successful Olympic city to also host the Paralympic Games. As part of this agreement, the IPC had to reduce the number of classification groups. One of the problems, however, with the creation of categories is in determining where the divisions of degree of disability occur. Should an athlete with a recent severe visual impairment compete against a person who has been completely blind from birth? Should athletes who have no use of a hand be placed in the same category as athletes who are unable to use their whole lower arm? And should intellectual disabilities be categorised? The issue is one of both fairness and good competition. As outlined in the previous chapter, the main reason for distinguishing different weight categories in sports such as judo and boxing is to make the competition fair and ensure that it is safe. As disability is defined via a scale of impairment, the IPC needs to ensure that the categories it chooses for sporting competition allow for this fair, safe and good competition. This is easier said than done.

IS DISABILITY A MEDICAL DIAGNOSIS OR A SOCIAL CONSTRUCT?

The typical conception of disability is that it is a medical problem or limitation that is a result of disease or illness. This model is exemplified by the World Health Organisation's (WHO) *International Classification of Impairments, Disabilities and Handicaps* developed in 1980. Such a model is driven by the medical profession, which seeks to eliminate disability through treatment or cure. Disability according to this view can be diagnosed according to a set of objective criteria and compared to the 'normal' person who has normal functioning and capabilities.

The problem with the medical model, however, is that the concept of a 'normal' person is based on a statistical mean and is a rare find in reality. Most people have limited capabilities in some aspects of their life, whether it is reading a number plate unaided from a set distance, catching or kicking a ball, or processing and remembering information. Equally, most of us have above-normal capabilities or talents in other areas. Some of our weaknesses and talents may have biological or genetic roots (such as short-sightedness or an ability to lay down muscle mass), and some may be environmental (such as lack of practice or opportunity).

In order to counteract the patronisation of and stigma attached to individuals that often comes as a consequence of the medical model of disability, some groups have argued that disability should be recognised as a social construction rather than an illness or impairment. Disability, they argue, occurs as a result of the way in which society is built and constructed. For instance, if all entrances to buildings have ramps and wide doorways, then a person using a wheelchair can enter the building as easily as a person who is able to climb steps. In this instance, we can eliminate disability through the way we design our environment since the wheelchair-user is not prevented from carrying out their intention of entering the building. A good illustration of this conception of disability can be seen in an episode of a 1970s

Figure 12.1 – Chorlton: a lone bipedal in a world full of wheels.

children's animation called 'Chorlton and the Wheelies'. Chorlton is a lone bipedal character in a world full of 'Wheelies', who travel on wheels (Figure 12.1). Since the environment is constructed for the benefit of the 'normal' Wheelies through the use of ramps, Chorlton feels disabled as he is not able to race up and down the ramps and travel as speedily as the others.

However, critics of the social model of disability have argued that while disability can be diminished or emphasised through the built environment, proponents fail to accept the conceptual truth that impairment is a necessary condition of disability. While it may be possible to adapt society in ways that increase the autonomy of everyone, it is still the case that some individuals will suffer from impairments in ways that others do not.

The WHO later replaced its original classification with the *International Classification of Functioning, Disability and Health*, which aimed to take into account both models of disability. It created a 'biopsychosocial' model by recognising impairments caused by biomedical limitations based on the 'normal' functioning of the human body, but also by including a reference to 'participation restrictions' caused by the way in which society is constructed (in the same way that opportunities to other minority groups are restricted).[2]

Nevertheless, Steven Edwards argues that this model remains deficient due to the way in which it still neglects the voice of the affected individual.[3] Many of those who are classified as disabled do not view themselves in this way because they feel able to aspire and reach life (or vital) goals. Vital life goals are not simply desires to do something (such as a bungee jump) but rather are part of what constitutes a meaningful life.[4] As such, it is possible for an individual to have an impairment but for it not to affect their ability to live a satisfying and fulfilling life. Sporting achievement is one way in which this is demonstrated.

WHAT ARE THE PROBLEMS WITH CLASSIFICATION IN DISABILITY SPORT?

Classification and handicaps (as in golf) in sport are designed to ensure fair tests and good competition. The use of age, weight and sex categories is based upon generalisations about ability and capability. It is easy to recognise that it would be neither fair nor worthwhile for an 18-stone adult male to box against a 6-stone eight-year-old girl (even the idea of such a fight is unpalatable). The difficulty though is in ensuring fair and good competition across all cases and in determining which are the relevant characteristics to use. As sporting ability is based on a whole range of genetic and environmental factors, it is difficult to separate out those that should be included in the concept of fair competition. For instance, the high jump is separated into men's and women's events as sex is judged to be a factor that gives men an unfair advantage. It is not, however, divided into different height categories, which arguably is a fundamental factor in being successful in this event. Competitors of average height are at a disadvantage when competing, through genetic factors that are not their fault, yet are neither compensated for this impairment nor afforded their own category. While different categories are used in elite able-bodied sport to a limited extent, they form the core of disability sport. The reasoning behind the use of classifications is to ensure that similarly impaired athletes compete against each other.

The *International Organisations for Sport for the Disabled* provide their classification rationale as follows:

> '[A] system has to be put in place to minimise the impact of impairments
> on sports performance and to ensure the success of an athlete is determined
> by skill, fitness, power, endurance, tactical ability and mental focus.'[5]

On this basis, it could be argued that disability sports are at least aiming to ensure fair competition that minimises the advantage provided by factors not determined by choice or desert: since success should arise from factors that do not result from the impairment from which a person suffers. Nevertheless, the fact that lines still have to be drawn means that individuals are subject to arbitrary distinctions. For instance, classification in the B3 ski class requires athletes to have a visual field of less than 40 degrees diameter or a low visual acuity.[6] An athlete who has a visual field of 41 degrees diameter may not be eligible unless they are judged to have low visual acuity (N.B. the definition of 'low' is unspecified). Furthermore, eligibility for competition is liable to change upon reclassification.

Reclassification is a notable problem in disabled-sport competitions, especially when athletes have trained and competed in one class to find themselves ineligible shortly before their event starts. The controversial reclassification of Victoria Arlen only days before the London 2012 Paralympic Games is an example of this. Although Arlen successfully appealed the decision at the time and went on to win a silver medal, her eligibility was again reviewed in 2013 where it was ruled that her impairment was not considered sufficiently permanent for her to be eligible for further competitions. This decision was based on medical evidence that suggested there was a possibility that, with intensive physical therapy, she might one day be able to walk again.[7]

The problem faced by the classification organisations is that is impossible to ensure that all competition is fair and provides equal opportunities for competitors to succeed while at the same time ensuring that it is worthwhile and meaningful. As Jones and Howe note, in Sydney 2000, 'there were fifteen 100m final races for men and eleven for women in athletics compared with the traditional dual male and female events at the Olympic Games.'[8] That these categories have since been reduced in order to increase the standard of competition and to make it more marketable as an entertainment spectacle highlights the difficulties in constructing fair and equitable groups that are based upon objective and relevant criteria. Jones and Howe make this point by arguing that it is impossible to ascertain the appropriate baseline function from which classifications can be fairly made.[9] This fact was all the more apparent in the case of Oscar Pistorius' attempts to compete in able-bodied competitions.

SHOULD PISTORIUS HAVE BEEN ELIGIBLE TO COMPETE IN THE OLYMPIC GAMES?

The difficulties in constructing fair and objective classification are exacerbated with advances in material and bio-technologies as has most recently been seen in the case of double-amputee Oscar Pistorius. Pistorius' times for the 200m were comparable with those of elite non-disabled runners although he differed from these athletes in his use of prosthetic limbs. Since his times were comparable, the question then was whether his abilities were too. In other words, had Pistorius not been a double-amputee would he have run similar or faster times than he was doing with the aid of prosthetic limbs? Unfortunately, there is no real way of answering this question as there is no control (a non-disabled Pistorius) to provide a comparison. All scientists are able to do is test his prosthetic limbs against the biomechanical and physiological norms of a human leg. Pistorius was subjected to tests that measured a range of movements that were deemed inherent to running, including forces, energy consumption and wind resistance. The IAAF (International Association of Athletics Federations) initially concluded that Pistorius' prosthetic limbs constituted an unfair advantage over non-disabled competitors due the fact that his prosthetics produced more recoil spring and less drag than a human limb. However, this judgement was overturned by the Court of Arbitration for Sport (CAS) on the grounds that insufficient variables had been tested. Indeed, the CAS questioned the validity of the testing procedure since:

> '[T]he IAAF's officials must have known that, by excluding the start
> and the acceleration phase, the results would create a distorted view

of Mr Pistorius' advantages and/or disadvantages by not considering the effect of the device on the performance of Mr Pistorius over the entire race.'[10]

Following further testing, it was judged that although the recoil spring from his prosthetics gave Pistorius an advantage over the latter stages of the race, this was offset by the fact that he was required to expend more energy in the initial acceleration stages and when running a bend. The IAAF ban was overturned and Pistorius was deemed eligible to compete against non-disabled athletes.

This case highlights the problems that sporting authorities are going to face on a more regular basis as prosthetic limbs and bio-technology becomes more advanced. There are already cases causing headaches to the IAAF, such as the German long-jumper with prosthetic limbs campaigning for inclusion in able-bodied events. His jumps are already comparable in distance with those of the best able-bodied competitors.[11] Again, it will be up to the authorities to determine what are the relevant criteria in performing the long jump and whether prosthetic limbs can be judged to be parallel in functional terms to 'normal' human limbs.

Elite sport is founded on the notion of ranking competitors on ability in equal competition. The difficulty is in determining what constitutes 'equal'. When inequality between competitors is hidden, for instance in terms of the financial and scientific support that an athlete might receive, it generates little controversy. However, when the differences between competitors can be visually seen, such as by wearing prosthetic limbs, questions are raised as to the fairness of the competition.

In the case of paralympic sport, I suspect that while the current ruling on prosthetic limbs in running is upheld and athletes using prosthetics are able to compete against those who do not, it is likely that this will change in the future, when athletes using prosthetic limbs and other bio-technology are frequently surpassing the achievements of 'able-bodied' athletes. The dissent from 'able-bodied' athletes, the media and the public will be so great that a ruling will be made to prohibit those technologies from competition in order to preserve the notion of 'natural' competition. We may then see a markedly different parallel Olympics whereby the terms 'abled' and 'disabled' no longer apply.

INDEPENDENT STUDY QUESTIONS

- *What is the difference between medical and social conceptions of disability and to what extent are they both used in sport?*
- *How can disability sport ensure fair but good competition when disabilities differ so much?*
- *What effect will advances in prosthetic and bio-technology have on elite sport?*

- *Can you give me a little bit on your background and what got you interested in the philosophy of sport?*
  - I have always been interested in sport, but didn't know there was a thriving field of study about it. Trained in bioethics – my dissertation was on *in vitro* fertilization and autonomy – I had the good fortune to stumble across the sport literature as I was researching a paper on performance enhancement. I realised immediately that I had found my place. Sport is a ubiquitous part of society, as well as a microcosm of it. This provides an opportunity to reach people who might not normally come into contact with philosophy.

- *What do you think is the most interesting problem in the philosophy of sport?*
  - The problem of equality, or perhaps more accurately, the problem of inequalities. In far too many cases, the outcomes of sporting events are determined by race, class, gender, and/or socioeconomic traits of the competitors rather than by their athletic abilities. The aspect that most concerns me is the cynicism that seems to infect every aspect of sport, primarily in assumptions that all players cheat whenever they believe they can get away with it and that all values are sacrificed in the quest for profit. Sadly, these assumptions are all too often true, but not universally so, and they overshadow instances of the values sport can confer.

- *What book or paper has influenced you the most and why?*
  - As an undergraduate, Alfred North Whitehead's book *Process and Reality* had great impact because it taught me how rewarding it can be to struggle with a difficult text. During graduate school, I loved everything by Martha Nussbaum because she took philosophy out of the classroom and engaged the world; she also showed that one can be amazingly prolific with hard work. And I've always loved John Stuart Mill, both for his philosophy and his autobiography.

Key Readings

Sailors, P., 'Personal Foul: an evaluation of the moral status of football', *Journal of the Philosophy of Sport*, 42(2) (2015), pp. 269–286.

Sailors, P., 'Mixed Competition and Mixed Messages', *Journal of the Philosophy of Sport*, 41(1) (2014), pp. 65–77.

Sailors, P., 'Gender Roles Roll', *Sport, Ethics and Philosophy*, 7(2) (2013), pp. 245–258.

INTERVIEW WITH A PHILOSOPHER

TAKAYUKI HATA

Takayuki Hata is a Professor at the Graduate School of Okayama University, Japan, in the Department of Education, Health and Physical Education. He is a past President of the Japan Society for the Philosophy of Sport and Physical Education. As a former track and field athlete, Takayuki now prefers to watch rugby and football.

- *Can you give me a little bit on your background and what got you interested in the philosophy of sport?*
  - I took part in athletics when I was at university where I was studying pedagogy and physical education. I became interested in the notion of existence in movement and sport as well as the meaning of movement and sport. That got me interested in the philosophy of sport.
- *What do you think is the most interesting problem in the philosophy of sport?*
  - I am interested in the notion of movement in the body in sport. I think the problem of 'being body and having body' is the most interesting for me in the philosophy of sport. Western philosophy tends to be the philosophy of study while East Asian philosophy is a philosophy of guidance. In East Asian philosophy, the practical interest in our life directs contemplation. The difference between the Western and East Asian philosophy is how the notion of existence is conceived and understood.
- *What book or paper has influenced you the most and why?*
  - Several works by Erich Fromm, especially *To Have Or To Be*. Also books on Zen philosophy, particularly by Daisetz Teitaro Suzuki, have influenced me. These seem to be the best places to start on understanding the relationship between sport and the self.

Key Readings

Hata, T. and Sekine, M., 'Philosophy of Sport and Physical Education in Japan: Its History, Characteristics and Prospects', *Journal of the Philosophy of Sport*, 37(2) (2010), pp. 215–224.

Ilundáin-Agurruza, J. and Hata, T., 'Eastern Philosophy', in McNamee, M.J. and Morgan, W.J. (Eds.), *Routledge Handbook of the Philosophy of Sport* (London: Routledge, 2015).

Sekine, M. and Hata, T., 'The crisis of modern sport and the dimension of achievement for its conquest', *International Journal of Sport and Health Science*, 2 (2004), pp. 180–186.

SPORT AND THE GOOD LIFE

13 WHAT IS THE VALUE OF SPORT?

Questions about value are essentially questions about priorities: what is important and what matters. When we decide that it is better to be kind rather than honest (in the case of telling a white lie to avoid hurting someone's feelings), or better to prioritise equality over freedom (in order to give opportunities to those who are disadvantaged at birth), we are making a value judgement. Although Graham McFee[1] asserted that the only genuine philosophical questions in sport are ones of ethics, he may have only been half correct. The branch of philosophy that studies value (also called axiology) includes ethical questions but it also encompasses questions of aesthetics: what is beautiful or how things affect our senses. So the study of value is concerned with what we believe to be good and right, and how we determine worth or priority.

ARE VALUES SUBJECTIVE OR OBJECTIVE?

Value can be seen as being either subjective or objective. Those who argue it is subjective see value as a matter of personal taste that is beyond the scope of disagreement. This view holds that if I value playing sport over going to my grandmother's funeral, it is as inarguable as my preference for vanilla over chocolate ice-cream. You might prefer chocolate but this is something that we just have to agree to disagree about. Subjective value then is merely a matter of preference. The contrary position is that value can be objectively determined by reference to an external authority such as God, or by recourse to biological or evolutionary facts, or even by the concept of rationality in that we must be consistent with the way we hold and order our values. An objective view of value maintains that value is not just individual personal preference such as whether we prefer the colour blue to green, but rather can be determined by external criteria. This seems a much more plausible way of understanding value as it reflects the way we generally discuss and debate issues of value, ethics and aesthetics; we are rarely content to simply agree to disagree as in the case of our preferences of ice-cream. However, the fact that an objective standard of value has never been agreed upon indicates that there is still space for some element of personal, subjective or non-rational value.

IS THE VALUE OF SPORT EXTERNAL OR INTERNAL?

In assessing the value of sport, there are again two contrasting views. An *externalist* will argue that the value of sport is found merely in the way that sport reflects the values that we hold in society and culture as a whole. There is nothing therefore special about sport itself, it is just a prism in that it allows us to see and measure our priorities more clearly. The same approach could be taken for other cultural activities such as theatre, music and art. An externalist would argue that all of these things are of value because they are ways of expressing other values, such as friendship, cooperation, health and well-being. An *internalist*, however, maintains that there are inherent values particular to sport as a practice. This view maintains that the value of sport is found within sport itself rather than as a vehicle by which to view or attain other values.

This highlights a key debate in the philosophy of sport: whether sport is of value in itself, or whether it is merely a means to achieving other things we believe to be important. Those things that we value as being good in themselves are said to hold *intrinsic* or *inherent* value. Those things that we value because they are means to other ends are said to have *extrinsic* or *instrumental* value. It seems reasonable to say that instrumental activities are not as valuable as intrinsically valuable activities, since we are only valuing them because they enable us to reach another higher value; they are only valuable because they act as stepping stones that enable us to get somewhere else.

WHAT ARE THE MORAL AND NON-MORAL VALUES OF SPORT?

Value can be further divided into moral and non-moral value. Moral values relate to moral qualities, such as: courage, honesty, fairness, freedom and respect. These are the types of values that are alluded to when people talk about sport being character-building or teaching fair play. Non-moral values are things such as: wealth, happiness, security, health and commitment. Kretchmar[2] argues that there are four primary non-moral values to sport and physical activity: health, knowledge, skill and fun.

- *Health*: Doctors, governments and public health organisations often cite good evidence that links physical activity to a longer and richer life. The more able you are in terms of aerobic and anaerobic fitness, strength and flexibility, the more likely you will be able to do other things that you value, such as play with your children and grandchildren, contribute to groups and activities, and lead the type of life that you enjoy.
- *Knowledge*: Humans are problem-solvers. We value understanding causal relationships as it enables us to develop and progress. As competitive creatures,

knowledge also allows us to develop effective and winning strategies. Knowledge of how to acquire and develop skill, how it has a bearing on health and other values provides us with tools that enable us to go beyond what we have already achieved.

- *Skill*: A particular type of practical knowledge or wisdom is manifested in skill; it is the ability to do or show rather than to know or understand (indeed many of the best athletes find it difficult to explain in words how they are able to execute skilful actions). We value performance and excellence in sport and physical activity because it is the demonstration of human achievement and possibility. While knowledge and understanding can help in skill-acquisition, ultimately it can only be developed through practice and commitment.
- *Fun*: It is commonly accepted that there is a link between enjoyment and motivation and therefore this value is emphasised in most teaching of sport and physical activity. Without it, it is difficult to acquire the other values, but it is also of value in itself since it provides us with satisfaction and a meaningful life.

As can be seen, all of these values are interrelated since each provides a rationale for another. We value fun because it is a motivating factor in helping us achieve skill, knowledge and health. We value health because without it we would be unable to acquire or demonstrate skill or have fun. We value knowledge because it helps in the acquisition of skill, health and perhaps even fun (if we know what others and ourselves enjoy), and we value skill because it exemplifies human achievement and is the manifestation of health, fun and knowledge.

HOW CAN VALUE BE ASSESSED AND PRIORITISED?

As has been indicated, we can hold a multitude of different values. Yet this raises the question of how to prioritise our values, especially when they might come into conflict. I might value both having fun and skill in sport but to achieve the latter might mean I have to sacrifice the former to some extent. Equally, if I am to achieve a personal best in a race, I might have to push my body through pain in order to do so.

The hierarchical view ranks value according to its worth: the higher up the hierarchy, the more worth a value holds. This is the model that Thomas Hurka used in his paper 'Games and the Good' when he attempted to explain the value that modern society places upon sport and game playing.[3] This model consists of differing levels of connecting values.

Hurka measures value through the Aristotelian concept of excellence or *aretē*. Each node in this hierarchy represents a different degree of excellence. Attaining a value on a particular level presupposes that one already has attained the degree of excellence that is necessary for the values contained in the hierarchy below. We can imagine, for instance, that a higher value represents the achievement of swimming half a mile. Being able to swim half a mile presupposes that one is able

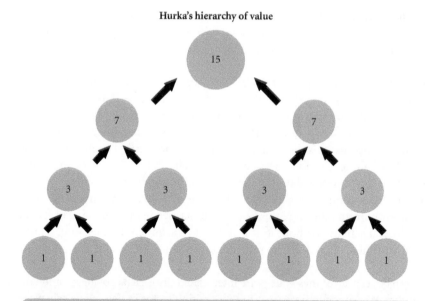

Figure 13.1 – Hurka's hierarchy of values.

to both keep oneself afloat without drowning (a lower value) and swim 30 metres (a mid-value). The ability to swim half a mile, however, is required to attain an even higher value of competing in a standard-distance triathlon.

Here we can see that excellence manifests itself in difficulty and mastery of skill. The model of hierarchy is one of means–ends. The higher up you go, the greater the skill required. It also explains why the greater the skill-acquisition, the more challenging the game has to become for it to be of any value. Hurka argued that complex games and sports are more valuable than those that require brute strength, e.g. weightlifting. Good games therefore are those that require a variety of skills and embody both practical and theoretical knowledge. This conception reflects Aristotle's belief that it is better to have a mastery of a variety of skills and knowledge that can be applied to other areas of life rather than to develop a narrow range of skill and ability.

Conceptualising value as a model of hierarchy provides us with one way of assessing or measuring it, and it can be useful in understanding skill-acquisition for example. However, it doesn't provide us with an answer for what value sport itself holds, if any. The hierarchy model appears useful in the example of swimming because it demonstrates how achievement, skill and excellence related to a particular activity could be measured and assessed. But its use becomes less clear the longer one looks at it since it seems to suffer from infinite regress and misrepresent some of the way in which we understand the notion of value. If we continue our hierarchy further, we then need to answer the question, 'Why is the ability to complete a triathlon of value?' One answer could be, 'In order to complete a double-triathlon' but now it appears as if we've missed the point. It may be the case that there are people who are never satisfied with their achievements and every accomplishment is merely a stepping stone on to the next, yet this seems to be a disappointing and demoralising way of recognising meaning and value in our lives.

In answer to this problem, Baier advocated three criteria that enable us to assess value: intrinsic value, satisfaction and coherence.[4]

- *Criterion of intrinsic value*: Activities that have intrinsic value are considered superior to those that have instrumental value; for logic suggests that if we could bypass the 'middle value' we would. For example, if we take part in weekly physical exercise classes merely because we want to maintain our weight, then if there were an easier way to do this (such as a 'magic pill'), we would take it. Some things only appear to have value because they enable us to attain other values. As such, things that have value in themselves are considered more valuable than things that lead on to the attainment of other values.
- *Criterion of satisfaction*: The ethical theory of utilitarianism holds that the highest value in life is pleasure or happiness. According to this theory, we should therefore do those things that maximise the most amount of pleasure or happiness and this will lead to a good life. However, one of the problems with utilitarian theory is that happiness or pleasure seems too narrow a value. This was exemplified by the American philosopher Robert Nozick[5] in his 'experience machine', a thought experiment that demonstrated why pleasure is not of ultimate value. Nozick hypothesised that if there existed a machine that gave us ongoing pleasure, few of us would want to live in it. We can apply an example of this thought experiment to sport. Imagine a machine that meant that sport was a constantly pleasurable experience and we always won. Every time we set foot on a golf course or on a football pitch we would feel an ongoing euphoria that culminated at the last hole or final whistle. What would our experience of sport be like? Arguably, it would be hollow and ultimately devoid of pleasure. The pleasure we get from sport is not from winning, but rather from overcoming the possibility of losing and the risk of failing. As such, satisfaction seems to be a better value than just happiness or pleasure.

Kretchmar breaks down the criterion of satisfaction into two further corollaries (consequences): the corollary of purity and the corollary of durability.

- *The corollary of purity*: The less harm that is caused in producing satisfying experiences, the better. This means that the satisfaction that one gets from playing and winning against an opponent of a similar level is preferable to the satisfaction that one gets from playing and winning against an inferior opponent. Kretchmar argues that while we may enjoy soundly and easily beating our opponent, it is not as valuable as the satisfaction of a hard-fought win.

- *The corollary of durability*: Long-lasting satisfaction is preferable to that which is temporary or erratic. Great sports teams and individuals are those that have a history of success, whereas short-term success is quickly forgotten. It is this type of satisfaction that comes from other values that we hold, such as dedication, commitment, determination, and the development of talent and potential.

Kretchmar defends the inclusion of these corollaries because they clarify the concept of satisfaction. The first corollary indicates that it isn't simply pleasure we value, since satisfying experiences come from also knowing that we have had to overcome challenge. The second corollary highlights that we prefer long-lasting satisfaction that is tied to other values to a short-term pleasure that might be associated with a quick 'high'.

- *Criterion of coherence*: Baier's third criterion is that of coherence. A meaningful life is one that makes sense on a wider scale and contains a narrative whereby who we are can be explained by what has gone on in our life before. One of the unique aspects of being human is the way we are able to view our self from a perspective outside the one in which we immediately find ourselves. We create stories that explain how we have reached our current situation, and imagine ourselves at various points in the future. This ability to create a coherent narrative about our lives is a valuable tool as it allows us to create the life that we wish to life. The fact that we are aware of our own existence and have the ability to project a vision of ourselves that is different to the self that currently exists gives us the freedom to be able to define ourselves in a multitude of ways. This means that humans can create goals and visions of the future that we can aspire to achieve. We can imagine ourselves standing on top of an Olympic podium collecting a gold medal, or raising the Champions League trophy at Wembley. Equally, we can remember the time when we were beaten on penalties in the county championship, or the time when we suffered injury during an important trial game. It is those memories and these goals that inspire many athletes to succeed and help them form a narrative to their lives. You only have to look at the enormous wealth of sporting biographies for evidence that supports this view. The criterion of coherence allows us to put together individual moments of satisfaction that are shared among a range of activities and events into a meaningful whole. It allows us to rank and evaluate our achievements as part of a bigger life narrative and ultimately is what makes life both meaningful and interesting.

HOW FLEXIBLE SHOULD WE BE IN OUR VALUES?

One of the ways to provide a rational justification of our values is to provide a cost-benefit analysis according to the evidence we currently hold. For instance, current evidence suggests that physical activity is good for health in terms of lowering blood pressure, reducing osteoporosis, reducing the likelihood of heart attack and stroke and improving mental well-being, among other benefits. Therefore, physical activity is of value because it provides a means for good health that is of value in itself. However, scientific or empirical evidence is insufficient on its own to provide justification for our values. We also need a normative element that provides a coherent and rational account of why the evidence is important. Consider, for example, someone who has smoked for many years. We might point to compelling evidence that suggests that they are significantly more likely to suffer lung and throat cancer, premature aging, yellowing teeth and skin and ultimately an early death. Their response, however, might be to argue that despite all these risks, smoking is a meaningful part of their life; they enjoy it, it forms part of their social activities and friendship group, and they're prepared to take the gamble of suffering some of the side effects. For the smoker, the benefits of smoking outweigh the drawbacks from not smoking and despite the scientific evidence they have produced a rational and coherent argument.

Kretchmar warns against excessive sporting values, which he terms: 'excessive survivalism, runaway individualism and oppressive rationalism.'[6] Excessive survivalism is an extreme focus upon health, addictive behaviour towards workouts and exercise, and the possession of an over-competitive attitude towards winning. Runaway individualism is the sole focus upon the self rather than community, with a strong advocation of individual rather than team-based activities, and an individualistic and egocentric morality. Oppressive rationalism is an obsessive fascination with breaking sports records and pushing the boundaries of higher, faster and stronger; and an over-reliance on the scientific method, at the expense of the spirit of playfulness.

As was noted earlier in this chapter, recognising and prioritising our values is not simply a matter of whim or personal preference. It is normative in that it shows what we think should be important for others too. At the same time we need to recognise that there is flexibility and room for disagreement. We need to strike a balance between being over-prescriptive in our values and being too tolerant of the values that are held by others. We ought to have a rational basis for the values we ascribe to but need to avoid being dogmatic. We need to be sensitive to culture and context. For example, it is often only when we have been immersed in a particular sport that we 'get it' and are able to appreciate its value. For Americans this might be the 'slow and tedious' game of cricket while for Europeans this might be the 'restrictive and autocratic' game of American football. Values may also change according to need and situation. Three core values that are often cited (for instance, in Maslow's hierarchy of needs) are food, shelter and warmth. But in modern society, when these are often taken for granted or provided by others such as the State, the values of leisure and freedom become more pronounced.

Understanding value is one of the most difficult tasks in philosophy, since it is an abstract concept that is axiomatic (self-evident). Values direct our priorities in life, which influence our actions. Recognising what is important allows us to set goals, provide us with meaningful experiences and work towards a fulfilled life. Moreover, it provides us with a foundation upon which we can make sound ethical judgements and encourage others to act in particular ways. Sport undoubtedly holds some value and can be a significant part of a good life. However, it is more difficult to assess whether the value of sport is intrinsic or instrumental. This question is explored further in the next few chapters, which consider the seriousness of sport and the part that risk and danger play.

INDEPENDENT STUDY QUESTIONS:

- *What is meant by subjective/objective, and intrinsic/extrinsic value?*
- *How can value be assessed and prioritised?*
- *To what extent can the different values of sport be ranked?*
- *What are the values that are most important to you and why?*
- *What part does sport play in your conception of a good life?*

14 IS UTOPIA A WORLD FULL OF GAMES?

It can be argued that Bernard Suits' seminal book *The Grasshopper: Games, Life and Utopia* comprises two parts: the first is an attempt to provide an analytic definition of game playing (as outlined in Chapter 2); the second is a more profound axiological consideration about the part that games play in a good life. In respect of the latter, Suits appears to suggest that the perfect life is one that consists solely of playing games.

This chapter will outline Suits' argument, his conception of play and its relation to work and games. It will continue to consider some of the issues raised in the previous chapter, regarding intrinsic and instrumental value, and asks whether Utopia is a world full of games.

WHAT IS THE RELATIONSHIP BETWEEN WORK AND PLAY?

Suits' book begins with a discussion between a Grasshopper and his two (worker ant) disciples who are concerned that he will starve to death as he has spent the whole summer playing rather than working to secure his future. The Grasshopper's disciples agree to provide him with food to last the winter on the proviso that he works to pay them back. Yet, the Grasshopper refuses, arguing that the only reason they are his disciples is because they admire his play ethic. In response, the disciple Skepticus argues:

> 'You talk as though there were but two possible alternatives: either a life devoted exclusively to play or a life devoted exclusively to work. But most of us realise that our labour is valuable because it permits us to play, and we are presumably seeking to achieve some kind of balance between work input and play output. People are not, and do not want to be, wholly grasshoppers or wholly ants, but a combination of the two; people are and want to be (if you will forgive a regrettably vulgar but spooneristically inevitable construction) asshoppers or grants. We can, of course, all cease to work, but if we do then we cannot play for long either, for we will shortly die.'[1]

In this passage, Skepticus highlights the commonly perceived relationship between work and play. Grasshopper argues that a perfect world, Utopia, would be one in which we would not have to work. Instead, life would solely consist of play.

Grasshopper's position can be explained by understanding the concept of Utopia. Utopia describes a perfect world. While many authors and literary works have attempted to articulate what this would look like in practice, Suits was the first to consider it in relation to game playing. His argument stems from the premise that in Utopia all instrumental activities have become obsolete. That is, the only activities that are left are those that are done for their own sake and not in order to attain some other goal. For example, if we only exercise because we believe it will allow us to stay healthy for longer, then we would be quite happy to substitute the exercise for anything else that had the same effect; a magic pill, for example. Equally, if we only work so we can afford to go abroad for our holidays, and if there was some other means to pay for these holidays, then we would not work. In this sense, work and exercise can be said to be instrumental: they are only done in order to reach a particular, other, end. Work and play are seen as diametrically opposed: while the value of work is said to be instrumental, the value of play is intrinsic. This is more commonly expressed in the phrase, 'work is doing what you have to do; play is doing what you want to do'. Suits' Grasshopper expresses a common conception of work in that it is only done because it gives us the time and resources to play. Eliminate the need for work and the only thing left would be play.

IS GAME PLAYING MORE VALUABLE THAN PLAY?

So far, the argument seems to suggest that play is the only activity left in Utopia. However, Grasshopper is very specific about what form this play takes. He claims that Utopia is not simply a life of play but rather a life of playing *games*: game playing is the ideal of existence.

The question that follows is how does Suits move from play as a primary value to the narrower category of game playing? Suits' disciple, Prudence, asks this very question: 'Why must a life freed from the necessity to work be identical with a life dedicated to games?'[2] Suits' answer is found in the first part of the book, in his definition of game playing, which states that a game is 'the voluntary attempt to overcome unnecessary obstacles'.[3] Using this definition, the fact that a game is deliberately designed to be inefficient (for example, using a club to get a ball into a hole) suggests we must value games for their own sake; they have intrinsic worth. If games were valued for instrumental reasons we would try to make the activity as efficient as possible in order to make the goal more easily attainable. If the sole point of golf was to get the ball in the cup, then there are far more efficient ways of doing so than using a club. One would be better off picking up the ball, walking to the hole and placing it in the cup by hand. Playing golf is not the same type of activity as washing clothes, for instance. The drive for efficiency in domestic chores, and the invention of various domestic appliances, highlights that washing clothes is not intrinsically valued in the same way as games. Games have a paradoxical quality in that we try to overcome obstacles that we have deliberately placed in our way. That games are inefficient by design means that they therefore must contain intrinsic value. Games exist purely so that they can be played. The value of games according to Suits is that the means and the ends are inseparable.

This is a view that is supported by Thomas Hurka, who suggests that we need to reject the Aristotelian or teleological view of value with its focus upon ends. Hurka argues it is the means of reaching the end rather than the end in itself that is of real value, and this is why games are the clearest expression of this.

> 'Game playing must have some external goal one aims at, but the specific features of this goal are irrelevant to the activity's value, which is entirely one of process rather than product, journey rather than destination. This is why playing in games gives the clearest expression of a modern as against a classical view of value – because the modern view centres on the value of process.'[4]

Accepting the value of game playing requires a particular psychological state, which Suits referred to as the 'lusory attitude' and which formed one of his four criteria for his definition of game playing. As outlined in more detail in Chapter 2, the 'lusory attitude' is the voluntary acceptance of the rules in order to play the game. It is required because the constitutive (fundamental) rules of games are arbitrary. Rules determine the means that are allowed in order to reach the goal: such as the use of the feet to play the ball in football. Without rules, the game would not exist. But the rules are non-binding. If we chose to pick up the ball in a game of football and run with it instead, the only consequence that follows is that we would no longer be playing football. It is the fact that we choose to follow the rules voluntarily, via the lusory attitude, which enables the game to exist.[5]

HOW SERIOUSLY SHOULD WE TAKE GAMES?

This non-binding nature of rules raises a question that Suits wrestled with: how seriously should we take the rules of games? On the one hand, rules are arbitrary and pointless; their only function is to allow the game to exist. In this they are trivial and absurd. However, the lusory attitude dictates that we have to take the rules seriously, for not doing so would be to condone cheating, if cheating is understood as the deliberate breaking of rules. When viewed objectively, with rationality and efficiency as the standard measure, games and sports are unimportant and insignificant. Yet at the same time they are of the utmost importance. Suits provides two examples to illustrate this paradox: Mario, the dedicated racing driver, and George, the dedicated golfer. Mario, the dedicated driver, is such a serious competitor that he will always follow the rules. All good and well, we might say. Mario is a good sportsman because of the seriousness with which he takes the rules. However, in his next race a child runs out in front of him. The only way Mario can avoid hitting her would be to break the rule that states *drivers must stay on the track at all times during the race*, but the seriousness with which Mario takes the rules means that he does not swerve and the child is killed. If this case were real, all sane people would be horrified. They would rightly argue that while it is right to follow rules in sport, these rules do not override other moral rules, such as the rule that states we should not kill innocent children. Rules in sport should be taken seriously but only if they are not compromising the following of other, more important, rules.

The second example that Suits provides is the case of George the dedicated golfer. George is so obsessed with golf that he neglects his wife and family. His wife complains that for George, golf is no longer a game but a way of life. This stems from his wife's belief that a game is something that is played after other more important aspects of life have taken priority. Suits, however, rejects this view. He argues that while it may be the case that golf has taken over George's life, it is not true that George is no longer playing a game. The problem for George's wife is that she views a game as something that should not be prioritised or valued above other things in life, such as spending time with and supporting his family. As Suits says, there seems to be something particularly problematic about games in that they are trivial and unproductive. Had George's life been taken over by doing good works or finding the cure for cancer, his wife may have been more sympathetic.

These two examples highlight the peculiar way in which we view games. We need to take them seriously in order to play them properly but at the same time we also need to recognise their pointlessness.

One way of resolving this paradox is provided by Andrew Edgar and his conception of the 'sportsworld'. When we inhabit the world of sport we are able to hold two opposing views without experiencing cognitive dissonance. For Edgar, the 'sportsworld' runs parallel to the 'artworld' since both allow us to suspend norms.[6] When we feel shock or sadness when a character we sympathise with is stabbed in the heart during the third Act, or when we appreciate Duchamp's urinal as a work of art, we suspend the norms and conventions of 'real life' and inhabit the 'artworld'. This is the same for the sportsworld. When we see our opposition as our enemy and attempt to foil their attempts to score by putting our 'body on the line' we inhabit a world whereby these actions and the effort they involve are highly important and meaningful. Those who hold a real hatred for the opposition and resort to hooliganism misunderstand the conventions of competition in the sportsworld. For Mario to adhere to the constitutive rules of racing and consequently run over a wayward child on the grounds that he didn't want to break the rules is to show a lack of recognition of the transient nature of the sportsworld.

IS GAME PLAYING ABSURD?

It is this aspect of working towards a voluntary chosen but trivial goal that leads Suits to argue that game playing is the ideal existence. On Suits' account, in Utopia there is no need for good deeds since there is no evil and wrongdoing. There is also no room for art since this is a product of the passions and emotions, and no need for science or knowledge-seekers (scientists and philosophers) since all knowledge has already been discovered. The only activity left is to voluntarily overcome unnecessary obstacles in order to reach unnecessary goals. In other words, to play games. This is demonstrated in Grasshopper's comment:

> 'What we have shown thus far is that there does not appear to be any thing to do in Utopia, precisely because in Utopia all instrumental activities have been eliminated. There is nothing to strive for precisely because everything has already been achieved. What we need, therefore, is some activity in which what is instrumental is inseparably combined with what is intrinsically valuable, and where the activity is not itself an instrument for some further end. Games meet this requirement perfectly. For in games we must have obstacles which we can strive to overcome just so that we can possess the activity as a whole, namely, playing the game. Game playing makes it possible to retain enough effort in Utopia to make life worth living.'[7]

As it is presented, it seems a compelling argument. However, there is a twist to the story that highlights the absurdity of Utopia as a viable concept. As illustrated in the case of George the golfer, his wife's annoyance stems from George spending his time on something trivial rather than worthwhile. It seems that while people are happy to play games for part of their lives, they need to believe that there is something more important that they ought to be doing instead. This is a psychological fact that Grasshopper reluctantly accepts:

> '... most people will not want to spend their lives playing games. Life for most people will not be worth living if they cannot believe that they are doing something useful, whether it is providing for their families or formulating a theory of relativity.'[8]

Suits' Grasshopper ends with a realisation that meaning in life comes from doing things that we think are worthwhile because they lead to a valuable end. As such it seems that contrary to our initial thoughts, instrumental activities are as valuable as intrinsic activities. As Hurka highlighted earlier, we often value the process of reaching a valued end as much as the end in itself.

CAN SPORT BE A PART OF UTOPIA?

There is a further flaw with Suits' conception of Utopia and this is due to the competitive nature of game playing, or as Tony Skillen said, the fact that 'sport is for losers'.[9] Both games and sport are by definition competitive activities, even if the competition is against oneself. A good game is one in which the level of difficulty is sufficient to maintain interest and motivation but is not impossible. A good game is one where the risk of failure is reasonably high. Indeed, Andrew Edgar argues that the definition of sport is a physical challenge at which we can fail.[10]

This then is the real problem with Utopia and one that Keith Thompson identifies in his paper, 'Sport and Utopia'.[11] He argues that Utopia is conceptually incoherent because life is based upon holding incompatible values. For instance, we may value both freedom and equality but promoting one will inevitably impinge on the other. Similarly, sport and games only give us satisfaction and pleasure when we have succeeded at a challenge at which we could have failed. It is the real possibility of failure that makes it a challenge worth undertaking.

This therefore renders Suits' Utopia an impossibility. Grasshopper wishes to argue that in Utopia there is no passion or emotion because there is no need to compete over limited resources, but that would make it a very dull world indeed. It is the passion and emotion experienced in life and in the playing of games, through sometimes succeeding and sometimes failing, that makes it worth living and which drives us on to do better in the future. Ultimately, Suits' Utopia is not a place where humans can live at all. And this may be why at the end of the book, Grasshopper accepts that Utopia is an impossible dream and resigns himself to his death.

INDEPENDENT STUDY QUESTIONS:

- Is it correct to define 'work' and 'play' as opposing concepts? What are the limitations with this understanding?
- How can we reconcile the way in which we need to take sport seriously but also recognise its triviality?
- Is Suits right to argue that game playing is the ideal existence because the ends and the means are inseparable?
- What are the problems with Suits' conception of Utopia? Is Utopia ultimately unintelligible?

15 WHAT IS THE VALUE OF DANGEROUS SPORT?

Sport contains risk: there are few people who have not suffered some kind of sporting-related injury, however minor. However, on the basis that sport is a voluntary and unnecessary activity done for its own sake, sporting risks can be said to be freely chosen. One might therefore ask, are the risks worth it? And is there any argument to be made for participating in a sport where the risks of severe injury or death are high?

This chapter will consider the value of danger in sport through providing a typology of various sports that distinguishes between the likelihood of harm and the severity of harm, and by outlining the debate that centres on the philosophical principles of autonomy, liberty and paternalism.

WHAT IS THE DIFFERENCE BETWEEN RISK AND DANGER?

In the English language, the terms 'risk' and 'danger' are often used synonymously but there are subtle differences. Risk is the assessed probability of a particular negative consequence of an action. In this respect, it is a subjective judgement based upon past experience. Danger is the existence of a particular hazard or risk. In this sense, it is an objective fact. So a danger might exist in the world but is not known and therefore not perceived as a risk. Nevertheless, despite this, the terms are often used interchangeably and there will be occasions when this will be the case here.

WHAT IS A DANGEROUS SPORT?

In order to evaluate the value of dangerous sports, a distinction needs to be made between dangerous sports and sport that contains danger. Dangerous sports can be categorised as activities that involve a significant risk of death or serious injury. So, while squash injuries may be common, the risk of severe injury is low and therefore it does not classify as a dangerous sport. In contrast, BASE-jumping

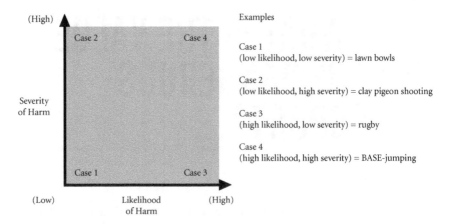

Figure 15.1 The axis of likelihood and severity of harm (adapted from Anderson, 2007)

has a much higher likelihood of harm, and that harm is more likely to be severe. Dangerous sports can therefore be defined as freely chosen activities requiring physical skill that contain both a high likelihood and a high severity of harm. This is shown in Figure 15.1.

As is illustrated by the examples provided for each case, different sports entail different risks and potential harms. The question that follows is whether there is any level of risk that should be prohibited. This requires balancing two different values, the right to autonomy and the duty to prevent harm. It can be theoretically framed as *libertarianism* versus *paternalism*.

SHOULD WE STOP PEOPLE FROM PARTICIPATING IN DANGEROUS ACTIVITIES?

This is a question that philosophers and politicians have wrestled with throughout human civilisation, but during the Enlightenment and the receding influence of the Church, the concept of individual autonomy – or the right to live one's own life as one saw fit – became more established. The right to autonomy is taken for granted in most countries today and the concepts of freedom and individual choice are core values of modern society. Over the last century, these rights have, in many areas, become increasingly progressive and now include the universal right to elect political representatives, rights to abortion and rights to same-sex marriage[1], as well as increasing discussion on allowing the right to die via assisted suicide. However, at the same time, there are increasing infringements on autonomy such as the ban on 'legal highs', curtailments on the freedom of speech, and calls for cycle helmets to be made compulsory.

One of the most widely cited advocates of individual liberty is the Scottish philosopher, John Stuart Mill (1806–1873). Mill argued that a person should have the right of authority over his own body even if they chose to act in such a way that could cause themselves harm. His claim is captured in this famous passage:

> '… the only purpose for which power can be rightfully exercised over any member of a civilised community, against his will, is to prevent harm to others. His own good, either physical or moral is not a sufficient warrant. He cannot be rightfully compelled to do or forbear because it will be better for him to do so, because it will make him happier, because in the opinion of others, to do so would be wise, or even right. These are good reasons for remonstrating with him, or reasoning with him, or persuading him, or entreating him, but not for compelling him or visiting him with any evil in case he do otherwise … Over himself, over his own body and mind, the individual is sovereign.'[2]

If we accept Mill's stance, then there would be few situations in which we could prevent someone taking part in a sporting activity that was dangerous. For instance, imagine a sport called 'BASE-jumping roulette', which involved participants choosing from a range of six parachutes, only one of which is in full working order. Let us imagine the likelihood of death or serious injury in BASE-jumping roulette is around 83 per cent. Following Mill's advice, although we may try to dissuade someone from taking part in this sport, we have no authority in physically preventing him or her from doing so, unless we could demonstrate that there was a direct risk of harm to someone else (for instance, if they were jumping on to a group of people below). According to Mill's stance, if someone chooses to subject themselves to this level of risk and danger then it is their prerogative to do so.

However, paternalists would argue that we do have a duty to prevent people from harm even if that involves infringing their liberty. The primary principle that paternalists work from is the prevention of harm rather than individual autonomy.

Paternalism comes from the Latin word 'father' and thus alludes to the way in which parents protect their children. It works from the presumption that people possess differing levels of wisdom. For instance, a father who stops his child running out into the road does so on the basis that he is able to judge the speed of oncoming traffic whereas the child is not.

There are several different types of paternalism; the most common distinction is between hard and soft paternalism. Hard paternalism is intervening to prevent someone from an action even if they are aware of the risks and likely consequences of their action. Soft paternalism is intervening in an action in order to be assured that the person is aware of the risks and consequences of that action. So for instance, a hard paternalist would stop someone from participating in a sport that is likely to cause them harm, whereas a soft paternalist would ensure that the person has sufficient knowledge to reach a decision about whether to participate, and would also try to ensure that any risks are minimised. In this sense, soft paternalism can be seen to overlap with libertarianism. John Stuart Mill accepted there were cases for paternalistic intervention but these were generally directed towards children and 'irrational' adults on the basis that they were not competent enough to make a rational choice.

When applied to the world of sport, soft paternalists would ensure that the level of education an athlete receives is sufficient to enable them to make rational and competent decisions. Examples of this could include: an instructor being satisfied that a kayaker has the ability to assess water conditions in relation to their level of skill; a coach ensuring that a player has the knowledge to tackle safely before being allowed to play contact rugby; or a doctor being satisfied that a boxer is able to make a rational choice about whether to continue the bout.

This last example highlights a difficulty that sporting and medical authorities have been increasingly forced to consider as the long-term effects of concussion are becoming known. The responsibility that a coach bears towards their athlete has been outlined in more detail in a paper by myself and Steve Olivier on coaching dangerous sport.[3] We discuss the scenario presented in the film *Rocky IV* in which aging US boxer Apollo Creed comes out of retirement to face his Soviet nemesis, Ivan Drago. His coach, Rocky, remonstrates with Creed not to fight on the basis that he will be significantly outclassed but reluctantly accepts Creed's choice to do so. During the fight, it becomes increasingly obvious to Rocky that Creed is suffering a brutal beating. Again, Rocky urges Creed to throw in the towel and again Creed refuses. The fight ends with Drago delivering a fatal punch.

Taking a libertarian stance, we suggest that Rocky was right in allowing Creed to continue despite his reservations. However, this conclusion is based on the presumption that Creed was of sound enough mind to be able to make a rational decision. While this may have been the case prior to the fight, the damage caused by repeated blows to Creed's head may have meant that he was no longer in a position to rationally assess whether to continue and therefore a more paternalistic approach may be justified.

It is a difficult balance that those involved in sport have to strike between allowing an athlete to risk suffering harm and preventing that harm. The clearest example of paternalism in sport is found in the area of performance-enhancing drugs. The primary reason for banning substances is the risk of harm to health, and classic cases of death from substance use in sport are cited in support of this approach. However, in his discussion on paternalism and the use of drugs in sport, Miller Brown argues that a paternalistic approach towards drug use in sport is contradictory to other values that we hold in sport:

> '... ironically, in adopting such a paternalistic stance of insisting that
> we know better than the athletes themselves how to achieve some more
> general good which they myopically ignore, we must deny in them the
> very attributes we claim to value: self-reliance, personal achievement, and
> autonomy.'[4]

Although authors such as Anderson[5] argue that the higher the risk of harm, the more justified paternalistic intervention becomes, as Brown indicates: if it can be argued that the value that comes from taking part in dangerous sport outweighs the risk, even if that risk is high, then intervention may not always be justified.

IS DANGER A NECESSARY AND VALUABLE PART OF SPORT?

Those who participate in dangerous sports will often cite various psychological and emotional reasons for doing so, including the desire for challenge, testing the limits of possibility, the quest for novelty, and the exhilaration that one feels as a result. The phenomenological (or raw-sense) experience of dangerous sport has been considered by a number of authors in the literature.[6]

One suggestion for the value of dangerous sport is that it allows the experience of the sublime. The sublime is often understood in relation to aesthetics in that it denotes a quality of experience. Edmund Burke distinguished the sublime from the beautiful by arguing that the sublime is awesome in a way that the beautiful can never be.[7] For instance, Carl Thomen argues that while we might be able to appreciate the aesthetic beauty of a high-board diver, it is only in dangerous sports such as big-wave surfing that we can experience the sublime.[8] The sublime occurs when we are aware of the power that nature has to compel and destroy us and the way in which it forces us to confront our mortality. Water itself is not threatening and can be easily overcome and manipulated by humans. However, even the best athletes recognise the power that an angry sea can have over the human will, and many accomplished surfers have suffered as a result. We experience the sublime through precariously balancing on the edge of a (real or metaphorical) precipice in the full knowledge that a slight slip would lead to certain death.[9]

Essentially, dangerous sports allow us to understand what it is to be human. They enable us to challenge our physical and mental limitations under conditions that we would not normally experience. This is also referred to as 'self-affirmation'. In taking part in dangerous sports we create a paradox whereby we both confront, and at the same time avoid, our mortality. As Leslie Howe asserts, risk and danger in sport is valuable because it amplifies:

> 'the imperative that operates in all sport to concentrate on the moment [and] to effect the crucial connection between awareness and embodiment. Risk sharpens the attention to detail and to one's priorities and values... Risk contributes to the clarification of who we are, what we value, and what we are willing to do about it. It is a valuable element in developing a knowledge of one's self.'[10]

On this basis, dangerous sports have value because they provide us with opportunities that are not afforded in other aspects of life but, more importantly, they enable us to experience a fuller range of human emotions and sensations.

Gunnar Breivik makes the argument that humans have evolved to seek out risk and the development of extreme sports comes as a direct result of a safer and more controlled society.[11] As both Breivik and Brown suggest, if we minimise risk in other areas of life, then we may well find ourselves subjugating the human attributes we value most, such as resourcefulness, imagination and authenticity. Preventing people from participating in risky activities may prevent the development of skills and capacities that enable us to flourish and live a good and worthwhile life.

INDEPENDENT STUDY QUESTIONS:

- What other examples of sports could be given for the four cases in Figure 15.1?
- What is the difference between Libertarianism and Paternalism?
- Under what, if any, conditions should people be prevented from harming themselves in sport?
- What is the sublime and how can it be understood in relation to dangerous sport?
- Is it a good argument to suggest that extreme sports allow humans the best capacity for self-affirmation?

16 ARE OLYMPIC VALUES WORTH ASPIRING TO?

The Olympics represents the foremost international multi-sports event and is named after Olympia, one of the original sites for the ancient Greek games, which were founded in 776 BC. Athletic competitions were a regular feature in ancient Greek society, with the Olympic Games being the most recognised. Even the ancient Greek philosopher, Plato, was a renowned wrestler and winner of several Olympic competitions. Although one of the commonly cited reasons for competitive physical training was the requirement for well-trained soldiers in the ongoing military battles that abounded during this time, the athletic training provided by the academies and gymnasiums was not merely to produce good soldiers but also good citizens. The original games evolved from the view held in much of ancient Greek culture that it was as important to cultivate the body as it was to develop the mind. They believed that there was a relationship between the body, mind and (moral) soul, and therefore training one element would positively affect the growth and development of the others.[1]

The modern Olympics, as any student of sport is able to recount, was born out of the romanticism of Pierre de Coubertin in order to restore pride to the French nation following the humiliating defeat of France in the Prussian war. This interpretation highlights the paradoxes and contradictions inherent in the Olympic movement. What we do know about de Coubertin is that he was both heavily influenced by ancient Greek philosophy and saw the need for a much greater level of physical education in the French schooling system. By circumstance, at the same time that de Coubertin was having these thoughts, the site of the ancient Olympic Games in Olympia was rediscovered and excavated by British and German archaeologists.[2] It was these events that led de Coubertin to propose an international athletic competition based upon ancient Greek Olympic ideals.

WHAT IS OLYMPISM?

The ancient Greek ideals revered by de Coubertin are often captured in the phrase 'Olympism'. This is defined by the International Olympic Committee as:

> '... a philosophy of life, exalting and combining in a balanced whole
> the qualities of body, will, and mind. Blending sport with culture and

education, Olympism seeks to create a way of life based on the joy found in effort, the educational value of good example and respect for universal fundamental ethical principles.[3]

This suggests that the Olympics Games are not merely a multi-sports event, but are founded on philosophical and ethical values. This passage from the Olympic Charter clearly addresses the fundamental philosophical question about what it is to lead a good life and what part sport should play within it.

The problem, however, is when greater scrutiny is applied to these fundamental values. The Olympic motto identifies the values of '*citius, altius, fortius*' (faster, higher, stronger) while the slogan of the Youth Olympic Games is 'excellence, friendship, respect'. The Paralympics holds the values of courage, determination, inspiration and equality, and the Olympic Charter also cites the values of peace, inclusion, tolerance and non-discrimination, and environmentalism. Such a broad swathe of values may have the effect of diluting Olympism's force, especially as the emphasis changes according to political and ideological context. As Jim Parry notes, it aims to be a universal set of values that applies to everyone regardless of nationality, race, gender, social class, religion or ideology while still allowing for cultural differences between nations.[4] However, this aim of striving for universality while holding on to a form of cultural relativism is both difficult in practice and logically problematic. It also creates difficulties for the oft-held notion that sport is outside the realm of politics, since the value of tolerance, non-discrimination and environmentalism are very much within the political sphere.

The range of values listed also highlights the tension between what we might call 'athletic excellence' and 'moral excellence'. The motto 'faster, higher, stronger' has become the dominant maxim in modern sport and clearly prioritises athletic performance above all else. A criticism of this focus is categorised by the 'technological attitude', whereby the only value is that of quantifiable performance. This has the effect of dehumanising those competing (since it treats the body as a commodity) and implicitly promotes morally problematic practices such as doping.[5] Focusing solely upon these athletic values ignores the moral values that are fundamental to the IOC's definition of Olympism. It is equally telling that for Paralympic sport the prominent values are moral ones. Such a difference in the focus of values supports the narrative of the 'super-crip' whereby individuals are celebrated for their courage and determination in triumphing over disability rather than their performances.[6]

It seems then that while Olympism aspires to a range of moral and athletic values, modern elite (and specifically able-bodied) sport demonstrates a greater focus upon the latter rather than the former. One reason for this may be the greater commercialisation and commodification of sport, and this is explored in greater detail in Chapter 30. A response to this concern may be to change the Olympic motto from its sole focus on athletic excellence to embrace a pluralistic range of values that recognise the ancient Greek values upon which the Olympics were founded.

WHAT CAN WE LEARN ABOUT OLYMPISM FROM THE ANCIENT GREEKS?

The question that Socrates and other ancient Greek philosophers posed that is reflected in the concept of Olympism was the question, 'what is it to live a good life?' For Socrates, the answer was found in the notion of *eudaimonia* or 'flourishing'. This concept is more easily understood when illustrated by an entity such as a plant. It is easy to identify a flourishing or dying plant. A plant flourishes if it is given the things it needs, such as light, oxygen and water but too much or too little of these and in the wrong ratio will lead to illness and death. Equally, humans have needs that, if satisfied, will enable them to flourish. Yet, as for the plant, it is important to strike an appropriate balance in meeting these needs. Too much focus upon one aspect of body, mind or soul will lead to a deterioration of the others. This is often referred to as the 'golden mean' as it depicts the optimum requirements for a flourishing life.[7]

A number of values have been identified as ancient Greek athletic ideals:[8, 9]

1. the pursuit of excellence (*aretē*);
2. the good life as one of moderation and self-control (*sōphrosynē*);
3. the duty to strive for an ideal beyond human imperfection (*eusébeia*);
4. to seek to improve one's body through athletic training (*askesis*);
5. the virtues of courage (*andreia*), justice (*dikaisosynē*) and wisdom (*sophia*);
6. the drive for competitiveness (*thymos*);
7. the notion of play (*paidia*);
8. the concept of beauty and goodness when applied to the body and soul (*kalokagathia*).

These ideals display a plurality of values that depict a human life that is worth aspiring to but also a set of values that can be specifically applied to sport. The overarching value is *aretē*, which points to the perfection of body, mind and soul. This explains why the ancient Olympians were seen as more than mere mortal athletes and were viewed as gods; such athletes personified perfection. It is important to recognise, however, that the pursuit of excellence was not simply about beating others in physical contests. For Plato, the body, mind and soul need to be trained and developed in the correct manner. In the same way that rhetoric should not simply be used as a way to win arguments, physical fitness should not be used simply as a way of defeating opponents. To excel is to develop the self in the right way with regard to other virtues. A true Olympian is not someone who revels in victory but someone who excels in their discipline. Heather Reid argues that the conventional view that athletic contests were originally developed as training for war is mistaken. Instead, sporting contests, such as running, throwing, jumping and wrestling, had no other purpose that the pursuit of excellence in these disciplines.[10]

Sōphrosynē can be translated as temperance or self-control. It is a dynamic but focused power that enables excellence through channelling one's energy towards a particular goal, and can be well exemplified in sport. This type of self-control allows for an aesthetic element within sport. As Reid notes:

> 'While modern sport is often characterised by excesses and 'winning ugly,' the ideal remains a harmonious tension between power and control.'[11]

Eusébeia can be translated as respect and a duty to strive for an ideal beyond oneself. While we must accept that perfection is an ideal that will never be attained we should however continually test ourselves against it. One way this can be done is by pitting ourselves against others who are also aiming for it, hence the value of competition with others.[12] One of the reasons that the olive wreath presented to winners in Olympia was to symbolise the notion of perfection but also the short-lived nature of victory.[13] Nevertheless, *eusébeia* does not endorse 'perfectionism' as is commonly understood today. Perfectionism in this context serves to offend other virtues. This can be captured by the ancient Greek concept of the 'golden mean', which argues that we must strive to avoid excess or deficiency. Perfectionism is to tip the virtue for the desire for excellence to excess, while in contrast to be content with mediocrity is to tip it towards a deficiency.

The golden mean can also be seen in the ideal of *andreia* (bravery or courage). *Andreia* is required to overcome the struggle of life against failure and sport is an example of this. It is not simply a gung-ho or foolhardy attitude (an excess) or an absence of fear but rather a virtue that allows us to discern where fear or caution is appropriate and when it can be overcome. *Andreia* enables us to pursue higher ideals even if doing so risks damaging ourselves in other ways, such as in terms of wealth or reputation. Sport provides an opportunity for us to develop *andreia* because it provides us with an artificial or manufactured struggle. While there is a risk that our failures will be public, or that we come to physical harm through injury, the nurturing of *andreia* allows us to strive for excellence despite the fear that we may fail in doing so.

Askesis refers to the development of the body through physical training. It has often been translated as 'asceticism', which is generally understood as deprived or penitential. However, the etymology suggests a much more noble conception as it is closely related to the term *ethos* from which we derive the word 'ethics'. *Askesis* is the sacrifice we must make in order to excel:

> '[A]sceticism enables us to escape from barbarism so that we might 'enter the stadium naked and unclothed, striving for the most glorious of all prizes, the Olympia of the soul.'[14]

Dikaiosynē translates as justice but needs further explanation. It applies to the adherence to a set of rules but also to a fair contest, hence our metaphor 'level playing field'. It can also relate to Plato's conception of a well-ordered and organised society that functions most effectively when the individual parts are utilising their best skills to fullest effect[15] and in this context may be a virtue that coaches and managers in particular aspire to.

Sophia (wisdom) is the ability to put knowledge and skill to good use and is the aspect of *aretē* that enables the goal of *eudaimonia*. It is the use of other virtues or ideals in a positive way (and can perhaps be seen as a forerunner for Kant's notion of 'good-will'). The concept of *sophia* demonstrates why the ancient Greeks believed in developing the body, mind and soul together and why there is a relationship between sport and philosophy. Reid conceptualises sport and athletics as a form of experiment: in the same way that a philosopher or scientist will attempt to solve a puzzle using a (rigorous and systematic) method, an athlete will attempt to solve questions about capability and excellence within a set framework (rules). A good athlete must have the courage to accept that the results are not always going to be what one expects (or wants) in the same way that a scientist must be willing to accept failure and disappointing results. Both must be open to new suggestions or hypotheses and both must be reflective about their successes and failures in order to continue to strive for excellence. The problem, however, as Reid argues, is that modern sport often prevents athletes from developing *sophia* since the focus is not on the pursuit of excellence but rather the pursuit of worldly goods such as fame and fortune.[16]

Perhaps the most controversial of the above ideals is that of *thymos* (or *thumos*). It essentially means 'heart' or 'guts' and can be viewed alongside courage, assertiveness and determination. It is an anger or indignation that rises to boiling point and hence is a powerful force if not tempered by other virtues. According to Socrates, *thymos* is irrational but can be channelled through *logismos* (rationality), *sōphrosynē* and athletic training into producing excellence. Our best understanding of *thymos* can be seen in examples whereby a competitor's drive to win allows them to succeed where all other measures indicates they will fail. It demands everything of the athlete who has nothing left to give at the end and can be illustrated by those athletes who at the end of their contest are left exhausted and spent. Rowing is a perfect example of *thymos* in action; it requires absolute discipline, focus and concentration in terms of maintaining stroke rate and rhythm and yet also demands sheer guts to push the body to its limit. We can also see *thymos* in sports such as boxing: boxers prepare themselves mentally and physically for this challenge, 'trash-talking' their opponent and are desperate for the fight to begin. Yet at the end of the fight, when their bodies are exhausted, they embrace and show a respect for each other that was not present before the start:

> '*Having discharged their* thumos *in the most direct way possible, the boxers can start behaving like ordinary, decent human beings again and no longer like savage warriors.*'[17]

Paidia is the basis of all sport and arguably forms a key pillar to the good life. Huizinga took his cue from the ancient Greeks (in particular, Plato) in arguing that humans are *homo ludens,* or man the player, and Bernard Suits later supported this by suggesting that Utopia would consist in playing games.[18] Seeing the world through play allows us to recognise what is valuable and important in life and recognising that play forms the basis of sport enables us to deal with failure and injury with a sense of perspective.

Lastly, *Kalokagathia* refers to the harmonious joining of both moral and physical beauty. This ideal encompasses many of the others in relation to sport and arguably should be the aspiration for all athletes since it is only achieved through bringing together other virtues, such as discipline, courage, modesty and self-control. For Plato, true athletic beauty is only attainable in conjunction with a virtuous soul.[19]

SHOULD ATHLETES ASPIRE TO OLYMPIC VALUES?

As noted, the concept of Olympism is designed to embrace a multitude of athletic and moral ideals. While there are criticisms as to how well these ideals can be formulated into a simple and all-encompassing maxim such as that expressed in the Olympic motto, ancient Greek philosophy, particularly exemplified by Plato's academy, demonstrates that athletic excellence is more than mere physical training and quantifiable performance. This seems to highlight, at the very least, a problem with a conception of elite sport that is focused purely on reducing the body to a machine in order to maximise its commercial value. That the ancient Greek philosophers such as Socrates, Plato and Aristotle were continually drawn back to the question of what it is to lead a good life allowed them to gain a perspective that is often neglected by those who focus purely on physical performance in sport. Olympic values that are founded on ancient Greek ideals such as *aretē*, *sōphrosynē* and *kalokagathia* provide an ideal conception of sport and what it is to excel within it.

INDEPENDENT STUDY QUESTIONS:

- *What is the modern conception of Olympism and what are its limitations?*
- *What are the ancient Greek ideals that are identified and how do they relate to the practice of sport that is seen today?*
- *To what extent is the modern Olympics founded on the values of the ancient Greek games?*

INTERVIEW WITH A PHILOSOPHER

RANDOLPH FEEZELL

Randolph Feezell is a Professor of Philosophy at Creighton University in Omaha, USA. He has written several books on play and the relationship of sport to a good life. He attended university on a full baseball scholarship. He has also played basketball and tennis at a competitive level, and has coached baseball at virtually all levels.

- *Can you give me a little bit on your background and what got you interested in the philosophy of sport?*
  - Two activities have been of central interest in my life: sports and philosophy. While I was at university on a sports scholarship I took a philosophy class and my life started to change rather dramatically. My athletic life faded into the background as I later worked towards a PhD in philosophy. When I was hired as an academic philosopher I had no idea that philosophy of sport existed as an area of serious study. At one point I stumbled upon a book by the noted American philosopher, Paul Weiss, *Sport: A Philosophic Inquiry*. It was a revelation to think that a real philosopher could write a whole book on sport! In the process of reflecting on Weiss's view of sport I discovered the fascinating work on play by Huizinga and Caillois. When I first began to study philosophy, I sensed that the reflective and athletic parts of my life were deeply antithetical; now, their marriage seems natural and extremely rewarding.

- *What do you think is the most interesting problem in the philosophy of sport?*
  - I wouldn't say there is any one problem that is most interesting in philosophy of sport; however, my reflections have always been quite personal. Regardless of the interest others might take in my work, I always felt that I was trying to figure things out about my own life. I spent so many hours playing and coaching these games, and my love for sports connected so closely with my identity, I wondered why I (or anyone) cared so much about sports. What concepts best represent or explain the attraction of sports? I began to think that the typical ways in which people talk about and conceptualise sport are incomplete, at best. Once one arrives at a deeper view of sport, it appears that certain things follow about the kinds of attitudes and behaviours that are appropriate for sports' participants. So the question about the nature of sports leads inevitably to questions about the value of sports and ethical questions about good conduct.

- *What book or paper has influenced you the most and why?*
  - This is a difficult question for me. As I mentioned, Huizinga's *Homo Ludens* was important for me early on. The work of Bernard Suits has been important, especially his paper 'The Elements of Sport'. I have returned to his analysis of the concept of 'game' many times in my writing. His book, *The Grasshopper: Games, Life and Utopia*, is wonderful. Additionally, the work of Thomas Nagel has been significant for me in thinking about sport, especially his essays in *Mortal Questions* and his book, *The View from Nowhere*. More generally, I have a long-standing interest in Buddhism, and this sometimes enters into my reflections rather obliquely. I make that connection more explicit in my book *Sport, Philosophy and Good Lives*.

Key Readings

Clifford, C. and Feezell, R., *Sport and Character: Reclaiming the Principles of Sportsmanship* (Human Kinetics, 2010).

Feezell, R., *Sport, Philosophy, and Good Lives* (University of Nebraska Press, 2013).

Feezell, R., *Sport, Play, and Ethical Reflection* (University of Illinois Press, 2004).

- *Can you give me a little bit on your background and what got you interested in the philosophy of sport?*

  - I had been an English Literature and Philosophy major in college. I had no idea that philosophy of sport existed. I was also a competitive cyclist. After graduating, I decided to devote the next two years full time to cycling in an effort to make the 1988 Olympics; the first time women would have a track cycling event. During those years I really started to love philosophy and decided to continue my studies. This softened the blow of missing the team (there was only one place and, rather unsurprisingly, the world champion got the spot).

  - In graduate school I gravitated toward ancient Greek philosophy and I found myself using my sports experience as a way to understand key concepts. I started to wonder if there was a connection between philosophy and sport. One day, while I was walking through the journal section of the library at the University of Massachusetts, I spotted the *Journal of the Philosophy of Sport* out of the corner of my eye. I remember opening the cover and reading the list of articles in wonder – there was such a thing as philosophy of sport! The next semester a course called 'Philosophy of Sport' showed up among the courses that graduate students would teach. I think it was a way of making sure I got a teaching assistantship. That course turned into my first book, *The Philosophical Athlete*.

- *What do you think is the most interesting problem in the philosophy of sport?*

  - Personally, I'm interested in the ability of sport to function as moral education. As for important questions for the field as a whole – there are many and I think it all begins with metaphysics. Until we understand what sport is metaphysically, it is difficult to make normative arguments about how it should be used and how practitioners ought to behave. I think that philosophy's job in the academy more generally is to think about and articulate these conceptual foundations and frame important questions for other disciplines like the social sciences. Sport is one of those things that society just seems to take as a given and to endorse (or reject) uncritically according to the status quo. It is up to the philosophers of sport to articulate how sport could and ought to function socially and to encourage a critical attitude toward the status quo. So I would say that the biggest problem in the philosophy of sport is not some individual academic issue, but rather trying to communicate effectively with the rest of the sport sciences, with practitioners, with the industry, and with society more generally.

- *What book or paper has influenced you the most and why?*
  - I still remember vividly sitting on a bench in a park in Cambridge, England, as a foreign exchange student in 1985, and reading a tattered black Penguin paperback of Plato's *Early Socratic Dialogues*. For the first time I realised that an academic future studying moral education was a live possibility for me. I was the first woman in my family to go to college and no one had a PhD, so I had never considered an academic career. It was Plato's dialogues that planted the seed for me. As far as the philosophy of sport, before I read any of the canon, I read John Jerome's *The Sweet Spot in Time*, which showed me a new way of thinking and writing about sport. Now that I have read most of the canon, I would say the most influential books for me have been Bernard Suits' *Grasshopper* and Drew Hyland's *Philosophy of Sport* – especially his theory of competition as friendship.

Key Readings

Reid, H., *Athletics and Philosophy in the Ancient World: Contests of Virtue* (London: Routledge, 2011).

Reid, H., *Introduction to the Philosophy of Sport* (Plymouth: Rowman and Littlefield, 2012).

Reid, H., *The Philosophical Athlete* (Durham: Carolina Academic Press, 2002).

SPORT, ART AND AESTHETICS

17 IS SPORT ART?

Despite contemporary discussion in the philosophy of sport being generally dominated by ethical issues, such as cheating, doping and fair play, many of the papers presented at the initial meeting of the Philosophic Society for the Study of Sport (later the International Association for the Philosophy of Sport) focused on the aesthetics of sport. This initial flurry of interest in the 1970s waned, however, as attention focused on to other areas. Recently, there has been a resurgence in discussion on this topic with special issues dedicated to this area in both the *Journal of the Philosophy of Sport* and *Sport, Ethics and Philosophy*, as well as books such as Stephen Mumford's *Watching Sport*[1] and Andrew Edgar's 'Sport and Art: An Essay in the Hermeneutics of Sport'.[2]

There are four positions in answer to the question, 'Is sport art?': David Best[3] argues that sport is not and can never be art; Chris Cordner[4] argues that some sport can be art; Stephen Mumford[5] and Jan Boxill[6] argue that all sport is art; and Andrew Edgar[7] argues that sport and art share a similar fundamental structure even though they are different concepts.

This chapter will begin by outlining a definition of aesthetics and its relation to art before considering some of the discussions that have occurred in the philosophy of sport.

WHAT IS THE DIFFERENCE BETWEEN ART AND AESTHETICS?

Aesthetics is contained within a branch of philosophy called axiology, which is the study of value. The other part of this branch is ethics. While ethics considers questions related to what we value in our relationships with others, and makes judgements about good or bad behaviour, aesthetics is a consideration of our values associated with sensory experience. This includes auditory and kinaesthetic experience but is often predominantly concerned with the visual. It asks questions about issues of taste and beauty, and the values we attach to them.

Before the question 'Is sport art?' can be answered, a distinction needs to be made between art and aesthetics. Although the terms are related, they refer to two different concepts. Aesthetics refers to sensory perception; what we find beautiful or ugly, intoxicating or horrifying, heartbreaking or sublime. Art in

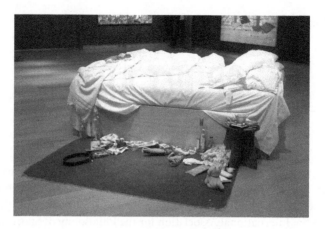

Figure 17.1 – Emin's 'My Bed'

contrast is the outcome of an intention to induce an aesthetic effect. It exists in order to express an aesthetic sensibility and to make a creative statement about the artist's perception of the world.[8] This means that there are things in the world that can invoke an aesthetic experience but are not art, such as a sunset, waves crashing against rocks, or the smell of freshly cut grass. Yet for something to be art there must be an aesthetic intention behind it. This explains why Duchamp's 'Urinal' and Tracy Emin's 'My Bed' (Figure 17.1) are art despite being 'merely' a urinal and 'merely' a bed.

DOES AESTHETICS PLAY A CENTRAL PART IN SPORT?

One of the questions first considered in the philosophy of sport was whether sport had anything important to say about aesthetics. The American philosopher Paul Ziff[9] argued that philosophers ought not to waste time considering the aesthetics of sport. He was notably forthright in his view:

> 'Research devoted to the aesthetics of sport can accomplish nothing. There is nothing there to be accomplished. Worse, it would not only contribute to the vaunted dreariness of aesthetics it could serve to delay even impede other possibly significant research.'[10]

His paper was in response to one by Paul Kuntz entitled 'Aesthetics Applies to Sports as Well as to the Arts'.[11] In it, Kuntz argued that sports have an important aesthetic value that can be appreciated by both the performer and the spectator. This is found in the beauty, joy and kinaesthetic empathy that we find in sport; 'it is the high emotional quality, like that of music, that makes sports worthwhile'.[12]

Kuntz cites Roger Bannister's account of running to provide support for this view. In it, Bannister points to the aesthetic element of sport as the key motivational factor for participating:

> 'I was running now, and a fresh rhythm entered my body. No longer conscious of my movement I discovered a new unity with nature. I had found a new source of power and beauty, a source I never dreamed existed. From intense moments like this, love of running can grow.'[13]

This account of sport's aesthetic value demonstrates that although competition is an important element in defining what sport is, it does not fully account for why people take part in it. An aesthetic account of the value of sport is exemplified in many sporting biographies like Bannister's and runs throughout sporting literature and is recorded in sporting memories. Kuntz wished to show that the aesthetic qualities that we ascribe to the arts, such as music, theatre and fine art, can be equally applied to sport. Sport provides similar meaning, affects our emotions and creates dramatic spectacle, albeit via a different means.

WHY IS SPORT NOT ART?

However, despite any aesthetic elements found within sport, it does not mean that sport is therefore art. David Best argues that those who think that sport is art are conceptually confused. Such proponents are conflating the two concepts. Best argues that neither is it correct to assert that sport is an art form in the same way that dance or literature or painting is an art form.

Best draws five areas of difference between sport and art: *means and ends, principal aims, types of expression, imagined and real objects*, and *subject matter*.

Means and Ends: Best argued that the means and ends in art are indistinguishable, whereas they are separate in sport.[14] In football, for example, it doesn't matter how a goal is scored as long as it conforms to the rules of that sport. The same is not the case for a painting. An original artwork by Monet, for example, is worth far more than a perfect replica, even if the two paintings are indistinguishable from one another. In art, the ends only make sense through understanding the means (how it is done, by whom and why). One of the criticisms levelled at much modern art is that it could have been produced by anyone. Yet the point is that it wasn't produced by just 'anyone' and that is what gives it value. In contrast, every goal scored is worth the same whoever scores it.

Principal Aims: Best maintains that the fundamental purpose of art is to be an aesthetic piece of work whereas this is incidental in sport. It is important to note here Best's distinction between the two different uses of the term 'aesthetic': the evaluative and the conceptual. Often we use the word to mean 'aesthetically beautiful', in phrases such as, 'he is an aesthetic athlete' or 'that team has many aesthetic qualities'. To use the word in this way is to evaluate the aesthetic merits of an object and is different from the conceptual use which, as outlined in the earlier definition, refers to the sensory effect in general. This explains how a piece of art can be disturbing or grotesque: the response we might have to it may not be pleasurable (or 'aesthetic' in evaluative terms) but its aim or purpose is still an aesthetic one. As the principal aim of a piece of art is an aesthetic one, it doesn't really make sense to ask 'what is the point?' since its point is contained in the fact that it is art. Artists might be asked to explain how they came to create their artwork, or a piece of art might be interpreted as making a particular statement, but fundamentally it is designed to be art and therefore to invoke an aesthetic experience. The principal aim of sport, in contrast, is different: it is to achieve the pre-lusory goal. Any aesthetic experience that comes from it is incidental.

Expression: The conventions of art allow for it to be an expression of the artist's perception of the world. Art is defined by the absence of rules, which allows it to depict an infinite number of conceptions of life. There may be rules for good technical drawing, creating a particular finish on a sculpture, or writing a compelling dialogue, but artists often aim to challenge conventions. Good art is often distinguished precisely because it expresses something new or in a different way. Sport in contrast, is limited by rules that mean athletes and players are constrained in opportunities for self-expression. Sport is defined by its constitutive rules. Indeed, one of the attractive features of sport is its ability to transcend differences and speak to people in a common language regardless of who is playing it.

Imagined and Real Objects: Art is a medium that is used to make a statement about the world or express a conception of life. Art is a representation of real or possible worlds, whether through paint, music or words. In a stage-play, for example, the actors are playing the role of another. The words they speak are not their own and they provide an account of a world that has been or could be. Sport in contrast, presents the world as it is; it is not a representation of an imagined or historical event. The blood dripping from an actor's nose is fake whereas for a boxer it is real. The pain that leads to a player being stretchered off the field has longer-term consequences, whereas in a play, the actor writhing around in agony happily walks off to the dressing room once off-stage.

Subject Matter: Art needs a subject matter – it needs to be 'about' something – but this can be anything the artist chooses. As we have seen, it can represent particular forms of life or express conceptions of the world. Art, therefore, can be about sport, as can be seen in Myron's bronze sculpture *The Discus Thrower* (Figure 17.2), or Jack Russell's cricket paintings. Sport in contrast, is not about anything other than itself; it exists merely as a regulated and competitive form of play or physical activity. Indeed, Best argues that 'the very notion of a subject of sport makes no sense.'[15]

The conclusion that Best reaches is that although it might be easy to find aesthetic qualities within sport (such as a beautiful goal in football, or the smooth and graceful running style of an athlete), it does not necessarily mean that it is art. For it to be art there must be an intention or recognition of it as an artwork.

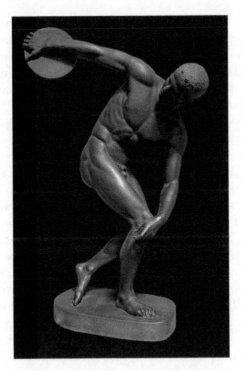

Figure 17.2 – Myron's 'The Discus Thrower'

WHAT ARE THE COUNTER-ARGUMENTS TO BEST'S DISTINCTIONS?

There have been several criticisms of Best's distinction of sport and art. Many argue that Best overstates his claim and that the differences are exaggerated or counter-examples can be provided.

Chris Cordner argues that counter-examples can be given for many of the differences between sport and art that are often cited. So, for the claim that sport is more physical than art, one can point to the examples of lawn-bowls and street dance. For the claim that art is creative whereas sport is not, the counter-examples of the Fosbury flop in high jump or the Cruyff turn in football can be provided. Those who claim that artists are motivated by a desire for self-expression and creativity whereas athletes are motivated by extrinsic rewards ignore examples such as Damien Hurst, who reportedly employs hundreds of people in five factories to create the artworks that earn him millions.[16] And while there are professional athletes who may participate for extrinsic reasons, most people take part in sport for the intrinsic pleasure and joy that it provides. Further counter arguments to Best's five distinctions between sport and art can also be given:

Expression: In rejecting Best's argument that only art can express a conception of life, Stephen Mumford suggests that this can be seen in sport too, for instance, in the contrasting styles of football demonstrated by teams such as Brazil and Poland. Brazil is famous for its flamboyant and ostentatious style that is exemplified in other depictions of Brazilian culture, such as the Rio de Janeiro carnival; while Poland, with its history of Soviet occupation and restricted liberty, is typified by a tightly structured, highly organised and austere game. Jan Boxill too, argues that both sport and art are media for self-expression and in both the ability to do so is hampered by a lack of skill. So an artist who lacks skill in painting will not be able to express himself as well as an artist who has been trained. Similarly, a footballer who possesses the skill to be able to control his body and the ball will be able to express himself in a greater way than a novice.

Principal Aims: Best may also be wrong in his claim that aesthetics is incidental in sport. Rule changes in sport are often driven by aesthetic considerations, such as the development of a faster-pace (20/20) version of cricket; and law changes in rugby union to allow advantage to the attacking side. Boxill argues that although sport requires efficiency of outcome, this does not overshadow the concern for beauty; it may be the case that beauty is not the sole aim in sport but neither is it in other art forms. She argues that, 'it is precisely these aesthetic qualities that account for the pleasure and meaning of sports to its participants and spectators'.[17]

Means and Ends: The distinction that Best makes between the means and the ends of sport and art are also exaggerated. The rules of the sport may provide constraints that limit what is possible but so too does a theatre script or musical score. A coach may stamp his creative direction on the way in which the sport is played in the same way that a director can provide a new interpretation of a classic dialogue. Equally, the existence of features such as 'goal of the month' indicates that all goals are not equal, and the popularity of players can often relate to their demonstration of aesthetic skill.

Imagined and Real Objects: Best's distinction between the imagined and real can also be countered since players will take on a role within a game. They may act as if they hate their opponent but then will shake hands and joke together afterwards. This can be seen in the bravado and hype shown by boxers before their fights or by rugby players on the pitch. Equally, football players like Vinnie Jones and Eric Cantona played up to their caricatures of 'bad boys', which enabled them to develop careers in acting. Similarly, a player who displays animosity to an opponent in a club game one week, shows friendship and respect to the same player when they are playing together for their national side a week later. Examples given by Bredemeier and Shields show that coaches and athletes alike recognise they have to 'act' out a particular role in sport. This is manifested in phrases such as, 'I have to change, I have to leave the goodness out and bring all the badness in, like Dr. Jekyll and Mr. Hyde' and 'I'm mean and nasty then ... I'm so rotten. I have a total disrespect for the guy I'm going to hit'.[18]

Subject Matter: Cordner argues that one of the central features that art and sport share is the space it inhabits, i.e. one that is beyond or outside 'ordinary' life. This conceptual 'playspace' is bounded by either formal or tacit rules as well as a physical space in which the activity is viewed: stadiums and arenas in the case of sport, and theatres and galleries in the case of art. It is 'outside' ordinary life because the rules that apply in these spaces are not the same as those that apply generally. For a member of the public to rush on stage in an attempt to prevent a character from being murdered, or for a spectator to jump into the ring to stop a boxing match in the same way they would attempt to break up a fight on the street, is to misunderstand the nature of those activities. As Cordner notes, the activities that take place within this space are self-contained and for their own ends. Although there may be a variety of motivations behind being a participant or spectator, the primary goals for both sport and art are contained within the activity itself.

Ultimately Cordner criticises Best for having an inherent intellectual bias towards the 'fine' or 'high-end' arts represented by particular types of theatre, dance, music, painting, sculpture and architecture. Best's arguments do not take account of many other forms of art, such as abstract or conceptual painting, and contemporary dance, music and theatre. These contra-examples render his argument that art has a deeper meaning or is a representation of something in the world, problematic. In many cases of modern or abstract art, it makes no sense to ask 'what is it about?' As such, art does not have a subject-matter in the way that Best believes.

DO SPORT AND ART BOTH REFLECT WHAT IT IS TO BE HUMAN?

These criticisms indicate that the distinctions between sport and art are much more blurred than Best supposes. Rather than being wholly different activities, sport and art share important similarities. Andrew Edgar goes further and argues that sport and art share the same structure; both provide us with a framework within which to consider metaphysical and ethical problems.[19] Both sport and art occur in the space between the real and the represented. We are able to grasp philosophical truths and test philosophical problems from the (non-real) worlds that art and sport inhabit. Both can tell us about human nature and the things that matter. Both art and sport highlight a deep responsiveness that we as humans have towards human activity that is founded in play. They may not contain an overt meaning that can be articulated through language and they may not express a particular conception of life, but they are an important part of a good life nonetheless. As Cordner argues, both art and sport are 'built upon a capacity for imaginative engagement'[20] with the world. This indicates that the concepts of sport and art overlap in a much deeper way than many of the superficial surface differences suggest. Ultimately, it can be argued that sport and art both reflect the essence of what it is to be human.

INDEPENDENT STUDY QUESTIONS:

- *What are the similarities and differences between sport and art?*
- *To what extent does the aesthetic matter in sport?*
- *How far can it be argued that athletes play a role in the way that actors do?*
- *What is meant by the argument that both sport and art tell us about life?*

18 DOES BEAUTY MATTER IN SPORT?

Sports that are judged on aesthetic elements such as creativity, beauty and fluidity are often viewed with a particular scepticism. After all, the critic argues, they are not *real* sports with clear objective goals. In contrast to a game of tennis, during which the ball is either out or in and a point and the winner is decided on objectively measurable criteria, aesthetic sports are often seen as being based on subjective judgement: how nice the dive looks, how creatively the figure skater performs, or how graceful the gymnast appears on the asymmetric bars.

This chapter seeks to discuss this criticism and will consider whether the differences between the so-called 'purposive sports' and 'aesthetic sports' are as great as first appears. It will consider the part that beauty and other aesthetic considerations play in sport and whether they form a necessary feature of good sport.

WHAT IS THE DIFFERENCE BETWEEN 'PURPOSIVE' AND 'AESTHETIC' SPORTS?

David Best first distinguished between what he called *purposive sports*, and *aesthetic sports*.[1] Purposive sports are those sports that contain a clear pre-lusory goal that is independent of the means to reach that goal; such as the team that has scored the most goals after 90 minutes, or the first person to cross the line. Purposive sports are often cited as exemplars of sport, such as football, cricket and tennis, but they also include track and field sports and most combat sports. They are the sports for which there is a clear measurement for winning. Aesthetic sports, in contrast, are those that focus upon and judge the movement of the body, and for which the pre-lusory goal is less clear and is wholly dependent on the means. Typical examples of aesthetic sports are gymnastics, figure skating, high-board diving and skateboarding.

The differences between purposive and aesthetic sports are often related to how the pre-lusory goal is achieved. For example, in football, a goal is worth the same number of points regardless of whether it was the result of several pin-point accurate passes and a spectacular half-volley from the edge of the box into the top right-hand corner of the net, or whether it came from a goalmouth scramble and a ricochet off a defending player. What matters in these purposive sports is that the pre-lusory goal is achieved within the rules, i.e. if the ball has crossed the goal line without a preceding foul. In contrast, the pre-lusory goal for aesthetic sports is less clear. In the parallel bars for instance, marks are awarded for specific elements such as swings, holds and dismounts. It is the way in which the competitor achieves these elements that gains or loses points: for example, it matters how a competitor gets into a handstand position and how well they hold it.

IS THERE A RELATIONSHIP BETWEEN BEAUTY AND SKILL?

At first glance, it may appear that aesthetic sports are judged subjectively. After all, as we saw in Chapter 17, aesthetics refers to judgements about sensory perception and emotional effect. The subjective view of aesthetics asserts that appreciation of beauty cannot be held to any objective standard. It is merely individual preference in the same way that some people prefer chocolate to cheese. However, even in this example there is some room for narrowing down food preferences. Although two people may differ when it comes to whether they like chocolate or cheese, the same cannot be said for whether they would prefer to eat faeces or rice. Anyone who stated the former would be categorised as insane or a joker. This dismissal of a pure 'anything goes' subjectivity can also be applied to aesthetic sports. Anyone who judges a belly flop into the pool as being aesthetically beautiful would not be taken seriously.

It is not simply the case that aesthetic sports are judged by the subjective preferences of the judges. The rules of sport will always dictate objective elements that the competitor needs to adhere to. So for aesthetic sports, such as gymnastics, figure-skating, snowboarding, skateboarding, surfing and high-board diving, it is the adherence to the rules of the sport that matter, not how beautifully or gracefully the performers carry out those rules. Marks are not awarded based on aesthetic qualities but rather for carrying out a series of movements in accordance with the judging criteria. One could imagine for example, a gymnast using a vault as a prop in a beautiful dance, but this would not score any points since it does not fulfil the rules of vaulting. The rules of gymnastic vaulting specify the points to be deducted for particular actions in take-off and landing as well as the points to be awarded for particular successful actions during the vault. It also includes point deduction for auxiliary elements such as starting before a flag is raised and using a spotter.[2] Points are not awarded for aesthetic beauty or for the emotional impact that a gymnastic performance might have, which explains why although some performances might have the crowd in raptures they may not necessarily achieve overall competition victory.

In this respect we might say that there are objective standards of beauty, and one of these is that beauty equates with skill. The athletes whom we often admire the most are the ones who make everything look easy. Such effortless smoothness often disguises a great degree of skill, as novices find out when they attempt to replicate such actions. That there is often an equation between beauty, elegance and simplicity is something that scientists and mathematicians have noted in their considerations of scientific and mathematical theory. The best solutions to problems are those that strip away all unnecessary excess and it is within this simplicity that we find an aesthetic beauty. Within sport, biomechanical efficiency is more likely to lead to a successful outcome and this is revealed through an aesthetic appreciation. Whether the reason is one of human nature or human culture, it seems that we simply prefer the look of biomechanically efficient actions. In order to highlight this further it is worth exploring the way in which points are awarded in 'aesthetic sports'.

It was suggested earlier that points are awarded according to the success of an athlete carrying out prescribed movements (for example, a round-off in gymnastics or a hardflip in skateboarding), yet such movements are valued precisely for the aesthetic beauty that they provide and would be explained by a correlation between skill and beauty. Falling on the floor, no matter how intentional, is not valued because it does not equate with skill, is therefore not beautiful and therefore will not be awarded points. There are obviously difficult judgements to be made however between badly executed (ugly) and difficult actions, and perfectly executed (beautiful) but easier actions. This is a judgement that both performers and adjudicators have to make but generally more points are awarded to the latter than the former examples. In high-board diving for example, a competitor will state the difficulty of the dive that they will attempt, with each dive being worth a pre-set number of points (generally, the greater the difficulty the more points may be awarded). These points are based on a perfect dive and points are deducted for anything less than this. As such, a diver will generally attempt the most difficult dive that they have perfected in order to gain themselves the most points.

There are, however, exceptions to the notion that skill equates with beauty. For instance, there are many examples of successful athletes who seem to have the most unattractive styles. The *New York Herald Tribune* said of the great distance runner, Emil Zátopek (Figure 18.1):

> *'Bobbing, weaving, staggering, gyrating, clutching his torso, slinging supplicating glances toward the heavens, he ran like a man with a noose around his neck. He seemed on the verge of strangulation.'*[3]

Zátopek, while certainly a skilful runner as demonstrated by his success, was not an aesthetically beautiful one by any stretch of the imagination. Yet, in 'purposive' sports, a correlation between skill and beauty is not important. As Paul Ziff points out, no matter how fine a forehand shot is produced in tennis, unless it travels over the net, bounces within the court and beats the opponent, it has no bearing on the success of the player who produces it.[4] Although there is evidence for the view that a correlation exists between what we find aesthetically pleasing and factors that contribute to success in sport, such as economy of effort and biomechanical efficiency (as can be seen by the examples of Zátopek and other successful, if ungainly, athletes), this relationship is not binding. An example of

Figure 18.1 – Emil Zátopek

coaches recognising that this relationship is not necessarily contingent can be seen in recent changes in coaching strategies in cricket. It used to be the case that cricket coaches attempted to mould a player's bowling action into a particular aesthetic standard; one that was judged to be biomechanically efficient. However, biomechanically efficient bowling will not always lead to success since it is arguably easier for the batsman to read and harder for the bowler to perfect. Coaches are now encouraged to work with the action as it is (no matter how 'ugly') in order to improve consistency and success rate, rather than worry about what it looks like (as long as it subscribes to the rules of bowling).

What this perhaps indicates is that although there are exceptions to the rule in non-aesthetic sports, there is an aesthetic value to sports performance that is based upon a relationship between beauty and skill. This is especially the case for so-called 'aesthetic sports' that are judged on movements that have been deemed to be of merit precisely for their aesthetic quality. That there are aesthetic norms built into the concept of 'vault' and 'dive' highlights the distinction between 'purposive' and 'aesthetic' sports, and was noted by David Best when he said:

> '[F]or whereas not any way of dropping into the water could count as even a bad dive, any way of getting the ball between the opponents' posts, as long as it is within the rules, would count as a goal, albeit a very clumsy or lucky one.'[5]

Even in non-aesthetic sports, whereby the victor is determined by the successful achievement of a particular goal (e.g. finishing the race first, or getting a ball into the net more times than the opponent), there does still seem to be a degree of correlation between skill and aesthetic appreciation. Moreover, it is this correlation that is appreciated most by spectators and promoters of particular sports, and is considered in more detail in Chapter 19.

IS SPORTING GENIUS AN EXAMPLE OF AESTHETIC BEAUTY IN SPORT?

While skill often correlates with that which we find beautiful, if the skill also contains pure originality, it is that which makes the performance great. This has led Teresa Lacerda and Stephen Mumford to argue that the genius should be considered a valid aesthetic category in sport.[6]

While they do not wish to provide a restrictively analytical account of genius, Lacerda and Mumford provide five characteristics: *creativity, innovation, originality, freedom,* and *inspiration for others to follow.*

Ultimately, they argue 'the genius is one who is able to break out from the existing chains of convention'[7] and provide the examples of Maradona, Schuschunova, Boklöv and Fosbury to illustrate this. Maradona demonstrated a vision and awareness in football that was unsurpassed. He was able to negotiate his way, seemingly effortlessly, past opposition players while continuing to keep control of the ball. Schuschunova's originality in developing new linking movements between set gymnastic moves brought a grace and fluidity to a routine that had not been seen before, while Boklöv and Fosbury developed new techniques in sport that enabled previous limits of human ability to be surpassed: Boklöv with the v-shape in ski-jumping, and Fosbury with his backward head-first jump in the high jump.

Although those who are considered geniuses in sport often demonstrate an aesthetic beauty, other elements such as creativity and freedom may play a larger role. Those who are able to work within the confines of the rules of sport yet demonstrate creativity and innovation may allow others to refine the techniques in more aesthetic ways. For instance, skateboarders, such as Rodney Mullen, have revolutionised what is considered possible on a skateboard, and yet are often criticised for being 'sketchy' or poor in style: in other words they do not have a natural aesthetic beauty. However, the fact that they inspire others to adopt and perfect the tricks they create is a demonstration of genius. It is the ability to be creative that generates the freedom for others to follow. For Lacerda and Mumford, it is the quality of genius that has the greatest aesthetic value in sport. The original always has greater aesthetic value simply because it is the original. They argue:

'Seeing something allows us to experience its aesthetic features but seeing it for the first time gives us something that is not in the subsequent encounters. The genius at work provides us with such experiences when

few others would be able to do so. This appreciation of the new – of novel successful strategies – is what rationally grounds our fascination with genius.[8]

What this discussion suggests is that beauty and other aesthetic qualities do matter in sport, although there are some sports in which these qualities have more influence on the outcome of the performance. While it is possible to win 'ugly' in 'purposive' sports, it is less easy to do so in the 'aesthetic' sports for the very reason that the label suggests. Nevertheless, aesthetic sports are still judged on objectively determined criteria and these often correlate to the degree of difficulty or skill involved. That there is often a link between skill and beauty supports the relationship between efficiency and beauty that is found in other areas of human life, such as mathematics and science. Yet beauty is not the only aesthetic quality that is appreciated in sport; the notion of genius uses creativity and innovation to push sporting performances to a new level that inspires others that follow. While quantifiable performance is often the sole measurement of progress in sport, it may be wise to bear in mind that the performances that are remembered are those that are based upon aesthetic or creative genius.

INDEPENDENT STUDY QUESTIONS:

- *What are the differences and similarities between 'purposive' and 'aesthetic' sports? Give examples to illustrate.*
- *How are aesthetic sports judged?*
- *Is it correct to suggest that biomechanical efficiency correlates with beauty in sport?*
- *How can the notion of genius be understood in relation to sport? Provide examples of your own to illustrate.*

19 IS IT BETTER TO BE A PURIST OR PARTISAN WHEN WATCHING SPORT?

WHAT IS THE DIFFERENCE BETWEEN PURISM AND PARTISANSHIP?

Sports fans are often separated into two types of spectator: those who value particular aspects of sport generally (such as aesthetic beauty or excellence of skill) regardless of who is performing those actions, and those who value particular teams or individuals regardless of their performance. Nicholas Dixon, who first distinguished between these types, describes them as follows:

> 'The 'partisan' is a loyal supporter of a team to which she may have a personal connection or which she may have sworn to support by dint of mere familiarity. The 'purist', in contrast, supports the team that he thinks exemplifies the highest virtues of the game, but his allegiance is flexible.'[1]

However, Stephen Mumford argues that Dixon's description of a purist is misleading. Dixon's purist seems to make a conscious decision to support a team or an individual based on the style of performance that they give and their allegiance will change according to whether the team or individual continues to uphold these standards. Dixon appears to be describing a fickle partisan with purist tendencies. In contrast, a true purist has no affiliation to a team or individual at all: they will value the action in its entirety regardless of who is carrying it out. As Mumford notes, 'A true supporter of the virtues of the sport could have no team allegiance because in any game or passage of play, which team plays virtuously could alternate rapidly.'[2]

On first inspection, it appears that the purist is the true sports fan since they value the intrinsic goods of sport, namely pure athletic excellence. They have no pre-determined allegiance and merely wish for a good game that demonstrates the highest levels of physical skill. In contrast, the partisan is merely interested in the result, however it is achieved. This is morally concerning since it can lead to an instrumentalist attitude that condones cheating and violence. As Dixon notes,

> 'When we teach children that playing the game fairly and to the best of our ability is more important than winning, the attitude we are nurturing is parallel to that of the purist, whereas the win-at-all-costs mentality that we discourage is more akin to that of the partisan.'[3]

Nevertheless, at a certain level of competition, partisanship may be understandable. For instance, those who support their local 'grass-roots' team are likely to have personal relationships with the players, who may be friends or family members. Wanting those players of which you already have personal knowledge to do well is akin to wanting friends and family to do well when attending job interviews, or going on a first date. Partisanship becomes more difficult to explain for those who support larger or more distant clubs to which the individual has no personal affinity. Many English Premiership football clubs, for example, have few 'home-grown' players and therefore even those people born in the locality are unlikely to share a common history and culture with the players representing their team.

Additionally, supporting a sports team may bring psychological benefits in that it offers protection against isolation since one feels part of a community,[4] which may be particularly the case for those who support their local club and are able to watch games at the grounds with others that they meet in the same environment on a weekly basis. This also provides an answer to why partisanship is generally directed towards teams and not individual athletes. Teams and clubs often have an identity, history and narrative that transcends the individual athletes that represent them.

In defending partisanship, Dixon suggests that an analogy should be made with 'love'. Unconditional love is morally commendable since we love regardless of whether the recipient achieves or fails in our expectations. The partisan who sticks by his team, and supports them week after week, despite them being relegated to a fourth division league, demonstrates a commitment and resilience that should be applauded. On this account, it is the partisan who is the true sports fan as they demonstrate an attachment and bond, and unconditional love that resembles the one we share with our family and closest friends.

A criticism of this view is that in the same way that love for an abusive partner is not healthy, unconditional love for a team that plays badly in terms of condoning cheating or violence, or that has a negative ethos, is unhealthy too. While unconditional love is generally regarded as virtuous, when it allows a person to be caught up in immoral practices or takes a purely instrumentalist attitude, it no longer remains so.

In contrast, the purist's position can be criticised for revering an abstract conception of excellence in sport that is impossible to attain, rather than the real (fallible) human sport that exists. This leads Dixon to argue that a purist cannot be a fan of sport since familiarity with sport will necessarily bring loyalty and commitment to particular people and teams. Attachment is a natural human emotion and only those who do not genuinely engage with or understand sport will fail to feel it. This view seems to hold merit as a detached observer who sees sport just as a series of aesthetically beautiful movements is arguably not watching sport at all. This is a criticism that is expanded on later.

Dixon, therefore, favours a 'moderate partisan' approach to watching sport. This mirrors his 'moderate patriotism' that is outlined in Chapter 26 and is based on a similar reasoning:

> P1: *Causing harm to others is immoral.*
>
> P2: *Favouring some within your community does not logically entail harm to others outside it. This can be called 'moderate partisanship'.*
>
> C1: *Therefore, 'moderate partisanship' in sport is not immoral.*

Most criticism for Dixon's argument is focused on his second premise. For instance, Tännsjö argues that partisanship is 'fascistoid' as it implies contempt for others.[56] Dixon disagrees and responds that Tännsjö's objection is actually with the purist rather than the partisan because it is the purist who admires athletic excellence above all else, and it is towards this that Tännsjö's criticism is directed.

A further criticism of Dixon's position is that partisanship offends the rule of impartiality since it favours some at the expense of others. Dixon responds by arguing that there is nothing morally objectionable about giving benefits to some as everyone is free to choose how to distribute their loyalty and fans do not owe their support to anyone. Partisan support is morally acceptable as long as it is not offset by negative attitudes towards others (e.g. hooliganism, racism and xenophobia). It is not incompatible to both respect and value one's opponents while also desiring that one's own team does well.

CAN SPORT BE WATCHED IN DIFFERENT WAYS?

In his book *Watching Sport*, Stephen Mumford focuses on the three main reasons people have for spectating: the aesthetic, the ethically educative, and the emotional.[7] Mumford concentrates upon the aesthetic element and argues that there are different aesthetic categories that can be appreciated in sport. As such, the term 'aesthetic' does not simply refer to a narrow conception of grace or beauty but involves a wider effect upon sensory perception. As Gumbrecht notes;

> *'Watching sports ... is a fascination in the true sense of the word – a phenomenon that manages to paralyse the eyes, something that endlessly attracts, without implying any explanation for its attraction. Through this ability to fascinate, sports exerts a transfiguring power, drawing his gaze to things he would not normally appreciate, like grotesquely*

overweight wrestlers, woollen caps with shields, or half-naked bodies that hold no sexual interest.[8]

Mumford maintains that while purists and partisans may appear to be watching the same game, their experience is fundamentally different. A purist seems to have an aesthetic appreciation that a partisan could not. Purists view sports for the aesthetic qualities that they provide, whether that is a demonstration of graceful movement and balance, sheer strength and power, or innovative techniques and strategy. In contrast, all the partisan is concerned about is victory and success no matter how it is achieved. The partisan has a competitive perception while the purist has an aesthetic one. Yet perhaps there is some philosophical defence for the partisan's experience of sport, namely that the sporting experience is better than it is for the neutral observer. The partisan's deep emotional involvement that is entailed in following their sport allows for a richness of sensory (aesthetic) experience. Both Dixon and Mumford agree; it is the purist who is missing the richness of the sport experience by adopting such a detached view and merely seeing it as a series of skilful and artistic performances rather than the sporting experience as a whole.[9] In this respect, one may argue that the total purist is not watching sport at all. As such, Mumford argues that most spectators hold both partisan and purist positions while watching sports and outlines three theories as to how this dual position occurs: the true perception theory, the mixture theory, and the oscillation theory:[10]

1. The *true perception theory* holds that while the purist and partisan see sport through different lenses, it is only the moderate spectator who watches it as it 'really is'. The problem with this theory, however, is that it does not account for the wealth of empirical evidence regarding perception and the way in which our visual processing system works.

2. The *mixture theory* suggests that the moderate spectator watches the game from both perspectives at the same time. This accounts for the way in which sensory data is cognitively laden and allows for a range of purist/partisan mixtures, similar to the way in which mixing yellow and red paint allows for different degrees of orange. Yet this suffers from a conceptual problem in giving no indication about how this mixed perception occurs.

3. Mumford's preferred theory is the *oscillation theory*, which suggests that the moderate fan switches between competitive and aesthetic perceptions of sport depending on what is happening within the game at any particular time. The advantage of this theory is that it does not need to offer a new way of watching sport and allows for a quantitative measurement of purist/partisanship, rather than the purely qualitative one suggested by the mixture theory. It would also allow for the fact that the degree of oscillation is dependent on what type of game it is and the importance of the competition. So, for instance, one could watch a pre-season friendly with a 60 per cent aesthetic perception, but a cup-final with an 80 per cent competitive perception.

On this conception, partisanship and purism are two ends of the same spectrum. Mumford suggests that the moderate partisan could have easily been called a moderate purist because they are actually oscillating between an aesthetic perception and a competitive perception. They are able to move between different ways of watching sport.

ARE PURISM AND PARTISANSHIP TWO ENDS OF THE SAME SPECTRUM?

Leon Culbertson offers an alternative 'picture' to Mumford's suggestion about how we watch sport.[11] He criticises Mumford's conception of partisanship and purism as being two ends of a spectrum and considers whether there are better metaphors that could be used. The purist/partisan spectrum does not account for other ways of watching a football match, such as as a gambler, commentator, statistician, or even as someone who has no idea about the sport at all. Mumford's response is that these examples are not of watching sport but rather merely seeing aspects of it. Yet Culbertson notes that if these are not examples of watching sport then neither is the true purist situated at the end of Mumford's spectrum, who merely sees the movement of bodies and does not watch sport itself.

Culbertson is also critical of Mumford's supposition that a quantitative account of perception, which is provided by the oscillation theory, is superior to a qualitative account. He suggests that this is a consequence of Mumford's dualistic foci whereby one either watches sport with an aesthetic perception or with a competitive perception. Culbertson argues that broadening out to other ways of watching sport will reduce the necessity for a quantitative account. Taking this view, watching sport involves paying attention to a variety of different aspects at particular times, and that involves more than the two aesthetic or competitive aspects that Mumford identifies. There are some cases when it is difficult to differentiate between a purist and partisan way of watching sport; for example, if the team that the spectator is supporting scores a skilful lofted volley into the top right-hand corner of the net. There is no obvious oscillation occurring here since the spectator is able to take an aesthetic and competitive perspective at the same time. As such, Culbertson rejects Mumford's notion that watching sport is akin to the duck–rabbit illusion (Figure 19.1), whereby one either sees a duck or a rabbit but not both. Watching a football match is not the same thing as looking at a painting. The football match is dynamic in that it is always physically changing whereas the painting is not. The duck–rabbit or Necker cube illusion that illustrates Mumford's oscillation theory is therefore misleading. Instead, Culbertson argues that watching sport is not merely a case of switching between an aesthetic and competitive perception but rather a more fluid change of focus upon some aspects of the game, bringing them to the foreground while relegating other aspects to the background.

Figure 19.1

The original question of whether it is better to be a purist or partisan when watching sport may have turned out to be a misconceived one. Arguably no true spectator is a total partisan or a total purist. The spectrum theory of watching sport is useful to the extent that it differentiates between those who place a greater emotional investment in their team winning and those who take a more detached perspective in wanting to watch a 'good game' but, ultimately, most sports fans and enthusiasts wish to see 'their' team win but do it by displaying a high degree of physical skill. Where the spectrum analogy fails is at the extreme ends since both the total purist and the total partisan are arguably not watching sport at all. The total partisan (e.g. the gambler) is only interested in the result at the expense of all else, whereas the total purist (e.g. the artist) is only interested in the movement of bodies. Neither of these extreme positions represents an interest in sport *qua* sport. Watching sport, and implicitly, understanding it, requires both a competitive and an aesthetic perspective: appreciating the purist elements that make it a test of physical skill, while taking a partisan interest in who wins.

INDEPENDENT STUDY QUESTIONS:

- *What does Dixon mean by 'moderate partisan' and why does he defend this position?*
- *What is the 'oscillation theory of perception' and why does Mumford prefer it for explaining how we watch sport?*
- *Is the spectrum analogy adequate for explaining the purist/partisan debate and are there others that may work better?*

INTERVIEW WITH A PHILOSOPHER

STEPHEN MUMFORD

Stephen Mumford is Professor of Metaphysics at the
University of Nottingham, UK, and is a former Head of
School and Dean of the Arts Faculty. He is past Chair
of the British Philosophy of Sport Association and
has written books on a range of philosophical issues
from sport to metaphysics. A huge football fan and
long-suffering Sheffield United supporter, he has also
travelled the globe to watch football at a range of
levels; from amateur grass roots to the biggest events.
While philosophy remains his true passion he says
that sport has helped him to think. Once he found the
philosophy of sport, it became easy to combine the two.

- *Can you give me a little bit on your background and what got you interested in the philosophy of sport?*
  - My main work is in metaphysics, primarily on causation, laws of nature, dispositional properties and the problem of free will. I discovered philosophy of sport by chance when I saw an advert for the annual conference of the International Association for the Philosophy of Sport. I submitted a paper and went along out of curiosity. A number of other philosophers I already knew were there and I found it immediately to be a friendly and welcoming group. Later I became Chair of the British Philosophy of Sport Association and was a regular at the conferences for a number of years, gaining some very good new friends.

- *What do you think is the most interesting problem in the philosophy of sport?*
  - The most interesting question in the philosophy of sport as far as I am concerned is the value of sport in general. I'm interested in why we play it and why we bother watching it. Why does it interest us, especially when it involves a number of what appear to be trivial or even meaningless achievements, such as getting balls in holes or over lines, running round in circles, fighting over nothing or jumping bars that one could more easily walk under? Is sport merely a money-making machine that has ensnared us or is it in some genuine way life-enhancing and edifying? I came to focus in particular on the question of why we bother watching sport because this is where the value of sport seems the most pressing question. People can play to get rich or to get fit. But when we watch sport it makes us neither rich nor fit and sometimes the opposite. So are we right to be so consumed by sport?

I explored these questions in my book *Watching Sport*, in which I tried to vindicate sports spectatorship to an extent. When we do it in the right way, there are good aesthetic, ethical and emotional reasons for watching sport. At its best, sport can point to some of the most valuable aspects of our existence. The fact that we participate in and watch it willingly, rather than treating it as a means to some other end, can reveal something about what we value for its own sake. At its best, sport reflects and is an expression of the human condition.

- *What book or paper has influenced you the most and why?*
  - Probably the book that most influenced my career was Gilbert Ryle's *The Concept of Mind*. I might not have been a professional philosopher had I not discovered it. It introduced me to the idea of dispositions and their importance to a variety of problems. Ryle used the notion to dissolve the mind–body problem whereas I've made my career working on dispositional accounts of various troublesome metaphysical problems. Even when I've written on philosophy of sport, I've found the concept useful. Sport can be seen as a contest of causal powers, for instance, of the individual athletes and teams, where stronger skills and abilities tend towards success. Weaknesses and liabilities tend to failure. Sport is all about the exercise of embodied empowerment so an understanding of dispositions is no small matter.

Key Readings

Lacerda, T., and Mumford, S., 'The genius in art and in sport: A contribution to the investigation of aesthetics of sport', *Journal of the Philosophy of Sport*, 37(2) (2010), pp. 182–193.

Mumford, S., 'Emotions and aesthetics: an inevitable trade-off?', *Journal of the Philosophy of Sport*, 39(2) (2012), pp. 267–279.

Mumford, S., *Watching Sport: Aesthetics, Ethics and Emotion* (London: Routledge, 2011).

- *Can you give me a little bit on your background and what got you interested in the philosophy of sport?*
  - I read English and Philosophy at a small university, which allowed me to be in sports teams that for someone with my modest frame and ability would have been denied had I been at a bigger university; but the real story begins when I took over from David Best to teach philosophical aesthetics to dance students. Although what I taught was called 'Human Movement', many of the examples seemed to come from sport: that is how I ended up in the field. I have always been very sceptical about the idea of the philosophy of sport (as I am about other notions of 'the philosophy of x') and most of my writing in this area has been on rejecting the notion of a philosophy of sport. I even voted against forming what later became the British Philosophy of Sport Association. However, my position meant I was under pressure to explain to my department why they should keep a philosopher on their books if there was no legitimate philosophy of sport. So, having deliberated for a time, I constructed a philosophy of sport course I could live with: it took a little while longer but finally the course had a shape that eventually appeared, some years later, as my *Sport, Rules and Values* (2004). (When people ask me about the book, I say that the publishers think it is about sport – and so did my Department – but it is really about rule-following, and ultimately about the nature of philosophy.)
- *What do you think is the most interesting problem in the philosophy of sport?*
  - It is no secret that I am a Wittgensteinian; and when Wittgenstein was asked for the title of the lecture course he was going to give, he said that – since the lectures would be on philosophy – the title could only be 'Philosophy'. I think he was dead right: at the centre of all endeavours in philosophy are questions about what philosophy is, and what it does.

Given this background, I would identify three related challenges for philosophy of sport:

- How can we explain what sport is, when all such explanations necessarily admit of exceptions?

- How can we appeal to the rules of particular sports, when rule-formulations necessarily admit of exceptions once they come to be applied in context?

- How can we explain what is valuable about sport, given the diversity of sports, and the diversity of occasions in which a particular sport is played?

- *What book or paper has influenced you the most and why?*

  o It is very hard to give a single answer: in one way, it must be Wittgenstein's *Philosophical Investigations*, which offers a revised way of thinking about philosophy, and especially about the project of philosophy. I think that everything I have every written that shows any insight could be traced back to something in Wittgenstein.

  o If I had to offer something about sport, it would probably be David Best's fundamental paper 'The Aesthetic in Sport', reprinted in his *Philosophy and Human Movement* (1978). It is a masterpiece of getting clarity using the tools of philosophy.

Key Readings

McFee, G., *Ethics, Knowledge and Truth in Sports Research: An Epistemology of Sport* (London: Routledge, 2011).

McFee, G., *On Sport and the Philosophy of Sport: A Wittgensteinian Approach* (London: Routledge, 2015).

McFee, G., *Sport, Rules and Values: Philosophical Investigations into the Nature of Sport* (London: Routledge, 2004).

ETHICAL QUESTIONS IN SPORT

20 WHAT IS FAIR PLAY IN SPORT?

Fair play is central to our notion of good sport. So much so, in fact, that the International Council of Sport Science and Physical Education (ICSSPE) declaration on fair play stated that 'without fair play sport is no longer sport'.[1] It is one of those concepts that is frequently used yet rarely deconstructed: everyone knows it is important but few are able to adequately define it. At its core, fair play must involve adherence to the rules of the game. This account, outlined in more detail in Chapter 3, is called formalism. However, fair play is often cited as being much more than following the (constitutive) rules. It also seems to reflect an attitude towards playing the game and towards others involved in the game. As such, fair play can be divided into two strands: *formal fair play* that is related to adherence to the rules; and *informal fair play* that is concerned with a 'spirit' or 'ethos' of the game. While the former is much easier to define and accept within any definitions of fair play, it is the latter that is more problematic and intangible. Heather Sheridan outlined seven conceptions of 'fair play': formalism, play, respect, social contract, rational norms, virtue, and ethos.[2] While these concepts differ they are not mutually exclusive and often overlap.

WHAT IS FORMAL FAIR PLAY?

Formal fair play refers to the written or constitutive rules of the game. These rules must be at the heart of a conception of fair play for without them the game could not exist. The difficulty is whether the formal rules are sufficient for an account of both sport, and of fair play. The primary criticism of the formalist approach is that it is so strict it doesn't account for the realities of the way sport is played. According to a formalist, unless a participant is abiding by the precise rules of the game, they are not playing the game. These criticisms are outlined further in Chapter 3. When it comes to fair play, a formalist would argue that anything goes as long as it does not contravene the formal (i.e. written) rules of the game. This would therefore allow behaviour that many would label as 'gamesmanship' or 'against the spirit of sport'.[3] For instance, imagine a striking and fielding sport whereby one of the teams fields an incredibly talented dog, which is able to run, catch and field balls. If there was nothing in the rules of that sport that stipulated all players must be human, a formalist would argue that the dog is therefore an eligible player. A formalist would argue that if the general consensus is that dogs should not be part of the game, then it is for the rules to reflect this. Until the rules do, the team that includes the incredible fielding dog is playing fairly. A further criticism of the formalist position is that rules are also always going to be open to interpretation. For instance, a rule that states, 'the referee may allow the game to continue after an infringement if she deems it provides the opposing team with an advantage', requires interpretation as to what would constitute an 'advantage'.

There are many instances of game playing that do not directly contravene the rules of the game but are questioned or frowned upon. In these cases, the formalist maintains that such issues reflect a defect in the rules rather than in the participants' attitude or behaviour. Equally, there are ways of playing a game that may formally break the constitutive rules but are accepted by all the parties involved. For instance, modified games are often played to ensure a greater level of fairness, enjoyment or simply due to practical constraints on time or space. The main criticism levelled against the formalist account of game playing is that it fails to recognise that sport is a human practice with a social and historical framework that changes and develops in different contexts and times. This is reflected in the continual development and alteration of rules, for a whole variety of reasons, not just to plug loopholes or limit deficiencies. Rules may be amended for aesthetic reasons to make the sport more appealing or marketable; for safety reasons; or for reasons that reflect changes in our cultural attitudes. As such, the rules will never be sufficient to account for all the possible ways the game can be, and is, played.

A formal account of fair play, therefore, is generally considered necessary but not sufficient for a definition. The concept of fair play is not merely playing in accordance with the rules but is also dependent on the attitude and values that are attached to the game. This leads on to an informal account of fair play.

WHAT IS INFORMAL FAIR PLAY?

Informal fair play encompasses the additional aspects of the game that are seen as important but that are not covered by the formal rules. It refers to the attitudes that we hold towards the sport and others involved in it, and the way in which these attitudes affect our behaviour when playing it. One aspect of this can be represented by Suits' term, the 'lusory attitude'. This attitude is one ultimately of playfulness and is exemplified in the 'amateur ethos' whereby sport is seen as being outside 'normal' life and 'non-serious'. Sport, on this conception, is intrinsically valuable for the same reasons that play is of value: because it is enjoyable, is a diversion from 'ordinary' life, allows us to expend superfluous energy, etc. As such, the primary value of sport is one of play, and 'fair play' is when this value is upheld.

The problem with this conception however, is that can be seen as idealistic and not a true representation of (modern) sport. To consider sport as 'non-serious' doesn't account for the seriousness with which many view it, and disregards the elite and professional spheres where playfulness is not at the core.

WHAT PART DOES RESPECT PLAY IN SPORT?

Other conceptions of fair play focus upon the notion of 'respect'. The term 'respect' is often used in relation to fair play and was at the heart of the ICSSPE declaration, which was written in conjunction with the IOC and UNESCO. This declaration explicitly defines fair play as: self-respect, respect for team colleagues, respect for opponents, and respect for the referee. This can be encapsulated as Butcher and Schneider's definition of 'fair play' as 'respect for the game'.[4] However, the issue then becomes one of defining the term 'respect'.

One way in which respect can be defined is by turning to the work of the German philosopher Immanuel Kant. Kant maintained that the right way of behaving is one that is based upon rationality (i.e. logic and consistency). He argued that things ought to be treated (given due respect) according to the type of thing that it is. So while it is perfectly appropriate to kick a ball, it is not appropriate to kick a cat or a person. He formulated two categorical imperatives:[5] 'always behave in ways that you would want everyone else to behave, and 'always treat people as ends rather than merely a means to an end'.[6] Kant argued that both categorical imperatives meant essentially the same thing. They can be summarised by the saying 'treat others how you would wish to be treated'. In sport, this can be understood by playing in a way that you would want others to play; for instance, not to cheat, not to be abusive, and to play in a way that allows the game to flow in accordance with the rules.[7]

Butcher and Schneider interpret Kant's first categorical imperative to suggest that sport should be treated in accordance with its interests. They state that, 'Sports are practices and practices are the sorts of things that can have interests'[8] and, 'Taking the interests of the game seriously means that we ask ourselves whether or not some action we are contemplating would be good for the game concerned, if everyone did it.'[9]

The main criticism of Butcher and Schneider's interpretation however, is that they do not actually specify what constitutes the interests of (the) sport. As Sheridan notes, a lack of clarity means that it is impossible to determine what constitutes fair play: for instance, whether proposed technological or technical innovations are in the interests of (that) sport or not.[10]

IS SPORT JUST A SOCIAL CONTRACT?

An alternative approach to fair play is to define it in terms of a social contract. There are various forms of social contract theory but they centre around the idea that people tacitly agree to behave in particular ways or act in accordance with particular norms on the basis that it makes life better for everyone. One of the first proponents of social contract theory was the philosopher Thomas Hobbes, who lived during tumultuous periods of the English Civil War and persecution in France. He believed that man's fundamental nature was 'nasty, brutish and short' and concluded that peace was enabled only through a free and mutual agreement to live by the rule of law. This form of social contract can be seen as a pragmatic one that produces beneficial consequences that people would rationally choose. When applied to sport, it means that the game is played in the way that we expect it to be played. For instance, I will not cheat on the basis that you will also not cheat, which means that our expectations about how the game is to be played are met. While not cheating may be core to playing the game, social contract theory also takes into account social or tacit norms. For instance, if a player from the opposition is injured, I will kick the ball out of play on the expectation that if one of my players were to be injured, you would do the same.

A more recent incarnation of social contract theory was presented by American philosopher John Rawls.[11] He argued that resources should be divided according to what people would choose if they didn't know what proportion of the resource they were going to receive. He called this the 'veil of ignorance'. One way to understand this is to imagine you have the responsibility of dividing a cake but everyone else gets the opportunity to take a slice before you do. If you divided it unequally, you are likely to end up with the smallest slice. By dividing it equally, the slice you receive will be the same as everyone else's regardless of which slice you are left with at the end. In sport, this means that we should act in a way that ensures everyone is treated equally according to what is fair. Therefore, everyone should agree to play according to the rules[12] and officials should be impartial in their application of the rules. It also means that competition in sport should be divided fairly according to certain, relevant, criteria, such as age, weight, sex and ability.

Sheridan criticises this conception, however, on the basis that it turns fair play into a negative concept: the absence of unfairness.

> "Fair play' is defined as the lack of unfairness, which itself is defined in terms of a breach of contract or agreement. Thus, 'fair play' is to simply do no more or no less than you said you would do.'[13]

Sheridan argues that a conception of 'fair play' needs to be more sociologically situated and take into account culture, history and tradition. Such a conception is one based upon a shared system of rational norms.

IS 'FAIR PLAY' A SET OF SHARED SOCIAL NORMS?

Loland's conception of fair play as a system of rational norms draws upon Rawls' notion of fairness but also encompasses a shared ethos of the game that is historically and culturally formed. Any given example or instance of fair play is therefore culturally and historically situated and is flexible within certain parameters. This may explain why notions of fair play and sportsmanship are difficult to define.

The example that Loland and McNamee provide is from differing expectations of acceptable behaviour following an injury to a player in a football match between Arsenal and Sheffield United:

'In accordance with the ethos of the game played at that level, a Sheffield United player kicked the ball out of play so that the injured player could receive medical treatment. It is normal, once the player has been taken from the field of play (or is able to continue) that the ball is thrown back to the opposition without challenge so that the state of affairs prior to the stoppage of play can be resumed. In this match, an Arsenal player threw the ball back in the direction of the Sheffield defence. Then a new player to the Arsenal team (a recent recruit from an African nation) intercepted the ball, crossed it to one of his teammates who instinctively (so it is said) struck the ball and scored. The referee blew his whistle and indicated a legal goal.'[14] [my emphasis]

This example highlights that there are particular ways the game is played that are outside the formal rules. However, it also shows that these may differ culturally and historically. The word 'normal' was highlighted as this term was culturally situated. Throwing the ball back to the opposition was normal in the British version of the game but is not necessarily normal elsewhere – hence information about the geographical citizenship of the intercepting player. Cultural differences are also not necessarily defined by large groups based on geography or religion. They can also manifest themselves within individual clubs or through the ethos of individual coaches. As such, a coach may say to her players, 'we don't play the game like that'.

Historical changes to expectations about how the game ought to be played can also be seen in the way that in the professional era, it has become less common for games of rugby to be stopped for injury (unless serious or head injuries). Physiotherapists are frequently seen attempting to assess injured players while protecting them from further injury caused by the ongoing game. While in previous eras the game was stopped in order for both teams to get back to full strength, the demands of entertainment for spectators and a fast-flowing game mean that this previous example of fair play has now become obsolete and the current ethos has changed.

In addition to the professionalisation of sport, the use of technology may have also changed the ethos of the game. If decisions about whether rules are being followed or broken is seen to be increasingly the responsibility of the officials – including television officials who have access to replays and other officiating technology – then it is less likely that the players themselves will feel a moral duty to own up to an infringement.[15]

'Fair play', therefore, can be seen as both adherence to the formal rules of the game but also a set of expectations and norms about how the game ought to be played. These norms demonstrate considerations about the meaning and values we attach to sport and to each other. It is a contested term but at the very least demonstrates that there are normative assumptions about the way that sport is played.

INDEPENDENT STUDY QUESTIONS:

- *Provide three examples of what you consider to be 'fair play'.*
- *What is the difference between formal fair play and informal fair play?*
- *To what extent is 'fair play' based on respect, mutual agreement or shared cultural norms and values?*

21 IS SPORT A MORAL EDUCATOR?

The French existentialist, Nobel Prize-winning author and part-time football goalkeeper Albert Camus once said that everything he learned about ethics he learned through sport. That sport is often seen to be a great moral educator was exemplified by the 19th-century British public-school system and has been extolled since. It is one of the most pervasive ideas in Anglo-American society. In essence, it is the view that playing sport makes good people.

That so many of our moral metaphors are sporting ones seems to support this view: phrases such as a 'level playing field', 'moving the goalposts', 'below the belt' and 'it's not cricket' all have easily recognisable moral connotations. Being a 'good sport' is probably the most widely recognised of them all; but what exactly does this mean?

This chapter will consider whether there are any good arguments to support the view that sport is a moral educator and a way of forming good character.

IS SPORT A MORAL EDUCATOR OR MORAL VACUUM?

One of the omnipresent ideas perpetuated by educationalists and politicians alike is that 'sport builds good character'. In the 19th century, character in this sense meant brave, honourable men capable of commitment to a cause.[1] Shields and Bredemeier define it as 'composite of four virtues: compassion, fairness, sportspersonship, and integrity.'[2] Such views support the notion that one of sport's primary values is its effect on moral character, and this endows its place within the education curriculum: sport is good because it creates good people. However, the evidence to verify this is far from conclusive. In fact, scholars such as John Russell argue that there is a range of evidence supporting the opposite: that being good at sport often correlates with lower levels of moral development.[3] Russell suggests two possibilities for this correlation: either sport does not provide the moral education that we often claim it does, and is morally neutral; or success in elite sport is actually more likely to occur with lower levels of moral maturity, and therefore sport can be said to be morally deficient. That elite sport may be more achievable for athletes who lack moral character is a radical suggestion indeed and antithetical to the common view about the morally educational value of sport.

One of the clearest examples of the lack of moral character shown in sport is the instrumental attitude that players and coaches appear to hold at the top of the game. Barely a day goes by without a high-profile story in the media about 'bad' or morally questionable behaviour by athletes, coaches or management. In his book *Why Sports Morally Matter*, Bill Morgan suggests that modern sport merely reflects the current attitudes and culture of wider society and argues that sport's current focus upon the 'free market' and 'external value' reflects the values of today's narcissistic, hyper-individualistic and 'win-at-all-costs' society.[4]

In their research on athletes' attitudes towards violence and moral reasoning, Shields and Bredemeier suggest that, for many, sport is viewed in a different moral sphere from other aspects of life. That is, behaviour that is acceptable in sport is not acceptable outside sport, and vice versa. Their study assessed the responses athletes gave to two (supposedly equivalent) hypothetical dilemmas. One concerned a coach who asked a player to break the rules in order to help win a game; the other asked whether it was better to break a promise to repay money to a rich man who didn't need it or give it to someone else who was desperately in need. Although there were a variety of responses to each of these scenarios, the most notable difference was that participants used different moral reasoning depending on the type of dilemma it was. Respondents gave a much deeper level of thought and consideration to the 'real-life dilemma' than they did to the 'sport dilemma'. Shields and Bredemeier concluded that: 'both athletes and non-athletes used lower-level egocentric moral reasoning when thinking about dilemmas in sport than when addressing moral issues in other contexts.'[5] This suggests that we hold different attitudes to how we should follow rules and what constitutes acceptable behaviour in sport compared with other areas of life. If this is the case, sport could be seen to present a 'moral vacuum' whereby 'anything goes'.

Although sport is a part of life, its arbitrary rules and separateness can make it seem otherwise. While it may be that computer games enhance the separation between 'real' life and an alternative world to its fullest extent – and therefore allows players to take upon alter-egos that behave in morally unacceptable ways that they would never consider in their 'real' life, such as violence, rape and torture – this can also be seen to a certain extent in sport too. For instance, Leslie Howe argues that sport is a space that allows the construction of a fictional world whereby one can play with one's identity and become a different moral character to the one you are outside of sport.[6] This construction of an alter-ego allows individuals to shift their moral compass and behave and rationalise their behaviour in ways they would not do otherwise. Howe argues that a diminished moral responsibility in sport does not occur because one is simply acting a part, but rather because the space in which they are playing allows them to *be* a different person, one who wouldn't be accepted in 'real' life. One of the clearest examples of this can be seen in Pam Sailors' analysis of Roller Derby for which players take on pseudo-names with particular personalities and character traits. For instance, Derby player Melicious states, 'A persona can deliver up an easy scapegoat for bad behaviour: 'It wasn't me who illegally elbowed Bloody Mary in the third jam, it was Melicious'.'[7]

Such a disparity in attitudes about what is acceptable in sport and what is condemned outside can also be seen in the way that spectators and players congratulate 'big hits' and 'knock-outs' in contact sports. In other spheres of life, such actions and their consequences would be seen as shocking and widely condemned, yet in sport they are applauded. The dystopia that is presented in the futuristic film *Rollerball* whereby competitors are routinely injured and substituted through physically aggressive (if not violent) conduct seems to all too closely resemble the attitude displayed in today's rugby or American football matches, whereby 'big hits' are celebrated and gleefully shared on social media. Coaches and players too, often view injured opposition as obstacles that have been eliminated in order to clear their path to success. The language of the 'big hit' rather than 'the successful tackle' suggests a moral legitimacy to this type of action.

Even violent behaviour (that goes against the rules) within sport is generally dealt with by the sporting authorities and not the law of the land. Many incidents within sport that would face legal prosecution outside are viewed as 'just part of the game' and rather than face a public court of law, hearings are conducted by governing bodies and the harshest sanction is a playing ban.[8]

It seems then that there are different standards of moral behaviour in sport compared with other aspects of life. If sport is a moral sphere of its own, it contradicts the notion that it teaches good moral behaviour that also applies to the 'outside' world. Yet at the same time, it is difficult to argue that sport is a moral vacuum, as despite some differences in acceptable behaviour (for instance, the moral acceptability of punching someone in the head on the street and in a boxing match), it simply isn't the case that 'anything goes'. Sport is a highly moral environment, from which many concepts are transferable and applicable to the non-sporting world.

IS SPORT A MORAL LABORATORY?

So, while there may be limited evidence to suggest that sport makes good people, sport may still be a place where morality and moral concepts can be usefully explored. Graham McFee suggests that sport should be seen as a moral laboratory; an environment that is conducive to understanding what constitutes moral issues and moral problems that require action.[9] For McFee, education is only education if one's state of mind has developed through an educative process rather than hypnoses or indoctrination.[10] The educative process includes the learning of (abstract) rules but, moreover, it requires an understanding of general principles in how and when to apply the rules. This in turn is learned through experience of these principles in practice and is dependent on how others around us have interpreted these principles.

McFee's premise is that morality isn't acquired through memorising particular rules (i.e. 'do not cheat') but rather is learned through the experience of applying those rules in different contexts. A criticism of research exemplified by Shields and Bredemeier is that it is based upon responses to abstract and hypothetical scenarios that by their nature do not contain the richness of a real situation, faced by a real individual who may experience real consequences. The advantage that sport has over other aspects of life is that it straddles the boundaries between the 'real' and the 'make-believe' world. As Suits rightly noted with his criterion of the 'lusory attitude', players must knowingly accept the rules of the game in order to be playing it, and recognise both its triviality but also the necessity to take the rules seriously. So while sport is 'apart' from 'real' life, it is nevertheless an environment in which moral problems are real and not hypothetical. A player is faced with a choice whether to lend a competitor some spare equipment so they are able to compete, or whether to force them to withdraw. The triviality of (certainly amateur) sport means that while the consequences are real, they are also temporary and inconsequential. While this position may be criticised for neglecting decisions in sport that have much more far-reaching and long-term consequences, such as the harm caused by doping or violence, it seems to correlate with the traditional values of sport and physical education championed by politicians and educationalists.

Sport's framework of rules provides a degree of clarity not provided in 'real' life. However, the fact that both players and officials need to interpret the rules and decide whether they apply to concrete cases highlights the moral dimension of sport. Concepts such as 'fairness' arise when there is disagreement over whether the rule has been applied correctly, or indeed whether it fits with our conception of the term in other spheres of life. As Reid suggests:

> 'Sport's potential as moral education lies in its ability to offer people the chance to work with moral concepts like fairness in practice, to test the concepts themselves, to confront others who fail to act on them, and even to explore one's own failure to act on them.'[11]

INDEPENDENT STUDY QUESTIONS

- Think of a variety of sporting heroes; are they admired because they are good people or because they are good athletes?
- What are the moral qualities that sport is often cited to teach and is there evidence to support this?
- To what extent does moral behaviour differ in sport compared to other aspects of life?
- Do you agree with McFee's claim that sport is a moral laboratory that enables us to test and apply moral concepts in a way that other aspects of life do not?

22 IS COMPETITION MORALLY ACCEPTABLE?

Arguments about the virtues or vices of competition abound within contemporary society. It is either seen as a way of developing excellence and motivation to succeed, or a model to foster corruption, nepotism, selfishness and despondency. These arguments also pertain to sport. This chapter will consider the definition of sport in relation to competition, its value and the different ways in which competition can be morally constructed.

Most definitions of sport include the concept of 'competition', despite the fact that there have been attempts in educational circles (which were particularly prominent in the late 1960s and early 1970s) to facilitate 'non-competitive' sports. The chief motivation behind such a drive is the fact that sport is considered a zero-sum game in that for every winner there will be at least one loser. According to some educationalists, these zero-sum games should be avoided as they diminish self-esteem in the loser and encourage arrogance in the winner. The contrasting attitude is that competition is good because it 'builds character' and teaches 'life lessons' in learning to deal with failure. While we will consider its moral status in more detail later in this chapter, it seems impossible to envisage sport without an element of competition, since such activity would be more akin to play or recreation. Sport, by definition, requires testing one's skills and making comparisons, even if the comparison is against your past achievements. Competition necessarily involves an element of ranking, measuring or comparison.

WHAT IS THE VALUE OF COMPETITION IN SPORT?

The value of competition is contested. It has been linked to the development of a variety of virtues and vices, such as: resilience, determination and commitment, concern for excellence, friendship, loyalty, leadership, arrogance, narcissism, ruthlessness and instrumentalism. The question, however, is whether there is any evidence of this causal relationship. Does taking part in competitive sport create strong, courageous and morally upstanding leaders or does it create obsessive and single-minded narcissists who will win at any cost? The fact that it is easy to find examples of both types of athlete suggests that this causal relationship is certainly not a simple one, if it exists at all. Furthermore, the direction of any causal relation is not clear either. For instance, Ogilvie and Tutko[1] have suggested that instead of building character, sport merely attracts those who already have strong characters.[2] Testing such theories empirically is incredibly difficult as it requires control groups and longitudinal studies that are often both ethically and methodologically unfeasible. The way in which philosophers can add to the debate is to provide conceptual clarity about what the term 'competition' entails, and to make some moral judgements about its consequences.

IS COMPETITION IN SPORT INHERENTLY SELFISH?

The German philosopher Friedrich Nietzsche argued that all living things were constantly involved in a struggle for power (he called this 'will to power').[3] This view mirrors that of the social biologists of the latter 19th century, which is represented in the phrase 'survival of the fittest'. In the same way that plants struggle against each other for sunlight and nutrients, and struggles for dominance and survival are played out between animals, humans too will compete for superiority. This Nietzschean view supports the notion of sport as a zero-sum game whereby everyone is competing against each other for victory and there is only one winner. It suggests that competition in sport is an inherently selfish activity. This view is reinforced in George Orwell's famous slogan: 'Sport... is war minus the shooting'.[4]

Robert Simon, however, argues that there is an important distinction to be made between selfishness and self-interest.[5] To be selfish is to act in one's own interest without regard for the welfare of others and is by definition ethically unacceptable. Acting in one's self-interest, however, is morally neutral. Consider the difference between:

- A player who refuses to take a turn in goal as part of a casual kick-around in the local park by stating that she'd rather go home and will take her ball with her.
- A player whose commitment to training and self-improvement ensures she is selected for a cup final where she scores the winning goal.

The first is an example of selfishness since the player is using the fact that it is her ball as a means to ensure that she doesn't have to play by the same tacit rules that everyone else is following (i.e. taking a turn in goal). She is therefore acting immorally. The second example, by contrast, is an action that although is in the player's self-interest is not a selfish one, since the action (i.e. scoring the winning goal) is also in her team's interest.

IS COMPETITION THE 'MUTUAL QUEST FOR EXCELLENCE'

Simon criticises the Nietzschean view of sport and argues that it is fundamentally dependent on cooperation. There is obviously the cooperation that is required between teammates but also cooperation between opponents. At the very least, opponents must accept that the game can only exist when all players agree on the rules and the means to play it.[6] The concept of 'fair play' generally prevents participants from taking a purely selfish attitude because it obliges players to abide by both the letter and the spirit of the game. Selfish players who disregard this concept find themselves criticised by others for not playing fairly or in the 'right spirit'.

According to Simon, good competition takes place when those involved accept the constitutive rules as a challenge to excel. He argues that the goal of good sport is not to win but rather to win well, by demonstrating excellence of achievement. The best way to excel is to compete against an opponent of equal skill and stature whereby victory is only possible by performing at the limits of one's ability. When we play those who are inferior to us it is of little challenge, and ultimately we will feel dissatisfied with an easy win. It is not good competition. This is emphasised by Delattre who notes:

> 'The testing of one's mettle in competitive athletics is a form of self
> discovery… [an opportunity] for concentration and intensity of
> involvement, for being carried away by the demands of the contest…
> This is why it is a far greater success in competitive athletics to have
> played well under pressure of a truly worthwhile opponent and lost
> than to have defeated a less worthy or unworthy one where no demands
> were made.'[7]

According to this position set out by Delattre and Simon, players have a moral obligation to provide the best possible competition for their opponents. It can therefore be seen as a cooperative venture whereby everyone gains by trying to meet the challenge set by an opponent. Games have little value when our opponent is not trying: it is no fun to play someone who isn't putting in any effort to win; indeed, such players are labelled 'spoilsports'. This conception of sport is not a selfish Nietzschean enterprise but rather a social contract. All participants recognise that they will gain the most if they tacitly agree to play to the best of their ability and provide a fair challenge to others:

> 'On this view, good competition presupposes a cooperative effort by
> competitors to generate the best possible challenge to each other. Each has
> the obligation to the other to try his or her best. Although one wins the
> contest and the other loses, each gains by trying to meet the challenge.'[8]

Competition, on this account, can be defined as a 'mutual quest for excellence through challenge'.[9]

CAN 'COMPETITION' BE RIGHTLY DEFINED AS 'COOPERATION'?

One of the main criticisms of Simon's view is that defining competition in terms of cooperation is to misrepresent the concept. Competition and cooperation are usually defined in mutually opposing terms. Our general understanding of competition is to attempt to win against others and yet it is now being defined in terms of cooperation and self-development. Simon responded to this criticism by arguing that his definition points to an ethical distinction rather than a conceptual one. Framing competition as a mutual quest for excellence means that we can *perceive* the competition as one where everyone benefits rather than a zero-sum game where winner takes all, as simple victory is not the sole outcome. Viewing competition in this way provides a defence against those who reject competition as unethical and advocate a form of 'non-competitive sport' that celebrates participation rather than winning. Simon argues that envisaging competition as a mutual quest for excellence allows us to see its value and to promote it as a part of a good life.

Simon's view is supported by consideration of the etymology of the term. The word 'competition' comes from the Latin *competitionem* which, stemming from the words *petere* and *com*, indicates the notion of 'striving' or 'seeking' *with* rather than *against*.[10] This leads to 'competition' being understood as a way of:

> '...questioning each other together, a striving together presumably so that each participant achieves a level of excellence that could not have been achieved alone, without the mutual striving, without the competition.'[11]

In response to this discussion, John Russell argues the debate over whether competition is morally good or bad is often predicated on different conceptions of competition. It is, he argues, comparing apples and oranges. He uses the terms *partisan success* and *non-partisan success* to illustrate this distinction. The former requires victory over others and is exemplified in zero-sum games whereby success is one-sided. This is demonstrated in competitions such as job interviews or court cases for which there are quantifiable winners and losers. Non-partisan success is illustrated by competitions in which everyone can succeed, for example in the production of knowledge or achieving a set pass mark in an exam, whereby one person's success does not denote another's failure. As we have seen, while sport is often initially conceived of as a competition that involves partisan success, it can also be constructed as one involving non-partisan success, as represented by the phrase 'mutual quest for excellence'. However, Russell's criticism of the non-partisan success conception of competition is that it neglects the very real partisan aspect in that you are seeking to overcome an opponent in victory. This leads Russell to extend Simon's phrase:

> 'Arguably, competitive sport is more accurately (if less elegantly) described as a 'mutually acceptable quest for excellence through ritualised partisan physical conflict'.'[12]

WHAT MAKES THE BEST SPORTING COMPETITIONS?

Simon suggested that good sport is when all involved are presented with a worthwhile challenge. A worthwhile challenge is one whereby you have to try your best to win but also that you have a chance of winning and of losing. At its purest, sport is supposed to be fair and meritocratic in that the means of winning are clearly laid out, the rules are the same for everyone and where victory is determined on performance rather than luck or partisan officiating. One of the formal characteristics of 'fair play' is that all competitors have a theoretical chance of winning even if, on paper, one side is stronger than the other. It is also one of the reasons why sport is so compelling.

In order to articulate what makes good sporting competition, Warren Fraleigh coined the phrase, 'the sweet tension of uncertainty of outcome'[13]. This suggests that the best sporting contests are those for which the result is uncertain and the contestants are evenly matched. Participants are required to perform to their utmost ability in order to obtain victory and spectators are provided with the emotional turmoil that comes with such uncertainty and dramatic spectacle. This sweet tension of uncertainty also indicates why the neutral supporter will often root for the underdog in the hope that the contest will be much more evenly matched.

Competitions in which all participants need to perform to their highest level if they are to win also drive up the overall standard of performance. Games that are unevenly matched might be useful for strategic and technical organisation but they are generally not good sporting contests and do not develop or illustrate excellence. As has been demonstrated throughout sporting history, sporting excellence is not an end state but rather the demonstration of what is possible at a particular moment in time. It is why few top athletes of yesteryear would be a match for those of today. There are many examples in sporting history whereby competition between two or more athletes or teams has pushed the possibilities of excellence in that sport to a new level, and the phrase 'standing on the shoulders of giants' is fitting. These competitive rivalries enable the standards of excellence to be continuously developed and are one of the reasons why Simon's conception of competition has merit despite its apparent contradictions. Moreover, in the most celebrated cases, these sporting rivalries are often based on mutual respect (though perhaps not friendship) and an appreciation of the intrinsic values of the game.

So while the practice of competition in sport may lead to a range of morally varied outcomes, the concept itself appears to be at worst morally neutral, and at best a way of developing excellence and human flourishing despite its partisan characteristics.

INDEPENDENT STUDY QUESTIONS:

- To what extent does sport necessarily involve competition?
- What is meant by the phrase 'mutual quest for excellence through challenge' and how can it be applied to sport?
- What is the difference between partisan success and non-partisan success in competition?
- What is suggested by the view that the actual practice of competition in sport may differ from the idealised concept of competition itself?

23 IS GAMESMANSHIP JUST ANOTHER SKILL IN SPORT?

Gamesmanship refers to actions that while not directly against the rules of the sport, are against the spirit in which that sport should be played. It is often called 'spoiling' in the sense that a 'spoilsport' is someone who ruins another person's enjoyment or intrinsic appreciation. As such, 'gamesmanship' is seen in negative terms. Yet, in the elite and professional sphere of sport, gamesmanship is often viewed as part of the game and a demonstration of intelligence and strategy. Gamesmanship demonstrates knowledge of the game and of the opposition and is often used to gain a psychological or material advantage.

WHAT IS 'GAMESMANSHIP'?

As has been outlined in Chapter 3, there is disagreement over whether a game is wholly defined by its formal (explicit) rules. Yet the fact we often talk about the difference between the 'letter' and the 'spirit' of the law (or rule) suggests that there are times when the written rules do not always stipulate the best, expected or correct way of playing the game. The term 'gamesmanship' is used to describe this gap between abiding by the rules of the sport and abiding by the 'spirit' of sport. It is behaviour that does not actually break a formal rule but is still questionable or dubious. By definition, it cannot be prohibited since it points to behaviour that is technically within the rules. It is also sometimes referred to as 'spoiling', although I would argue that this term is slightly broader and covers any behaviour that ruins a game, including cheating, professional fouls and illegal or criminal acts. It is also considered the polar opposite of 'sportsmanship', which is behaviour that goes beyond the rules of the game and demonstrates respect to the opposition and the game itself, or makes the contest better or fairer than it would have otherwise been. Gamesmanship is often defined as the attempt to gain a psychological and competitive advantage through the manipulation of rules, but it is still difficult to fully describe. There are several different types found in sport but the most common ones are time wasting, psychological intimidation and pedantry. These are illustrated in the four cases below:

Case 1: 'The Time-Waster'
Joseph is playing tennis. He was leading in the final set of the match 4–1 but his opponent, Jacob, has recovered his form, taken the last three games and is now serving to go 5–4 ahead. Joseph is concerned about Jacob's sudden renaissance and so purposely delays Jacob's serve (the weakest part of Jacob's game) by holding his hand up and turning his back on the court. The umpire warns Joseph not to continue to time-waste but it nevertheless coincides with Jacob producing a double fault and allowing Joseph to take the final set and win the match.

Case 2: 'The Sledger'
Lucy walks out to bat in a game of cricket. As she approaches the wicket, one of her opponents says loudly to her teammates, 'Oh, this one's nothing to worry about, she couldn't hit a ball if it was placed on her bat; she was out last week for a duck'. It is true that Lucy didn't score any runs in her last game and has been performing below par for the season and these comments strike home. They continue throughout the time she is in bat, have the effect of unsettling her and ultimately contribute to a quick dismissal.

Case 3: 'The Pedant'
At an under-12s football tournament, the coach of the tournament favourite notices that one of the lower-level sides is fielding a player who had not been registered within the designated time of 48 hours prior to the tournament. Although the organisers are aware of this fact and are prepared to accommodate for the sake of the team being able to compete, the coach points out that this contravenes a regulation in the rule book and maintains they should be disqualified from entering. The tournament organisers are reluctantly forced to agree.

There are two questions that we can consider from these cases. First, should these examples be treated the same and for what reason? Second, is gamesmanship morally wrong?

All of the cases described above are attempts to provide one player or team with a competitive advantage, all cases are successful and none of the cases breaks the formal rules of the sport. Yet they do seem to differ. Cases 1 and 2 are attempts to psychologically affect the opponent's ability to play to the best of their ability by putting them off their game. It is clear that skill in sport is not simply being able to carry out particular biomechanical movements, but the ability to do so within the pressure of a competitive environment. It therefore involves additional cognitive skills. Case 1 states that Jacob's serve is the weakest part of his game and Jacob may well have double-faulted even without Joseph causing a short delay. Equally, Jacob's serve could have been delayed by a sudden gust of wind. The umpire is aware of the tactic of time-wasting and has the power to issue sanctions if necessary. As such, this type of behaviour seems to be the least morally problematic. Joseph's actions are testing Jacob's mental capacities to perform in a high-pressure situation and this involves the ability to concentrate without being distracted by external factors.

Case 2 seems similar to the first yet differs in the way in which it is personally directed. In some respects, it could be argued that the ability to ignore personal comments is another part of the skillset required for competitive sport, yet there is a line that seems to be drawn over what is and isn't acceptable. Examples of 'sledging' in sport are frequent, and particular notorious examples seem to occur in cricket, which provides opportunities for this behaviour to occur since a lone batsman is required to stand among a group of opposition players. In the case given above, although the comments are truthful they are also related to the sporting performance of the player involved. In this sense, they are fairly innocuous. Other real examples, however, are much more vindictive and may be personal and/or false comments about sensitive issues and family members. The line perhaps should be drawn between making comments directly related to the game, and making comments about aspects incidental or unrelated to the game, such as someone's sexuality or family members.

Case 3 seems to be a clear example of unsporting behaviour. It is gamesmanship in the sense that a coach is using the rules in a way that can be said to go against the 'spirit of sport'. That it is an amateur tournament for children suggests the focus is on participation, fun and enjoyment and not the 'win-at-all-costs' attitude that the coach seems to be displaying. Moreover, preventing a team from competing is also likely to limit the opportunity of others (including the coach's team) to participate and enjoy the tournament as the games involving the disqualified team will no longer occur.

There may be an argument at the professional level of the game to ensure that the rules are adhered to since, rightly or not, the focus of the game is much more directed to outcome (and financial consequences) than enjoyment. Moreover, in the professional sphere, the management and support staff are paid to ensure that they are aware of and abide by the rules. Nevertheless, at all levels, when examples occur of athletes putting the good of the game first – such as going beyond the rules to help opponents – it is celebrated as a demonstration of good sportsmanship and playing in the right 'spirit of sport'.

IS GAMESMANSHIP MORALLY WRONG?

The difficulty with gamesmanship is that according to the formalist argument, it is perfectly legitimate behaviour. Formalists argue that since the rules set out the parameters of the game, and can be changed accordingly, it is up to the rule-makers to ensure that the rules are changed so that gamesmanship does not occur. Consider the recent case of 'time wasting' in rugby union. If a team was ahead and there were only a few minutes of time to be played, that team would attempt to keep possession of the ball by leaving it at the base of a ruck. While aficionados of the sport may argue that maintaining possession this way requires skill, it effectively stopped the game and ran down the clock. Once teams became particularly adept at this strategy, a decision was taken to change the law to ensure teams had to play the ball within five seconds or lose possession.

The formalist argument on purely logical grounds may seem reasonable. After all, the rules of sport are arbitrary and if the game is not being played in the way that those involved believe it should be, then the rules can be changed accordingly. However, critics of this stance maintain that the constitutive rules of sport cannot stipulate all possible ways in which the rules could be interpreted. Graham McFee argues, 'no rule (or law) can deal with *all* cases ... one cannot, for instance, resolve *all* difficulties in a particular sport by making new rules for that sport.'[1] This fact can be also be demonstrated outside sport by the millions of pounds spent on court cases and judicial review that often focus on the interpretation of a particular linguistic term. Simply put, language requires interpretation. McFee's solution to the problem is to provide officials with more jurisdiction for interpreting the rules, and that includes the 'spirit' that it was written in. This would reduce the occurrence of gamesmanship because actions deemed contrary to the 'spirit of sport' would be over-ruled by the officials.

The initial question set out in this chapter was whether gamesmanship should be seen as a skill in sport. If we take the definition of gamesmanship as the attempt to gain a psychological and competitive advantage through the manipulation of the rules, then it does indeed suggest a degree of skill in terms of knowledge of the game and the formal rules of the game, knowledge of the opponent in understanding their psychological limitations or weaknesses, and knowledge of how both of these factors can be manipulated in order to provide oneself with an advantage. Possessing this degree of knowledge and being able to apply it would normally be commended. Nevertheless, gamesmanship does generate a degree of moral distaste. Much of this arguably comes back to questions regarding the value of sport as part of a good life.[2]

Leslie Howe suggests that a moral equivalent of gamesmanship is seduction, in that the decisive move is taken by the target of the would-be seducer. She argues that in the same way that it is the recipient of the seductive behaviour who determines whether the seduction is successful or not, the success of attempts at gamesmanship is determined by the gamer's opponent. As such, it is a test of the recipient's personality and resolve rather than a test of the rules:

> 'If the gamer's behavior is within the rules, it cannot be unfair, and the competitive failure of the target is not the result of unfair advantage. It is because the target did not pass one of the fundamental aspects of competition: the test of psychological strength and preparedness.'[3]

Despite this, Howe later suggests that gamesmanship only makes sense in the wider context of good sport. Sport, she argues, is not simply about a test of athletic skill but also character. This is reflected in John Russell's analysis of sport. He argues that in many ways, the values we often celebrate and aspire to in sport are incompatible:

> 'There is no straightforward natural alliance with sportspersonship and competitive sport in the way that there is for non-competitive sporting

activities... Indeed, moral virtue and competitive sport seem to be in an uneasy tension... there is good reason to believe that striving for excellence or playing one's best can for some individuals, and perhaps for most individuals at least some of the time, require motives that are morally disturbing or even destructive of personal character.[4]

Both Russell and Howe identify a problem at the core of sport that is exemplified by the concept of gamesmanship: is gamesmanship a legitimate part of sport that demonstrates and tests the abilities and character of those participating in it? The answer depends, as McFee suggests, on the context and particulars of the sport in question. In the case of the children who are prohibited from playing on the grounds of a technical rule-infringement, such behaviour by the coach demonstrates a lack of understanding of the primary value of that particular tournament. However, in the case of the tennis player who attempts to psychologically rile his opponent on a crucial point, while it may demonstrate a ruthlessness and lack of compassion for his opponent, it may be seen as a legitimate action in that particular contest. The issue of how we should act towards others is further discussed in Chapter 26.

INDEPENDENT STUDY QUESTIONS:

- *What examples of gamesmanship have you come across in sport? Why are they good examples of the concept?*
- *What is the formalist's view of gamesmanship?*
- *How does McFee criticise this view?*
- *Do you agree with the view that gamesmanship demonstrates skill in sport? If so, does this mean it is morally acceptable?*

24 WHAT IS WRONG WITH DOPING IN SPORT?

Performance-enhancing drug use is generally regarded as the most problematic issue in sport and it frequently dominates discussions in the sports media. Two of the most notorious examples are the 1988 men's Olympic 100m final, after which six of the eight finalists (including Ben Johnson, Linford Christie and Carl Lewis) were subsequently found guilty of doping offences; and the more recent scandal involving the cyclist Lance Armstrong, who finally admitted to doping after years of denial. Doping scandals are found in all sports, from athletics to martial arts to football to boccia.[1]

WHAT IS 'DOPING'?

Doping is a term that covers a wide range of substances and methods that are designated as illegal in sport. The World Anti-Doping Agency (WADA) is the body that administers and enforces what is considered doping. The WADA Code defines doping as:

'• *The presence of a prohibited substance or any residue or markers for a substance in an athlete's sample;*

• *The use or attempted use by an athlete of a prohibited substance or a prohibited method;*

• *The refusal or failure to submit a sample without compelling justification;*

• *A repeated violation of the requirements for availability during out-of-competition testing;*

• *Tampering with any aspect of doping testing or control;*

• *The possession of any prohibited substance or method;*

• *The trafficking or attempted trafficking of any prohibited substance or method;*

• *Any interference, complicity in or covering up of anti-doping procedures or anti-doping rule violations.'[2]*

It is clear then, that doping does not simply refer to using a particular banned substance; it also alludes to a reasonable suspicion that a doping infringement may have taken place (as indicated, for instance, by repeatedly missing tests or interfering with the process). This explains why there are many cases of athletes, coaches and support staff who have been found guilty of doping offences but who have not tested positive for a banned substance.

WHAT IS MEANT BY 'STRICT LIABILITY'?

WADA enforces a strict liability rule. This means that regardless of the reasons or excuses that a person gives for violating an anti-doping rule, they are still liable to be found guilty:

> 'It is each Athlete's personal duty to ensure that no Prohibited Substance enters his or her body. Athletes are responsible for any Prohibited Substance or its Metabolites or Markers found to be present in their Samples. Accordingly, it is not necessary that intent, fault, negligence or knowing Use on the Athlete's part be demonstrated in order to establish an anti-doping violation.'[3]

The reason that the 'strict liability' rule exists is that most athletes plead innocent when faced with doping charges. When the consequences are so serious (usually a ban of several years and often the end of a career), it is unsurprising that athletes are unwilling to admit their guilt. However, this may mean that occasionally genuine cases of innocence are found guilty. One of the most famous cases in this respect was the Scottish slalom skier Alain Baxter, who won a bronze medal at the 2002 Winter Olympic Games. Baxter tested positive for the banned substance methamphetamine. He claimed that this was from a shop-bought nasal inhaler that contains slightly different ingredients in different countries; the US version contained methamphetamine whereas the UK one did not. Baxter claimed he naïvely and wrongly assumed that since the make of the inhaler was the same, they would be the same product. He argued that since this was an innocent mistake it was therefore not an example of cheating and he was not guilty of a doping offence. Unfortunately for Baxter, his argument was not accepted and he was stripped of his medal and received a ban from competing. Ironically, Baxter's appeal at the Court of Arbitration for Sport argued that the banned substance wasn't a performance-enhancer and would have had no effect on the outcome of the competition. The IOC, however, claimed that it was right to enforce due punishment because of the precedent it would otherwise set.

Nevertheless, there are other athletes who have claimed their innocence after a positive test result and have been acquitted. Tennis player Greg Rusedski was cleared after he tested positive for the banned substance nandrolone, believed to have come from electrolyte tablets that were sanctioned and supplied by the Association of Tennis Professionals (ATP). The Royal Society of Chemistry[4] later suggested that over 70 per cent of the positive test results for nandrolone could actually be due to a chemical breakdown of the urine sample and not from taking illegal supplements. This doubt led to Rusedski successfully appealing his case and him being cleared.

WHAT SUBSTANCES AND METHODS ARE PROHIBITED?

There are a variety of substances and methods that appear on the WADA list but they fall generally into specific categories.

Prohibited substances:

- Anabolic agents: for example, steroids such as testosterone and nandrolone.
- Peptide hormones and related substances: for example, Human Growth Hormone (HGH).
- Beta-2 agonists: this includes the active ingredients in asthma inhalers for which athletes require a Therapeutic Use Exemption (TUE).
- Hormone antagonists and modulators: these substances were developed after testing for androgenic anabolic steroids became more effective, and include myostatin inhibitors (which enables the production of muscle) and anti-oestrogenics.
- Diuretics and other masking agents: these include substances that have no positive effects on athletic performance but disguise the presence of another prohibited substance. Diuretics are also used to enable short-term weight loss in sports that are categorised by weight.

Prohibited methods:

- Enhancement of oxygen transfer: this includes blood doping, erythropoietin (EPO) and haemoglobin modification.
- Chemical and physical manipulation: i.e. any attempt to tamper with a doping sample or any unnecessary intravenous infusions that might affect a doping sample.
- Gene doping: although there are few, if any, known examples in athletes, this covers any modification at a genetic level.

Substances and methods prohibited in competition:

- Stimulants: for example, amphetamines.
- Narcotics: for example, pain-relieving substances such as morphine and codeine.
- Cannabinoids: these are plant-based substances that are frequently used as a recreational drug.
- Glucocorticosteroids: these are powerful anti-inflammatory drugs.

Substances prohibited in particular sports:

- Alcohol: this is banned in sports such as shooting, archery and bowling, but also in motorsports.

186 PHILOSOPHY OF SPORT: KEY QUESTIONS

- Beta-blockers: these are banned in the above sports but are also prohibited in other sports in which concentration and fine-motor judgements are a factor, such as snooker, darts, golf and bridge.

WHAT ARE THE CRITERIA FOR BANNING SUBSTANCES?

Essentially, a substance or method is banned if it fulfils two from three criteria: (1) that it is harmful to health, (2) it is performance enhancing, and/or (3) that it is against the 'spirit of sport'.

WHAT IS THE 'ARGUMENT FROM HARM'?

Not all drugs are bad, as we know every time we take ibuprofen to alleviate aches and pains. And not all bad things are illegal, as we also know every time we smoke a cigarette, have one drink too many, or find ourselves suffering an injury from over-training. Yet there are some things that are on the prohibited list because they are deemed to cause severe health problems. The obvious examples are steroids and amphetamines. There are many well-known stories about former Eastern-bloc athletes who have had sex changes (such as shot-putter Andreas Krieger) because they were forced to take large quantities of hormone supplements when competing for the USSR or East Germany. Although some of these stories are exaggerated, there have been historical cases of athletes suffering severe health problems through the overuse of certain substances. WADA's role, therefore, is to ensure that the athletes are protected from these risks.

The argument against the use of particular substances in sport is a paternalistic one, which restricts a person's choice on the basis that doing so protects them from harm. This argument is set out in greater detail in Chapter 15. The paternalistic argument in doping stems from the assumption that sport is a healthy activity. It can be expressed in two ways:

Argument A:

P1: Anything that risks the health of those involved in sport should be prohibited.

P2: Substance X [e.g. steroids] risks the health of those involved in sport.

C1: Therefore, substance X [e.g. steroids] should be prohibited.

Argument B:

P1: Anything that risks the health of those involved in sport should be prohibited.

P2: Individual athletes do not always know or understand the health risks involved in using particular substances or methods in sport.

C1: Therefore, individual athletes should be protected from the risk of harm by those who have expert knowledge (such as WADA) about the risks posed by particular substances or methods in sport.

There are, however, counter-arguments. First, the danger of substances is sometimes overstated. Most harmful effects occur after prolonged and excessive use and arguably many serious athletes are able to discern appropriate dosages without suffering long-term side effects. Equally, it has been argued that if these substances were legal then better research and development could increase their safety and ensure that they were used in a way that minimised the risk of harm.

A further counter-argument focuses on the issue of autonomy and rejects the paternalistic principle. This argument states that the decision to take performance-enhancing drugs is one that an athlete should make for themselves because they have the absolute right to decide what happens to their body even if they are potentially causing themselves harm. Elite athletes already make sacrifices in other areas of their lives, for example, in sacrificing relationships and family duties, and limiting financial, educational and career opportunities. So perhaps success in elite sport requires a further sacrifice of long-term health.

The response to the libertarian argument is generally concerned with coercion. Athletes often start at a young age and are highly influenced by those around them, such as coaches and managers. If the coach promotes a product or substance, there is substantial pressure on these athletes to accept this advice. Sport, even individual sport, is a social and communal activity that involves a range of different people and associated power relationships. Young or aspiring athletes may be easily swayed by those in positions of authority, such as coaches, managers and physicians, and are influenced by peer-pressure from other teammates. This is amplified in a goal-orientated, competitive environment where performance and results matter. The environment within which an athlete trains fosters their attitudes, outlook and wider values and affects their choices and behaviour. Nowhere can this be seen more than in the elite cycling culture of the late 20th and early 21st centuries. The accounts of many of those involved in doping at that time point to a culture in which it was 'normal' to receive blood transfusions and illegal supplements. Indeed, many argue that it was impossible to compete at the elite level without accepting many of the questionable and illegal practices that went on. The other notable point is that becoming 'a fully fledged doper' was a gradual process that took advantage of the closed culture of cycling. Athletes were typically given legitimate nutritional supplements in oral form before being encouraged to undergo more dubious procedures, such as an injection of these supplements or receiving intravenous drips. It is perhaps understandable that once an athlete had become used to receiving a 'legitimate' injection, they acquiesced when other illegal methods were used.

These extracts from David Millar's biography highlight the ease with which he went from taking 'legal' supplements to doping:

> 'The big fad at the time was for Italian 'recovery' products... These were all supposed to keep your blood healthy and to maintain your oxygen-carrying capacity at its highest… There was nothing 'wrong' with 'recovery'. It was not illegal, and far from doping, it was a simple injection that gave my body the vitamins it couldn't replace through eating alone... [The first time I doped] I was so accustomed to syringes by now that the sight of them didn't perturb me in any way. I'd been injected scores of times… and it was probably the easiest and the most anti-climactic injection I'd ever had. It was less like the stereotypical idea of doping than the injectable récup ['recovery'] I'd grown so used to.'[6]

What Millar's account indicates is that environment that surrounds an athlete can have a great influence over their decision-making. Millar also suggests that he ended up doping due to the pressure of being part of a successful team and the loyalties he felt towards it. The idea that humans will generally conform to the behaviour of others around them and will be influenced by those in positions of authority is borne out in the literature of those such as Asch[7], Zimbardo[8], Migram[9] and Glover[10], among many others. Those supporting the anti-doping rules argue that it is necessary to protect athletes from this type of harmful and coercive environment. Unscrupulous coaches may not care too much about the long-term health of their athletes if their athletes are excelling at their sport. While there may be some athletes who are freely willing to suffer ill-health in order to obtain victory, there are many others that are not, and it will be these athletes who will be either coerced against their will or forced out of the sport altogether.

WHAT IS WRONG WITH ENHANCING PERFORMANCE?

Sport in many ways is dependent on the enhancement of performance – we expect and hope for records to be broken and players to demonstrate ever-increasing skills. So the enhancement of performance cannot be bad in itself. The last few decades have witnessed the creation of thousands of jobs in performance analysis, sports psychology, nutrition, strength and conditioning, recovery and therapy, and many other areas; all of which have performance enhancement as their *raison d'être*. This suggests that it is not the enhancement of performance that is morally problematic but rather the way it is done; particularly the way it affects fairness and justice. A clear example of this can be seen in the development of swimming costumes, which has been called 'technological doping'. During the late 2000s, records in swimming events were broken at a rate previously unsurpassed. The cause was a new type of swimsuit that increased buoyancy and reduced drag. While there was nothing physically harmful about these swimming costumes it caused embarrassment to the governing body, FINA, because it indicated that records were being broken solely due to the developments in clothing technology. This highlights the crux of the issue of performance enhancement. There is a perception that sporting performance should be a consequence of natural talent, hard work and the ability of the human body. It should not be due to technology. If swimming races are tests of the human ability to swim a set distance as quickly as possible, then records set using technology that enables them to swim faster becomes meaningless. Swimmers might as well fit motorised propellers to their feet. The difficulty that governing bodies face is in deciding where the limit lies between fair and unfair performance. One of the ways in which this has been addressed is to attempt to define the essence of the sport, and determine whether a particular substance or method contravenes that essence. An example to illustrate this is the case of Casey Martin, an American golfer who suffered a painful condition that meant he needed to use a buggy to get around the course; a method that was prohibited in the rules of the game. Although the US Supreme Court eventually ruled in Martin's favour, the PGA and many prominent professional golfers argued that the ability to walk between holes was an essential part of the game of golf and to allow a golf buggy was to eliminate an integral test of fitness. This argument can be framed as follows:

P1: Sport S requires a test of Y.

P2: Technology T negates the test of Y.

C1: Therefore, technology T should be prohibited in sport S.

A further problem with the polyurethane swimsuits was that they were only available to a handful of sponsored athletes, which left others at a clear disadvantage. Again, this is premised on the idea that sporting performance should be the test of natural talent, hard work and motivation, not access to technology. The problem with this argument, however, is that modern sport is saturated with inequality in terms of access to resources. It is not surprising to note that the most successful sporting nations are those that are the most affluent and have the best research and development facilities.

WHAT IS THE 'SPIRIT OF SPORT'?

Both the criterion of harm to health and fairness of performance enhancement are based upon some fundamental values about sport, i.e. that it is part of a good life. These assumptions form the final criterion for WADA's definition; that doping is against the 'spirit of sport'. This comprises eleven attributes and values that are believed to be the essence of what is valued in sport:

- *ethics, fair play, honesty*
- *health*
- *excellence in performance*

- *character and education*
- *fun and joy*
- *teamwork*
- *dedication and commitment*
- *respect for rules and laws*
- *respect for self and other participants*
- *courage*
- *community and solidarity*

These elements are an indication of why we value sport so highly and what we should strive to preserve. However, critics argue that this list is vague and contradictory: many athletes aren't having fun when they have to put in another hour's training on a cold and wet evening. Similarly, they ask, 'is it not an example of courage and commitment to give everything, including long-term health to your sporting success?' Some on WADA's board have admitted (off the record) that this list is an idealised version of (amateur) sport and therefore is problematic at the elite level. Nevertheless, WADA still wishes to maintain that there are intrinsic values of sport that this list points to, and that these should be protected from the threat faced by doping.

WADA is certainly not without its critics or exempt from criticism, and some of these have merit, particularly ones that focus on the draconian measures involved in testing and invasions of privacy. The main problem that WADA faces is that the multi-billion dollar industry that sport has become means that there are those who have vested interests in ensuring a win at any cost. While many people are involved in sport because there is something that they find valuable at the heart of it – that is categorised by WADA's 'spirit of sport' – the money and prestige offered at the top may mean that some athletes are coerced into making decisions that are not necessarily for their own good, while others become disillusioned and give up altogether. As in many other areas of sport, it is a difficult balance to strike between the right to freedom and liberty versus the protection from harm. Currently, most in the sporting world favour the latter over the former.

INDEPENDENT STUDY QUESTIONS:

- What are the criteria that are to decide whether a substance or method should be banned in sport?
- What are the arguments and counter-arguments that focus upon the issue of harm to health? Which is the most persuasive?
- Should an athlete have the absolute right to decide what happens to her body if she is aware of the risks? Justify your answer.
- What is the purpose of the 11 criteria that form the 'spirit of sport'? What are the advantages and disadvantages of this list?

25 DO ELITE ATHLETES DESERVE HERO STATUS?

Newspaper column inches and internet pages abound with lists of 'Greatest Sporting Heroes' while towns, cities and countries across the world proudly acclaim their illustrious athletes with honours, placards and statues. Most of us can identify athletes whom we have admired and whom we have attempted, to lesser or greater degree, to emulate in our own sporting achievements. The questions this chapter will consider are whether athletes should be held up as role models and whether our worship of them is excessive or morally acceptable.

WHAT IS A HERO?

Common definitions of 'hero' refer to a person admired for bravery, courage, acting in a way that is considered exceptionally good, achieving something considered outstanding or unsurpassed, or who demonstrates other noble qualities. It may also be someone who is admired for a lesser reason; because they have a particular skill or quality, or have been influential at a personal level. There therefore seem to be two conceptions of heroism: an objective one suggested by the former, and a subjective one suggested by the latter. These two conceptions allow for individuals to argue that 'my mum is my greatest hero' despite that individual not fulfilling any objective measurement of heroism.

While there may be individuals within sport who have a profound effect on others at a personal level (for instance, a coach, teammate or administrator) this chapter is ultimately concerned with the 'objective' conception of a hero, i.e. an athlete who possesses particularly exceptional skills and/or qualities, or has demonstrated outstanding courage or bravery, that is not demonstrated or shared by the majority of the population.

SHOULD ATHLETES BE HELD UP AS ROLE MODELS?

Heroes are generally considered to be role models; that is someone who sets an example for others to follow, and whose behaviour should be emulated. Although the definition of a hero includes the possession of exceptional skills and qualities, there is also an assumption that such a person is also morally good or virtuous. This contrasts with the notion of the 'anti-hero' (in literary genres) who, while possessing exceptional powers or skill, does not exemplify the moral qualities that are expected from heroes.

The notion that being an athlete also involves being a role model is often accepted without question.[1] However as David Hume noted, just because something is the case, does not mean that it ought to be so.[2] This is known as the 'is–ought fallacy' or 'Hume's Guillotine'. Indeed, many athletes reject the notion that they should be considered as role models simply because they are good at their sport:

> *'I'm not a role model. I'm not paid to be a role model. I'm paid to wreak havoc on the basketball court. Parents should be role models. Just because I dunk a basketball, doesn't mean that I should raise your kids!'*[3]

Athletes and sports stars are often considered role models primarily because they demonstrate exceptional skills or qualities in sport, not because they demonstrate notable moral qualities. Yet there is an expectation that because they are admired for their sporting skills, they have a duty to also demonstrate moral virtues. Carwyn Jones takes this view in arguing that simply because athletes *are* influential to those who admire them they therefore have a duty to set a good example.[4] Jones draws upon Alasdair MacIntyre's virtue theory in support of his view.[5] MacIntyre's neo-Aristotelian ideas attempted to overcome a key criticism of Aristotle's virtue ethics (in that what is considered virtuous behaviour or a 'good person' alters over time and between different cultures) by situating virtues within an historical and cultural context. As a result, MacIntyre places virtues within a 'practice'. A practice is a cultural community that contains its own internal goods with a tradition and history. MacIntyre uses the example of chess to illustrate a practice but it could also include football, science, or the Church of England.

One problem with MacIntyre's conception of virtue is that accepted norms and required virtues within practices may differ, and this is particularly the case for sport, which, while it may be considered a practice in its own right, also contains other practices, i.e. particular sports. One could, for example, highlight the different attitudes and behaviours towards officials as seen in the practices of cricket, football and rugby. In cricket, it is (or at least was) expected that a batsman would 'walk' if he 'nicked' the ball even if the official had not spotted it. In rugby it is expected that players accept referees' decisions without question, and in football, it is commonplace for players to surround and intimidate officials if they disagree with a decision. While the normative virtue in some sports is one of absolute honesty, in others players are expected to play to the official.

Nevertheless, MacIntyre's theory maintains that humans have a capacity to recognise moral standards beyond those of a particular practice. This leads Jones to argue that athletes should not conform merely to the accepted or tolerated ethos within their immediate peer group but demonstrate virtues that are valid

in a wider context. Jones suggests there are plenty of ways in which athletes
can be moral heroes: refusing to engage in cheating or deception; standing
up to corruption, violence and bad sportsmanship; and rejecting any form of
racism, sexism or homophobia. These are virtues that are commended within
wider society. This, however, indicates that athletes should not be considered
role models solely because they are athletes, but rather they should exemplify
virtues and character traits that should be shared by everyone, regardless of their
athletic status.

ARE SPORTING VIRTUES COMPATIBLE WITH MORAL VIRTUES?

While we might accept that there is a set of moral virtues that everyone ought
to cultivate in an attempt to become a good person, it still does not address the
assumption that there is something specific to being an athlete that is deserving of
hero status. Indeed, it could be argued that the requirements for sporting greatness
are antithetical to those for moral greatness. Consider the following example:

Player A (let's call her Shona) is bolshy, irritating, arrogant, and frequently on
the receiving end of penalties and infractions when playing sport. She is a referee's
worst nightmare, winds up the opposition and dismays her teammates and coaches.
In many ways, she contradicts the traditional virtues exalted in sport: she is often
guilty of gamesmanship and will attempt to break rules to secure an advantage, is
dishonest, undermines authority and has a tendency to retaliate with aggression
and violence. But she is also incredibly committed, hard-working and will suffer
for her team. Though she is a player who requires effort and 'management' to
reduce her liability, she is valuable and appreciated, primarily because she can
make the difference between winning and losing a game.

What Shona's case illustrates is that sporting success is not a direct consequence
of virtuous behaviour. Human character is complex and while there are elements
of an individual's character that are unsavoury, there are other aspects that are
commendable. Moreover, the emphasis that we place on one virtue (e.g. honesty)
may be to the detriment of another (e.g. commitment). It may be that the
requirements of being a good athlete – single-mindedness, absolute self-belief,
dedication to sport to the detriment of other values such as family and friendship –
do not correspond with those required to be a good person – moderation, modesty,
humility, etc. The very attributes that make someone great may also make them
selfish or conceited.

Equally, there are numerous examples of athletes who have been lauded as
paragons of virtue who have later been exposed as possessing particular vices.
Ironically, the very athlete that Jones focuses on as a notable exemplifier of moral
virtue was later (after Jones' paper was published) revealed as having cheated on
his wife. Similarly, the story of Lance Armstrong is perhaps a key illustration of the
complexity of the human character and the discord of virtues. While Armstrong

was found guilty of a degree of cheating that surpassed most other forms in sport, he has nevertheless raised millions of dollars for cancer research through his LiveStrong Foundation. He also demonstrated many other contemporary virtues, such as the ability to get people to work as a team, loyalty, determination and commitment.

IS ADMIRATION FOR ATHLETES A FORM OF FASCISM?

A philosophical criticism of our admiration for athletes comes from Torbjörn Tännsjö, who argues that it is a form of fascism. Tännsjö interprets fascism to mean admiration of strength and contempt for weakness. When we admire athletes, we do so because they are able to demonstrate a sporting skill that the majority of the rest of us do not possess. For Tännsjö, this admiration for athletes is ultimately based upon an admiration for physical strength. Furthermore, he argues, if we admire athletes for their strength then this correspondingly means we must feel contempt for those who are weak. Tännsjö uses the term 'fascistoid' to assert that the way we admire athletes bears a resemblance to fascism.

> 'While nationalism may be dangerous, and has often been associated with fascism, what is going on in our enthusiasm for individual athletic heroes is even worse. Our enthusiasm springs from the very core of fascist ideology: admiration for strength and contempt for weakness.'[6]

Tännsjö identifies three forms of contempt we feel as a consequence of this fascistoid ideology: *aggressive contempt*, where weakness is viewed as something that must be eliminated or eradicated (exemplified by the abhorrent actions of the Nazis, who literally eradicated those they saw as weak); *negligent contempt*, whereby we treat those who are seen as weak as non-entities and therefore ignore them; and *paternalistic contempt*, which manifests itself in a form of pity and causes us to aim to help others we see as lesser than ourselves. I would also argue that there is an additional form of contempt that falls between aggressive and paternalistic contempt and reveals itself through the ridicule or mockery of others.

Tännsjö's argument stems from the premise that we admire athletes because we see them as exemplifying the excellence of physical strength. This also leads him to conclude that if we value physical strength it necessarily means we value the performances of men over women and able-bodied over disabled athletes. While women and disabled athletes may not, in today's contemporary society, be subject to an aggressive form of contempt, they are subject to the paternalistic contempt of pity; in essence we feel sorry for them. He then makes two further steps in his argument. First, in suggesting that because we value the excellence that athletes demonstrate, we value the athletes themselves. Second, in valuing those who demonstrate excellence we necessarily place lesser value on those who do not:

> 'When we celebrate the winner, we cannot help but feel contempt for those that do not win. Admiration for the winner and contempt for the loser are only two sides of the same Olympic medal.'[7]

Tännsjö considers objections to his argument. The first objection is to note the similarity between sport and other human activities, such as the arts and sciences, and ask whether the same conclusion holds. Tännsjö responds that there is something particular to sport, that it is based upon physical strength, which means that there is a qualitative difference in the way we admire athletes compared to those in the arts or sciences. While we might admire the (subjective) skill of artists, writers, composers or performers, we only care about the results of athletes, which are based upon objective measurements and comparisons with others. Such ranking and comparison in sport has an inherent fascistoid element that is not shared by the arts and sciences.

Tännsjö's thesis is soundly rejected by Claudio Tamburrini, who argues that by separating out excellence in sport (measured by physical strength) from other types of excellence found in the arts and sciences, Tännsjö himself is guilty of elitism and gender-bias.[8] Tamburrini states that the admiration we have for athletes is not merely that of physical strength; it is much wider than Tännsjö suggests and encompasses other excellences such an self-sacrifice, dedication and courage. Tamburrini also rejects Tännsjö's assumption that admiration for winners necessarily leads to contempt for 'losers'. Such an assumption neglects the fact that we admire athletes who have achieved a level of success despite having to overcome other barriers (such as poverty, death of a loved one, illness, disability) even if they do not ultimately win gold. We admire athletes for a variety of reasons and often the 'story' behind their success makes us admire them more. As Tamburrini notes, excellence can be demonstrated in many ways.

If we accept Tamburrini's conclusion that successful athletes are often admired because they demonstrate other excellent qualities that are equally valued, then the admiration of athletes is not necessarily morally unacceptable. However, this precludes an excessive admiration or 'hero worship' for athletes that is based upon seeing them as symbols of strength. Tännsjö may be correct in arguing that there are many examples of the excessive admiration of athletes; this can be seen in the wider media's and fans' treatment of athletes and teams, which demonstrate sycophantic support while they are winning but will denigrate and vilify them upon losing.[9] While athletes who demonstrate outstanding accomplishment and skill in sport may be rightly admired for doing so, it does not mean that there should also be an expectation upon them to demonstrate a moral excellence beyond that which is expected of everyone else. While particular athletes may find themselves in the public eye to a far greater extent than the 'common man', they will undoubtedly be as flawed in their character as the rest of us.

INDEPENDENT STUDY QUESTIONS:

- *Which athletes do you most admire and for what reasons?*
- *Does admiration equate with the notions of heroism and role model?*
- *In what way should we expect an athlete to be a role model?*
- *Is Tännsjö right in arguing that our admiration for athletes is fascistoid?*

26 IS IT WRONG TO BE PATRIOTIC IN SPORT?

It seems reasonable to assert that most people support their national teams in sporting events and patriotism more generally is regarded as being a characteristic of a good citizen. However, the notion that it is right to favour one's compatriots at the expense of others is not without criticism. This chapter will consider the broader concept of patriotism and its moral standing before discussing whether patriotism in sport should be viewed as morally mistaken.

WHAT IS PATRIOTISM?

While there are various degrees of patriotism, ranging from an unquestioning allegiance to one's country to a more muted acknowledgement that one is part of a particular community, patriotism essentially describes a loyalty towards the country with which you most identify. While for most people this is their country of birth, for others it may be an adopted country that has either shown them particular kindness, has welcomed them as their own, or has values and a history that they share. Nick Dixon defines it as 'identification with, and a special concern for, the well-being of our own country and our compatriots'.[1] Fundamentally, patriotism demonstrates a sense of belonging.

Simon Keller's analysis of patriotism focuses upon this concept of loyalty.[2] He notes that there are different types of loyalty depending on the type of object that is being recognised and distinguishes between derived and non-derived loyalty and serious and non-serious loyalty. There are certain things in the world to which one is loyal out of a rational choice. There are other things, however to which loyalty is determined by circumstance or relation. Derived loyalties are those that stem from fundamental values. Non-derived loyalties are just happenstance. If a person loves a country from a derived loyalty it suggests a degree of choice and it does not equate directly with patriotism. So, you could love Sweden because of the values that it represents, or France due to its culture and cuisine. However, when one is patriotic, one loves a country for being *one's* country, not due to a rational decision based on a sharing of fundamental values. Similarly, you may be loyal to a particular political party because it represents the views and values that you share, but this differs to the loyalty one feels towards one's family which stems simply from the fact that they are your family whether or not you agree with their fundamental values and principles. (Hence the paradoxical truism that however much a person might denigrate his own family, only the foolhardy would repeat those sentiments back to him.) In respect to one's family or one's country, one does not choose the object of loyalty.

The loyalty a person shows in sport may be either of these types. You may be loyal to a particular team or club because it exemplifies the values that you hold, for instance, its policy on racism or homophobia. However, you may also be loyal to a team simply because it is your home club. This type of loyalty is the type that exemplifies itself in patriotism. So while you may appreciate the style of play of another country's football team for instance, you nevertheless support your own country, merely because it is your own country. As Keller notes, the identification with a country comes first, patriotism comes second. While the question 'should I be interested in politics?' naturally leads to one that asks, 'which political party should I support?', when asking whether it is right to be patriotic, it makes no sense to then ask 'which country should I be patriotic towards?'

Keller also distinguishes between serious and non-serious loyalty. Patriotism is generally a serious loyalty that involves a degree of respect and deference to national anthems, flags and other symbols. While burning a national flag may, just be an indication of pyromania, it also is likely to cause great offence and outrage. National symbols are representative of one's identity and are often considered as sacred as the lives of the individual citizens of that country.

Patriotism is also taken so seriously that it leads individuals to believe that it is worth sacrificing their life for their country and the eulogies of those who have done just that exemplify the status of patriotic martyrs. The seriousness with which patriotism is taken is the source of some criticism since it allows governments to utilise patriotic feeling in order to mobilise troops in unjust or unnecessary wars. Unquestioning loyalty to one's country may lead individuals to sacrifice their lives and the lives of others without sound justification.

Justifying loyalties is a further element of Keller's analysis and stems from whether a loyalty is derived from particular values or principles. There are some objects of loyalty that require defence through explanation, such as the loyalty we might show towards musicians or bands, film directors, and sports stars; and some things that by the virtue of the thing it is, do not require justification, for example, the loyalty we show to family members and religious icons. The loyalty we show towards our country is of the latter type; patriotism is often expected without any justification.

> 'To be a patriot is to have a serious loyalty to country, one that is not characterised by the phenomenology of choice, is essentially grounded in the country's being yours, and involves reference to (what are taken to be) valuable defining qualities of the country.'[3]

IS PATRIOTISM A VIRTUE?

The question of whether patriotism is good or bad is dependent on wider ethical principles. Typically, the debate around patriotism has been framed by universalism and communitarianism.[4] Universalists maintain that ethical decisions need to be made from an impartial and objective perspective that sees and treats everyone equally. In contrast, communitarians recognise that as individuals we are part of a community and therefore hold particular social roles and allegiances. Proponents of the former view include Paul Gomberg, who is known as a hard universalist. Gomberg insists that patriotism is a vice because it necessarily values some human lives over others, i.e. it values the lives of those who happen to live in the same country more than the lives of those who do not.[5] This, he argues, is intrinsically immoral. Conversely, Alasdair MacIntyre is a communitarian who argues that the communities of which we are a part, and with which we identify, deserve a greater share of our attention and effort.[6] As such, MacIntyre maintains that patriotism is not just a virtue but is a central virtue: it is a loyalty-exhibiting virtue that is exemplified by marital fidelity, love of one's own family, friendship and loyalty to sports teams. Not being patriotic means being alienated from one's community. While these positions represent the extremes of the debate, there are others who fall in between. These include: Marcia Baron[7], who takes a soft universalist position in recognising that there are some instances when favouring those communities of which you are a part over others is understandable; Martha Nussbaum[8], who takes a cosmopolitan position in arguing for a soft (educated) communitarianism; and Stephen Nathanson[9], who calls for a moderate patriotism.

The central criticism of the hard universalist position is that it neglects what it is to be human and does not value the human characteristics of loyalty or kinship: arguably, hard universalists don't understand humanity at all. A hard universalist would not see anything wrong (or odd) about choosing to save a stranger from drowning over one's mother. If we did not favour particular people over others then we could be accused of being morally insensitive or amoral. For instance, few would argue it is morally wrong to choose to spend more of our money and time looking after our own children rather than those of strangers. Being a parent suggests that we have particular duties to particular people, and looking after our own children is one of those duties. The question, however, is whether we have similar duties towards our countrymen.

There are two responses to this criticism. First, hard universalists would argue that being part of a community is not a valid excuse for discriminating in favour of those within that community at the expense of those outside. It is an attempt to defend nepotism. Second, even if being a member of a particular community, such as blood relations, does condone the positive treatment of some, it does not necessarily follow that patriotism merits the same behaviour as family kinship.

Keller criticises patriotism for being a form of bad-faith; in maintaining a belief that the holder knows to be false. He highlights the example of the sports fan who protests vehemently to the referee about a 'bad' decision and who will not admit the bias of his perception towards his team, even when 'at heart' he knows the facts are otherwise. This he argues is the case for the blind patriot too:

'Out of patriotic loyalty, she is motivated to believe that her country has certain features, and she marshals the evidence in ways that support this

belief; but she cannot maintain the belief in its full-blooded form if she admits to herself that it is not grounded in an unbiased assessment of the evidence; so she does not make this admission.'[10]

IS PATRIOTISM IN SPORT MORALLY INNOCUOUS?

The debate around sporting patriotism hinges on the issue of whether supporting one's country in sport is any more or less morally problematic than supporting one's country in general. While Bill Morgan[11] highlights the beneficial consequences of patriotism in sport, Nicholas Dixon[12] follows Nathanson in arguing for a moderate patriotism, while Paul Gomberg maintains that all forms of patriotism are morally unacceptable.

Morgan takes a positive view of patriotism in maintaining that an affiliation with a country is part of our individual identity and narrative about who we are and where we come from. International sporting events are a safe and positive way of constructing, reinforcing and challenging narratives about ourselves.[13] In this respect, Morgan allows for a space in which we can criticise, question and feel shame about our country's shortcomings while still loving it and respecting others. He argues that, 'sports are a morally rich language of nationalism'.[14] Evidence that supports Morgan's position can be found in examples where international sporting events have opened up diplomatic channels between countries that were previously closed. For instance, during the Cold War, representatives from the US and China continued to face each other in table-tennis competitions: after the 1971 World Championships held in Japan, the American player Cohen approached the three-times men's singles World Champion, Chinese player Zhuang Zedong, to ask if they could practise together and exchange skills, strategies and techniques. The Chinese player, fearful of his coaches and the Chinese government, declined the invitation and reported the incident to his manager who in turn reported it to those above him. When the incident was relayed to Chairman Mao Zedong, he agreed that this player could practise with the American. This small incident ultimately led to a new channel of communication – 'ping-pong diplomacy' – between the two nations and paved the way for renewed dialogue.

Nevertheless, there are equally other examples of patriotism that has spilled over into violence and hostilities, such as the many incidents of football hooliganism that stem from patriotic fervour. There are also other morally problematic examples such as the jeering of golf and tennis players, the moral disregard for athletes' well-being[15], and the chanting of fans. Carwyn Jones and Scott Fleming argue that many patriotic chants have racist overtones:

'Chanting at [sports events] is an audible and visible manifestation and celebration of national identity and ethnic pride. However, it is only a short step from these behaviours to their much more sinister and pernicious cousins, xenophobia and racism.'[16]

In response to these morally concerning examples of patriotism in sport, Nicholas Dixon argues that while such incidents are unacceptable, sporting patriotism itself is not necessarily morally wrong.[17] Dixon argues that while we might support those representing our country in sport, it does not logically follow that we therefore hate or feel contempt for those representing other nations. Patriotism can be a force for moral good if it is not vilifying the other. A feeling of pride in the sporting success of one's nation is for Dixon 'morally innocuous'. He utilises Nathanson's defence of a 'moderate patriotism',[18] which indicates a non-serious conception of patriotism in the sense that one recognises both the serendipity of being born in a particular country at a particular time, and that success in sport does not demonstrate a moral or axiological superiority over others. This view suggests that sport can be a moderating force, since it allows for contests to be fought between nations in a non-serious[19] sphere and thus avoids the wars and horrific consequences that follow. However, moderate patriotism is criticised from both sides: MacIntyre argues that moderate patriotism is not patriotism at all, while Gomberg argues that moderate patriotism is conceptually impossible. Both criticisms maintain that when 'push comes to shove, one must fall on to one side of the fence or the other'. Dixon responds to MacIntrye's moral relativism by arguing that it leads to unpalatable consequences for sport. If MacIntyre stands by his view that each community (or nation) has its own internal goods and values, it implicitly condones practices such as the doping that was prevalent in the former Soviet Union and East Germany. Similarly, Dixon rejects Gomberg's assertion that patriotism is a zero-sum game, in that supporting one's country means denigrating all others. Dixon maintains that a moderate patriotism in sport does not logically lead to harm to other countries. Sport in this regard differs from access to limited or natural resources such as land mass, labour and raw materials, which are often the primary reasons for patriotic wars.[20]

In response, while Gomberg concedes that Dixon is correct in noting that in most sporting situations patriotism does seem to be morally innocuous, he nevertheless maintains that trying to be moderately patriotic inevitably leads to jingoism. Gomberg draws an analogy between being a little bit patriotic and being a little bit pregnant. They are conceptually impossible. As a result, when one demonstrates patriotism in one area, such as sport, it is easy for it to be appropriated and applied in others. When large populations share patriotic feeling and identification it allows Governments to manipulate these emotions to support war. For Gomberg, patriotic feeling in sport can be harnessed as a tool for more Machiavellian purposes.

Ultimately, Dixon's and Gomberg's conceptions of patriotism differ. Dixon views it as a scale whereby one can be excessively patriotic (jingoistic) at one end (which is morally wrong) but also moderately patriotic and sit towards the centre of this scale. In contrast, Gomberg views patriotism as being dichotomous: either one is patriotic (which is morally problematic), or one isn't.

The solution to this argument may be to accept a non-serious conception of patriotism that avoids falling into bad-faith, whereby one supports one's home nation in sporting events based on the view that it is just a fortune of circumstance and recognising that had circumstances been different, one's loyalty would lie elsewhere. A non-serious conception of patriotism allows us to take a partisan interest in the outcome of sporting events whilst acknowledging such a patriotism is insubstantial and tenuous.

INDEPENDENT STUDY QUESTIONS:

- *What does Keller mean by 'derived' and 'non-derived', and 'serious' and 'non-serious' loyalty and how do these relate to patriotism?*
- *What is the difference between a Universalist and a Communitarian position on patriotism?*
- *Is Gomberg correct in arguing that innocuous moderate patriotism in sport inevitably leads to immoral consequences such as support for patriotic wars?*
- *Does a 'non-serious' conception of patriotism in sport overcome MacIntyre's and Gomberg's criticisms of moderate patriotism?*

27 CAN YOU RESPECT SOMEONE YOU'RE TRYING TO BEAT?

Respect seems to be a pertinent concept in sport as can be demonstrated by the stock phrases, 'Don't give them too much respect', 'I respect him as a player' and 'They should have shown a bit more respect'. When players are accused of not giving enough respect, or showing too much, the implication is that the level of respect afforded to the opposition affects how the game is played and, ultimately, the final result.

This chapter will consider what is meant by 'respect' and the way in which people, and opponents in sport in particular, should be respected.

HOW IS RESPECT CONSIDERED IN ETHICAL THEORY?

One of the key ethical theories that focuses upon the notion of respect is Kantian ethics. The German philosopher, Immanuel Kant, argued that the most important part of morality is a good will. It is the intention to do right and to treat others well that is central to acting morally. Kant articulated his ethical theory through categorical imperatives based upon rationality and *a priori* truths. As noted in Chapter 4, *a priori* (analytic) statements are true by definition, such as 'all triangles have three sides' or 'all footballers play sport', in contrast to *a posteriori* (synthetic) statements that are true by appealing to (scientific) evidence, such as 'all the cars parked on my street are Renaults' or 'England won the women's Rugby World Cup in 2014'. Kant aimed to ground morality in a priori truths on the basis that it requires no further or contestable evidence. This is achieved through Categorical imperatives which provide moral guidance about what is the right way of acting regardless of aim, outcome or consequence. They are directives for good (moral) behaviour. Categorical imperatives contrast with hypothetical imperatives as hypothetical imperatives take into account the consequences in directing action. Hypothetical imperatives allow some discussion of whether the particular consequences are desirable or not. So, while a hypothetical imperative might maintain, 'If you want to get the 'fair play' award then you ought to play fairly' – to which a response may be 'I don't care about a 'fair play' award' – a categorical imperative would merely state, 'You ought to play fairly'. For Kant, one should act in accordance with a categorical imperative because it is what reason and rationality require. From this perspective, it makes no sense to ask why one should play fairly in the same way that it makes no sense to ask why one should be good. Playing fairly and being good are simply things that ought to be done because they are good in themselves.

WHAT ARE KANT'S CATEGORICAL IMPERATIVES?

Kant formulated two categorical imperatives (which he argued ultimately expressed the same thing):

> *Act only on that maxim [rule or principle] which you wish to be universal.*

> *Act in such a way that you always treat humanity, whether in your own person or in the person of any other, never simply as a means, but always at the same time as an end.*[1]

The notion of respect is relevant to Kant's theory because it stems from a good will; that is, a desire to act in a good and proper way. We act out of respect for a rule or principle when the motivation for doing so is consistent with what that rule or principle requires. For example, imagine that Cain and Abel are playing football together. Cain does not respect the rules of the game or the principle of fair play and tries to repeatedly foul other players in an attempt to get the ball. However, Cain's incompetence means his attempts are unsuccessful and despite his efforts he plays the entire game without committing a foul. Abel on the other hand is a far superior player but respects the rules of the game and the principle of fair play. When an opportunity arises to commit a professional foul on an opponent in order to save a certain goal, he chooses not to. While neither Cain nor Abel broke the rules of the game, it is only Abel who can be said to have acted out of respect for the rules.

Kant's first categorical imperative states that a rule is morally good if we would want everyone to follow it. Cain's action is not rational according to this imperative because he could not possibly want everyone else to act in the same way. No one would want to universalise a maxim along the lines of 'attempt to foul other players' since the game would descend into anarchy and become unplayable. In contrast, Abel's action based on the maxim, 'do not commit a foul even if the other team are likely to score' could rationally be universalised.

There are criticisms of Kant's first categorical imperative, most notably, that it can yield false positives. For example, a coach could hold the maxim, 'I will beat my players if they do not obey my commands' and be happy for this maxim to be universalised (and for all coaches to beat disobedient players). Kant's response to this was that immoral maxims are irrational and inconsistent since we would not be acting in respect of the moral law that it is based upon. In this case, it is legitimising the principle of causing harm to others, which would not itself be universalisable.

This criticism is also be overcome by turning to Kant's second categorical imperative. Kant's second categorical imperative states that we should treat others as ends and not merely as means to ends. In other words, we should not use people purely for our own aims. We need to recognise that others have hopes, dreams, desires and fears, in virtue of the fact that they are human, like us. This stems from Kant's notion of respect, which notes that different objects in the world deserve to be treated in different ways according to the type of thing that object is. For example, while it is perfectly appropriate to sit on a chair as a means for us to rest, it would not be appropriate to sit on our grandmother, or any other person for that matter. Grandmothers, and other people, deserve to be treated in accordance with the fact that they are persons – that is autonomous, rational, moral agents. Note that Kant argues that we should not use others as *mere* means. This does not signify that we should not take up offers from others to help us reach our goals, or that we should not assume their consent in being used as means in particular roles. For instance, when athletes attend a training session, they do so in the belief that they can use their coach's knowledge and expertise to make them a better player. The coach's job is to facilitate an athlete's development, i.e. to be used as a means to an end. However, the coach should also be recognised (respected) as a person in her own right and therefore not used *merely* as a means to another's end.

WHAT DOES 'RESPECT' MEAN IN RELATION TO SPORT?

In relation to sport, the notion of respect and Kant's second categorical imperative presents several challenges. Sport is antagonistic in that is it is a competition for scarce resources: there are winners and losers, first and last places. Furthermore, there are many instances when athletes seem to be used merely as a means to a fulfil an end, whether that end is to enable a manager to seek promotion on the back of a team's success, ensure a sponsorship deal, or keep shareholders happy.

Tuxill and Wigmore distinguish between two types of respect for persons: recognition respect and appraisal respect.[2] 'Recognition respect' is to treat something appropriately according to what it is. They argue, at the very minimum, this requires us to not impinge on the actions of others: to keep our distance and let others get on with living their lives in the way that they choose. Yet they also maintain that to do so will probably involve a degree of restraint, self-sacrifice and courage on our part. The degree of self-sacrifice involved in acknowledging the goals and ambitions of others is disputed and it is this that accounts for the two concepts of respect. For instance, Downie and Telfer have interpreted Kant's maxim to suggest that it is not sufficient to merely avoid being a barrier to the goals of others; instead we should actively treat the ends of others as if they were our own.[3] This positive conception is known as 'appraisal respect' and stems from the ability of humans to 'step back' from their own perspective and see the world from the position of another. It involves identifying with others' aims and ends. Feezell provides the example of a parent whose child is on the bench in a basketball game.[4] As a parent (rather than a neutral spectator), they immediately identify with how their child feels – that he is miserable about not being able to play. Yet appraisal respect requires identifying with relevant others too. As such, the parent also identifies with the coach's perspective and sees that it is not possible for everyone to play at the same time and that the child does not have the same ability and physical skill as the other starting players. 'Appraisal respect' attempts to provide an objective account of another person's perspective. The criticism of this conception is that it is impossible to treat the ends of others as if they were our own as Downie and Telfer advocate, when the ends of others may either conflict with another person's ends, or the ends are not morally acceptable to begin with.

The issue of respect is further discussed in relation to the three case studies below.

Case 1: 'The Ambitious Manager'

The ambitious manager of the amateur side North West Vikings believes the team can win promotion this year. His selection policy is based purely on individual performance linked to winning outcomes and thus ignores other factors such as commitment to training, being a paid-up member of the club and ensuring everyone gets a chance to play. This results in some players being left 'on-the-bench' or not being selected at all.

Case 2: 'The Trash-talking Boxer'

Zac has been boxing for several years and has the opportunity to fight in a title-winning contest. His opponent 'trash talks' Zac's ability and character in an attempt to intimidate him before the fight. Zac is considering whether to do the same.

Case 3: 'The Ruthless Scorers'

At the beginning of a match in the early rounds of a Cup tournament, it becomes clear that the two sides are manifestly unequal. After the first quarter, the better team is already significantly ahead. The only result that matters in terms of a team's progress in the Cup competition is the result, not the final score, but the stronger team takes advantage of their sporting superiority and continues to run up the score to thrash their opponents.

According to Kant's second categorical imperative, we should never treat others merely as a means to our own ends. In Case 1, the ambitious manager is clearly violating this maxim. His aim is to get the team promoted, and while this may also be the goal of others too, it is primarily being achieved by using others merely as a means to reach this end. The fact that this is an amateur team (with membership fees) suggests that the main reason for players to join it is to play that sport. The manager is not demonstrating respect for his players by acknowledging the ends that they seek – that is, their desire to play.

The issue of 'trash-talking' or 'sledging' was touched upon briefly in Chapter 23 but it is more pertinent to discuss it in relation to the concept of respect. However, it is not clear whether 'trash-talking' in itself violates either of Kant's categorical imperatives. Kant's first imperative argues that we should not follow any maxim we could not universalise to everyone. On this, it may be argued that because there is a culture and tradition of 'trash-talking' in boxing it presumes that boxers are happy to accept such a maxim as universalisable. Equally it is not so straightforward to argue that 'trash-talking' contravenes Kant's second categorical imperative either. 'Trash-talking' one's opponent does not necessarily indicate a lack of 'recognition respect' unless it could be demonstrated that it impinges on another's freedom to pursue their goal. In Zac's case, his opponent's behaviour may fulfil this criterion since he states that its purpose is to intimidate Zac and arguably reduce his ability to win the fight. It also does not fulfil Downie and Telfer's requirement that Zac's opponent should be assisting Zac in his aim of winning the fight if his intention is to reduce Zac's chances. On this, it could be argued that Zac's opponent offends Kant's fundamental principle of acting in accordance with a 'good will'.

Concerning Case 3, there is significant debate in the literature on the ethics of 'running up the score'. It primarily focuses upon the notions of embarrassment, humiliation and hubris. Kant's first categorical imperative appears to rule out causing pain and embarrassment to others on the basis that a rational person would not wish such a maxim to be universalised. However, Nicholas Dixon argues that continuing to 'run up the score' does not demonstrate a lack of respect towards one's opponents. Indeed, he maintains that losing in sport (even by a significant amount) does not reduce the value of one's personhood or disgrace you as an athlete. Moreover, 'easing up' would demonstrate a lack of respect towards one's opponent since it would diminish the possibility of allowing the other team to play the game as well as they could. The principal aspect of Case 3 is the way in which the team conducts itself and sees the opponents. As Dixon notes:

> 'Mocking, taunting, and gloating at outmatched opponents is despicable. The sportsmanlike victors should thank the losers for the game, and console them for their obvious disappointment.'[5]

All of these cases highlight the importance of recognising others as persons rather than merely viewing them as players (objects). Yet as Tuxill and Wigmore note, doing so may reduce the ability to pursue one's own goals.[6] Depersonalising others in sport is often used as an effective technique to carry out actions that, when personalised, are morally problematic, especially in contact sports such as rugby and boxing. While this problem has led authors such as Bredemeier and Shields to conclude that sport is a sphere in which it is morally acceptable to depersonalise others, such a solution seems unpalatable.[7] As Tuxill and Wigmore argue, 'the cure seems worse than the disease'. Not only does it violate Kant's second categorical imperative but it also demonstrates a lack of respect for oneself as an autonomous being. A more fruitful solution to the problem of other people and their aims in sport may be found in the type of sport it is, and in the way it is played. Tuxill and Wigmore conclude that while it might be impossible to demonstrate a positive 'appraisal respect' in sport because of conflicting aims (i.e. you both want to win), it may be possible to fulfil the criteria of 'recognition respect' to a greater or lesser degree depending on the sport. For instance, in parallel sports such as athletics, all competitors are able to pursue their goals without being directly hindered. How fast a competitor runs has no effect on how fast their opponents run. However, 'invasion sports' necessitate an attempt to thwart one's opponent's efforts in reaching their goals. Contact sports such as boxing go further in this limiting behaviour. This clearly seems to contravene Kant's second categorical imperative and Tuxill and Wigmore conclude that the degree of respect afforded to others in sport diminishes when comparing parallel sports, striking and fielding games, invasion games, and contact and fighting sports.

Yet such a pessimistic approach need not be necessary. After all, the basis of Kant's notion of respect for others stems from seeing others as persons, acknowledging their aims, and acting with a 'good will'. Robert Simon's conception of sport as a 'mutual quest for excellence through challenge' points to a way to achieve this in all sports.[8] On the basis that we participate in sport voluntarily, then even in contact sports it can asserted that the fundamental aim of those participating is to participate in that sport. The notion of 'winning' only makes sense within the context of the sport itself. Moreover, the rules of sport are designed to require considerable self-discipline and self-restraint to ensure that all participants have an equal opportunity to achieve their aims. If played with an appropriate attitude, i.e. with a good will, then it is possible to respect someone you are trying to beat.

INDEPENDENT STUDY QUESTIONS

- *What is the basis of Kantian ethical theory?*
- *What are Kant's two categorical imperatives? Provide an example for each.*
- *Is Dixon right to suggest that there is nothing necessarily wrong with 'running up the score'?*
- *Is it more difficult to respect opponents in sports such as boxing rather than sports such as sprinting?*

28 CAN VIOLENT SPORTS BE ETHICAL?

This chapter considers whether there are some sports that are morally unacceptable because they are violent. It highlights the differing definitions of violence and distinguishes between the related terms, *assertion* and *aggression*, before assessing the part that intention to harm and harmful consequences play in our understanding of the term.

WHAT IS VIOLENCE?

Violence appears to be endemic in some sports such as boxing, martial arts and rugby. However, defenders of these sports often maintain that they are not violent at all. They may involve displays of physical power but that does not make them violent. The question then becomes one of definition. In order to determine whether particular sports are violent or not, we first need to be clear about what we mean by the term. This is more easily said than done as there are many definitions that have been offered, ranging from common understandings of the word, such as, 'actual injury caused by intentional force', 'potential injury caused by intended action', 'threats to harm', 'violation of human rights', to less common interpretations, such as, 'sudden extensive and radical changes'[1] and Levinas's view that violence is manifest in an attitude we have towards others (denoting a contempt or lack of respect).[2] Despite the lack of consensus about the definition of the term, at the very least the word's connotations suggest that it is something morally negative. When we label an action as being 'violent', we seem to be making a moral judgement that the action is unwarranted or excessive in some way. This can be seen in rejections to claims that a particular sport is violent; the defence is often that it is not violent but rather a display of 'controlled aggression' or some other morally neutral phrase. Such discussion highlights the importance of clearly defining terms and the normative ethical judgements that are contained within them. By most definitions, violence refers to a physical force that goes beyond psychological or emotional pain. While some theorists argue that violence does not have to be physical, certainly when it comes to sport, it points in the direction of physicality. Indeed, it doesn't really make sense to talk about non-physical violence as Ronald Miller identifies:

> 'The phrase 'physical violence' is redundant. Violence is just the physical overpowering of a person or object with the intent to injure or destroy. There is no such thing as non-physical violence.'[3]

In his paper 'Violence and Aggression in Contemporary Sport'[4] Jim Parry highlights the paradox that the ethical acceptability of physical force on another person differs according to context. Demonstration of physical force is necessary for many sports, yet the same actions are unacceptable when seen in wider society. A fight on a Friday night in a town centre is likely to be broken up by the authorities (even if all parties involved are consenting), whereas the same acts in a designated MMA cage are accepted. This begs the question of whether both are examples of violence or whether there is a qualitative or conceptual difference between them. One way of answering this is to consider both the intent of the person demonstrating the physical force and the consequences of their action. Separating action on these grounds is one way of distinguishing between the terms 'violence', 'aggression' and 'assertion'. Following Parry's classification, they can be defined as follows:

> *Assertion: To defend oneself and to affirm one's rights. Essentially, it is a reactive force to prevent one's being or space being encroached [upon].*

> *Aggression: To force your will or being on others. It is vigorous, offensive (as opposed to defensive) and proactive.*

> *Violence: Forceful and vigorous action but with an intention to cause harm or damage. It is this intention or recklessness with regards to the consequences that distinguishes the action from aggression or assertion.*

ARE THERE DIFFERENT CATEGORIES OF VIOLENCE?

In his analysis of this issue, Michael Smith provides a typology of four categories of violence in sport:[5]

> *'Brutal body contact: Covers an expectation that participants in the sport in question are likely to suffer minor injuries, and will possibly suffer major injury, through bodily contact with the opposition. However, the likelihood or risk of severe injury is constrained by the rules of the sport. This applies to sports such as rugby, wrestling, martial arts and American football.*

> *Borderline violence: Applies to actions within sport which although are generally prohibited by the rules, are an accepted part of the culture and history of the game. Actions are left to the preserve of the game-officials as to whether and what sanction should be given. Examples are fighting in ice hockey, two-footed challenges in football, and kicking and punching in water polo. In these cases, it would be inappropriate to go outside the game in order to sanction or penalise [actions].*

> *Quasi-criminal violence: Applies to severely harmful or injurious actions that are not usual or frequent occurrences, and are not an accepted part of the wider culture of the game. They are dealt with by officials at the top of the game, such as a disciplinary panel or hearing, and are typified by*

longer-term bans or sanctions. As Parry notes, these types of offences are also more frequently being investigated outside sport and are leading to more criminal prosecutions. Examples include punching, stamping, biting and gouging.

Criminal violence: Covers actions that cause severe or long-term injury or death and are so far beyond the rules and boundaries of the sport in question that it is only appropriate [for it] to be dealt with by an external court of justice. Examples could be where a wrestler continues a strangulation hold on their opponent despite attempts by the referee to stop the bout, or where a boxer continues to punch an unconscious opponent on the ground.'

Cases in the first, third and fourth categories are reasonably clear-cut, since the first category contains actions that are not considered violence, while the third and fourth are viewed as such in criminal law. The problematic cases appear to be found in the second category and result in the question of whether or not these types of actions should be considered to be violent. One of the main difficulties in coming to a conclusion about this is that these actions and behaviours are culturally and historically bound. This explains how the same action in differing contexts can be considered in a different moral light.

CASE STUDY: IS FIGHTING IN ICE HOCKEY VIOLENT?

The primary aim in ice hockey is to score by hitting the puck into the net, yet the emergence of fighting is considered by many as an entertaining and acceptable part of the game (it is generally even included as part of ice-hockey video games). There are even unofficial roles in teams for rough players (called 'enforcers' or 'Goons'). Smith cites a player who provides this defence for fighting in hockey:

'I don't think that there's anything wrong with guys getting excited in a game and squaring off and throwing a few punches. That's just part of the game. It always has been. And you know if you tried to eliminate it, you wouldn't have hockey any more. You look at hockey from the time it was begun, guys get excited and just fight, and it's always been like that.'[6]

This player seems to be wrong on at least one count. Fighting is not part of the constitutive rules of game. Rule 46 of the National Hockey League states that the act of fighting is a game infringement and details penalties that referees are able to enforce. Fighting contributes nothing to the goal of the game (unless you count a degree of psychological intimidation) and only occurs as an act of aggression towards the opponent. Can it be argued that it is an intention to cause unwarranted physical harm to another? This is more difficult to ascertain as players are already highly protected in their clothing and therefore there is an acknowledgement that the physical harm inflicted would be less severe than if they weren't wearing padding. Nevertheless, there have been significant injuries caused through fights, and cases of players being knocked out. There are also tacit (unwritten) rules about how fights take place. As the quotation suggests, players are expected to remove their gloves and fight with their fists. It is a legitimate way, defenders argue, of players releasing pent-up aggression rather than being an intention to hurt their opposition. Yet this argument doesn't hold for other sports in which players may be equally prone to frustration; no one has advocated that javelin throwers should be allowed to release their frustration as a result of a foul throw by using their opponents as targets. Sporting excellence requires athletes to channel their energies into the legitimate goals of the game, rather than becoming distracted by a desire to hit a member of the opposition. The fact that fighting is outside the rules of the sport, and demonstrates a lack of self-control and unacceptable physical aggression towards another goes some way to suggesting that it is an act of violence and therefore morally wrong.

IS 'INTENT TO HARM' THE KEY ETHICAL FACTOR IN DEFINING VIOLENCE?

The difference, according to Parry, between morally acceptable aggression and morally unacceptable violence lies with the intention to harm. According to this view, a contact sport such as rugby is not violent since the primary goal is to get a ball over the try line, not to cause harm to the opposition. While it may be common for players to suffer injury as a result of a tackle, this is an unintentional consequence of the rules of the sport and no points are awarded for how hard a player might be hit. As such, it is perfectly feasible to imagine a great game of rugby whereby all players end the game injury free. Played in this spirit, barring any unintentional injury, the game would still be a good one. In contrast, according to Parry's distinction, boxing is a violent sport as its primary purpose is to cause harm by attempting a knock-out. To be 'knocked out' is, by definition, to suffer some kind of (potentially life-threatening) injury. Consequently, Parry argues that as participants intentionally aim to harm others, boxing (and other violent sports) should be banned.

Parry's argument against boxing can be laid out as follows:

P1: Intentionally harming others is morally unacceptable.

P2: Boxing is the intention to harm others (via a 'knock-out').

C2: Therefore, boxing is morally unacceptable.

P3: Activities that are morally unacceptable should be prohibited (banned).

C3: Therefore, boxing should be banned.

A counter-argument can be given on two points: first, the intention behind boxing (and perhaps other combat sports) is not to harm your opponent, but rather to score points and win the contest. Although a knock-out renders a competitor unconscious, this is an unintended consequence of a punch to the head. Indeed, if the objective was to harm the opponent then feasibly a boxer could continue punching her unconscious competitor while they were on the floor. Yet, fights are stopped if boxers are seen to be suffering or at risk of harm. In boxing, points are awarded according to where blows make contact not on how hard they are. This therefore challenges Parry's argument that the intention behind boxing is a violent one.

The second, related defence is that actions in sport are constrained by rules. The rules of sport ensure that an action is proportionate and legal according to that sport; so while a player is not allowed to make contact with another person in netball, they are able to physically tackle them in rugby. And while competitors are not allowed to punch opponents in the head in rugby, they are allowed to in boxing. Even the most violent sports, such as cage fighting and mixed martial arts (MMA) are constrained by rules and are based on the notion of consent. Competitors are not allowed to bring weapons into the arena, and are barred from biting, gouging and head-butting among other actions. And there does seem to be a limit to what is acceptable even in the most macabre of sports. The precursor to MMA, Vale Tudo ('anything goes'), was forced to adapt and implement rules or risk being banned by the authorities. One could feasibly make the point that a sport without rules is not a sport at all. Ultimately, it seems that the point of all of these sports is to win the contest through fair and rule-bound means, and these means might involve a degree of physical contact, but that does not make them violent and morally condemnable. In many respects, boxing is championed as a sport that requires considerable self-discipline and respect, as well as other positive character traits. If violence were the primary aim of the activity then it would be far easier for those involved to conduct unorganised and unsolicited fights. Instead, credibility and moral acceptability is given to those sports by virtue of rules that prohibit particular actions.

This is not to say that there are not cases of violence in non-violent sports but these are dealt with by the rules of that sport, e.g. red cards, disciplinary panels and bans. Parry himself gives an example of a rugby player attempting to wrestle the ball away from his opponent. If it is within the bounds of the rules then it is acceptable; if it goes beyond the rules – if a player bites an opponent, for instance – then it is not.

DO CONSEQUENCES MATTER IN DETERMINING VIOLENT ACTIONS?

Although the focus so far has been on the intent to harm, consequences are also important when judging what is morally acceptable. It appears to be the case that

Figure 28.1 – A 'tip-tackle' in rugby.

as sports become more professional and our society becomes increasingly risk-averse rules are changed to ensure that there is less opportunity for actions that are likely to cause harm (deliberate or unintentional) to participants. Even as recently as the late 1990s it was legitimate for rugby players to 'ruck' a player out of the way by treading on them. Indeed, coaches were heard urging their players to give the opposition a 'good shoeing' if they did not release the ball at the bottom of a ruck. The law has since been changed so that players are not allowed to make contact with their opposition by use of the foot. If a player does not release the ball in the tackle as the laws require, then it is up to the referee to issue a penalty against them, not for the opposition to do so. Similar law changes have occurred with the tackle so that an immediate red card is issued if during a tackle a player's hips are brought above their head (Figure 28.1). This is regardless of the intention of the tackler and was introduced to reduce the likelihood of injury to players if they landed on their neck and shoulders.

Although it has been suggested that an intention to harm another person is the key moral factor in determining acceptability, consequences also play a part. There are cases where there is no deliberate intent to harm but the action could be seen as being reckless or negligent. Parry defines a reckless action as one for which there is no primary intent to harm the opposition but there is an awareness of the risk of injury. An example could be a bowler in cricket who deliberately bowls a 'bouncer' or a 'bodyline' ball whereby the ball is pitched short and subsequently is aimed towards the batsman's head. The intention behind such an action is usually one of intimidation rather than to cause harm (on the expectation that the batsman will duck or move out of the way), but if the batsman does not react quickly then there is a risk of injury. While this tactic may be officially frowned upon by those involved in the game as being against the 'spirit' of cricket, and led to a slight rule change that states a bowler is not allowed to bowl more than two of these balls per over (six balls)[7], it is nevertheless still viewed as a legitimate part of the game.

Negligent actions are defined as being those that a reasonably competent adult could foresee would cause the risk or consequence of injury or harm. Anthony Duff defines it as, 'choosing to take an unreasonable risk, failing to notice an obvious risk or acting on the unreasonable belief that there is no risk'.[8] An example could be when an experienced martial artist practises a move against an inexperienced and junior opponent who is not sufficiently skilled to be able to safely react to it. Arguably the experienced athlete should have been aware of the risk involved.

Including the consequences of an action in determining whether that act is morally acceptable or not overcomes a limitation of merely focusing upon the intention. Since it is only the individual who is truly aware of their intention (and perhaps even they are not fully cognisant of what this may be), an inference is often made that considers context, body language and past history. If a player is accused of a violent act but denies it, arguing that there was no intention to harm, then applying the concepts of recklessness or negligence allows for an appropriate punishment to be given, even if intent cannot be determined. The footballer who suffers ligament injury as a result of a late challenge for the ball cares little whether the action was intentional or not. The act can be said to be reckless if a reasonable person could foresee the consequences of making that challenge in that way, at that time, regardless of conscious intent.

ARE 'VIOLENT SPORTS' MORALLY WRONG BY DEFINITION?

It seems reasonable to suggest that 'violence' when ascribed to human behaviour is a morally negative term. Phrases such as 'he is a violent player' or 'she has violent tendencies' are moral judgements on a person's character. In the same way, labelling a sport as violent is also to ascribe a moral category. Those who categorise sports such as boxing, MMA, ice hockey and rugby as violent are generally making a moral judgement about their acceptability and place within human society. Yet just because a sport is labelled as violent does not make it so. To be violent is to lack control and self-discipline with either an intention to harm or a recklessness towards harmful consequences, yet all sports require adherence to the rules that oblige participants to remain in control and be aware of the rules. Furthermore, governing bodies are increasingly making the safety of participants a priority and are changing the rules accordingly. There may be some sports that we find morally distasteful because they point towards some of our base instincts in using physical force to overpower another, but this does not necessarily make those sports violent.

INDEPENDENT STUDY QUESTIONS:

- *What sports are often labelled as violent and why?*
- *What is the difference between violence, aggression and assertiveness?*
- *What are Smith's four types of violence and to what extent do they fit with other conceptions of the term?*
- *Which is more important when labelling an act as violent, and why: the intention to harm or a recklessness that leads to harmful consequences?*

29 SHOULD SPORT BE USED AS A POLITICAL TOOL?[1]

Keeping sport free from political interference is an understandable, if naïve, sentiment. This view holds that sport exists within its own logical space, irrespective of the moral, cultural and political values that participants may hold outside this space. However, the fact that sport is nevertheless part of a wider human society means such a view is arguably untenable. Moral, and subsequently political, decisions will inevitably affect sport in one way or another. This chapter will consider to what extent sport can be considered separate to other spheres of life, whether it should be used as a political tool to facilitate other normative values, and if so, how should such decisions be made.

CAN SPORT SEPARATE ITSELF FROM POLITICS?

The modern Olympics were originally conceived as a method of displaying athleticism and challenging the limits of human physical endeavour and ability and yet they were established on the back of the embarrassing French defeat in the Prussian war. From the outset, they were envisioned as a way of restoring national and political pride. If the modern Olympics were solely about the capability of the individual, then they could have followed more closely the ancient Greek model whereby individuals represented themselves rather than their country. Historically, the modern Olympics have been a stage upon which international political relations and grievances have been acted out. Up until Barcelona in 1992, at least 10 out of 24 games had been affected by political disputes or boycotts, and the Games have often been used to promote particular political ideologies and/or demonstrate athletic, economic and military superiority. Politics is, and always has been, infused in the Olympic Games despite protestations to the contrary. Despite this, the IOC continues to maintain its detachment from political affairs. In its statement expelling the US athletes who gave the Black Power salute on the podium in 1968, it stated:

> *'The basic principle of the Olympic Games is that politics plays no part whatsoever in them. US athletes violated this universally accepted principle … to advertise domestic political views.*[2]

However, the IOC contradicted its own position when it banned South Africa from competing between 1964 and 1992 due to South Africa's policy of apartheid. This contradiction of moral positions was also demonstrated in the attempt of the campaign group, Atlanta Plus, who in the late 1990s protested against the IOC's decision to allow the participation of countries that did not permit women to compete in their teams. Atlanta Plus argued that allowing such discrimination against women contravened the moral ideals that the Olympics sought to exude, but this was rejected by the IOC on the grounds that Atlanta Plus was orchestrating a politically motivated attack on the religion of Islam.[3] As noted in Chapter 16, the IOC aims to hold the difficult position of maintaining a set of values that applies to everyone regardless of nationality, race, gender, social class, religion or ideology while still allowing for differences in political and moral beliefs between nations. In aiming to ensure that no one is discriminated against on the basis of these differences, the IOC attempts to reconcile mutually incompatible values.

The IOC's position is similarly replicated in other sporting bodies. For instance, the International Cricket Council (ICC) outlines stringent deterrents to prevent countries from pulling out of tours unless they do so on grounds of safety and security, or on the orders of national governments. When faced with increasing pressure over England's fulfilment of their cricket tour to Zimbabwe in 2004, during a time of political unrest and controversy over the actions of President Mugabe, the ICC argued that it is not for the governing boards to make political or moral judgements. The ICC president at the time, Ehsan Mani, stated that it would be unacceptable to cancel a fixture on moral grounds and that it is not appropriate for cricket to judge between countries and regimes with different cultures and values.[4]

It appears that there is an inherent contradiction within the positions of both the IOC and the ICC, which aim to take a culturally relativist view of morality. The strongest criticism of relativism is that it ultimately collapses in on itself. Arguing that all moral positions are equally valid is to take a moral position that is implicitly universal. Moreover, both the Olympics and the game of cricket do emphasise particular moral values: for example, the concept of fair play, good sportsmanship, abiding by rules and cooperation with others. These things may well be practical necessities to enable sport to exist (see Chapter 3) but they are still promoted as moral values. For instance, cheating is not something to be avoided just because it would irreparably damage the game, but because it is held to be morally wrong. The problem for international sports organisations such as the IOC and ICC is that they aim to be representative of all their members when these members may hold conflicting moral values. It is therefore unsurprising that these organisations attempt to rescind all moral positions when controversial issues arise.

HOW SHOULD A CLASH OF POLITICAL AND MORAL VALUES BE RESOLVED?

For many individual athletes, political involvement in sport is a positive thing. There are many athletes, coaches and support staff who are funded, directly or indirectly, by governments on the basis that sport is a social and political good because it encourages others to participate in healthier lifestyles, fosters a national pride, motivates the workforce, and so on. From this, it can be argued that the involvement of politics in sport is not inevitably a negative one.

However, a question as to what is the morally acceptable course of action for an individual athlete to take when a clash of political and moral values and sporting competition does occur. For instance, when Sebastian Coe decided to compete in the Moscow Olympics in 1980 he went against the wishes of the British government, who had withdrawn the GB team in support of the US during the Cold War. As a result, Coe's coach (who was also his father) was summoned to the Foreign Office. While Coe, and several other British athletes, were allowed to compete, and did so under the IOC flag, the US government took a more authoritarian position and refused to allow any of its athletes to take part. The question that arises is how much power should a government have over individual athletes in relation to wider political events, and to what extent should individual athletes be able to reflect their own moral views on these matters, even if they are representatives of a national team.

At first sight, one may suggest that it should be up to the individual athlete to make the decision about their representation in politically sensitive sporting events. However, the problem with placing the sole responsibility onto individual athletes is that they are subject to issues of conflicting interest. At the very least, most athletes are aware that they are not irreplaceable and someone is always waiting in the wings to take their place. For example, if someone was selected for England's tour to the USA, but disagreed with their foreign policy and made the decision to stay at home, that person would know that the team would still go with a full squad; someone else would be drafted in their place and that athlete may never regain their place in the national side. It requires significant moral courage for an athlete to make a decision that involves considerable personal sacrifice.

The cricketer Stuart MacGill made such a sacrifice when he pulled out of the Australian national tour of Zimbabwe in 2004 on moral grounds. At the time, it was suggested there were other players who shared MacGill's beliefs and toured reluctantly but who were not prepared to sacrifice their position in the team. The courage and conviction that is needed to take such a stance may be one that most athletes believe to be too great. Indeed, there have been suggestions that MacGill was only able to take the position he did because he was at the end of his international career and therefore his actions would not affect his future in the same way it would for a younger player. Perhaps the most we can legitimately and reasonably ask is for athletes to be sufficiently reflective and critical to consider the morality of participating in sensitive competitions, be willing to express any reservations, and to lobby others to make a collective decision about a team's representation, but not to expect them to make a solitary act of boycotting the event if it will ultimately affect their sporting career and achievements.

If we accept the conclusion that individual athletes should not be left with the final decision about whether to represent their nation in politically sensitive sporting competitions, then who should be making these decisions? Perhaps consideration can be given to the role of a sport's governing body or team's management.

The case against governing bodies making such decisions rests on two issues: whether they have a vested interest in maximising profit for their sport, or whether governing bodies should represent the views of their athlete members rather than the views of other institutions. Both of these could factors could cause conflict when making a moral decision on a political matter. It is unsurprising that the England and Wales Cricket Board (ECB) did not wish to renege on their fixture with Zimbabwe in 2004 when they were faced with a fine of two million dollars, in addition to lost television revenue and other media coverage. But this leaves the question: if athletes wish to participate or withdraw from participating in a politically sensitive competition, does their governing body have a duty to support the athletes' decisions rather than the wishes of the government, the media or the general population?

If we take a pragmatic line when resolving these issues, we can propose the following: 1) international sporting committees are unable to reach unanimous moral positions regarding political matters if they are to represent conflicting cultural values; 2) it is unreasonable to ask individual athletes to sacrifice their highest aspirations in a political act that may have little positive effect; 3) it is also unreasonable to expect national governing bodies to make moral decisions that may conflict with other valued interests.

Yet this means we are still no closer to being able to answer the principal question of who should be making the moral decisions regarding participation in politically sensitive sporting competitions. Perhaps the only other institution to which we can turn is the national government.

SHOULD GOVERNMENTS PREVENT TEAMS FROM COMPETING IN POLITICALLY SENSITIVE SPORTING EVENTS?

The British Government is often reluctant to take an unequivocal position in politically sensitive sporting situations. For instance, although the British Government expressed their opposition to England's cricket tour of Zimbabwe in 2004, they were unwilling to become directly involved in the surrounding discussion and certainly in the decision-making process. Peter Hain, the government minister at the time, left the burden on the players' shoulders:

> 'If other governments will not back our own Government's stand, then it is still important for English cricket to show some moral backbone. The idea that cricketers or cricket officials are absolved from moral decisions simply seems to me to be wrong. We all have to take moral decisions in the jobs that we do.'[5]

Yet, as indicated by the arguments set out previously, this seems to place the ECB and its players in an impossible situation; a position highly criticised by Lord Coe who maintains that sport and its players should not be shouldering the burden of the Government's moral conscience.[6] Peter Hain implied that though the British Government disapproved of any action that may be seen or used as an act of support for the Zimbabwean authorities, it was prepared to let the players and the ECB suffer the consequences of cancelling the fixture, which may have entailed a multi-million dollar fine and a suspension from international test cricket.

The British Government's view is that decisions on political matters in sport are outside its remit. However, this seems to be inconsistent with the belief that the Government does have moral decisions to make regarding the place of, and participation in, sport in society. This can be seen with the enforcement of physical education within the school curriculum and the funding of sporting events and athletes. That there is a Minister for Sport seems to indicate that there must be areas of sport that the Government believes it should be concerned with. It is perhaps here that a distinction can be made and where sport can be legitimately used as a political tool: between athletes and teams that represent themselves, and athletes and teams that bear the name of their nation. A team that plays under the England name is as much a representative of that country as is their Government and therefore the Government should be able and willing to prevent national sides from taking part in competitions of which it disapproves. In contrast, we would probably hold that the Government should not be using individuals representing themselves or local club teams as political tools because they are not direct representatives of that government. Old Trojans 2nd XV from Barnsley, for example, should be able to determine for themselves whether it is morally acceptable to tour a particular country, although others, including the government and the media, should be at liberty to express their disapproval. The England hockey team, however, should not have such authority. Despite this, apart from a few isolated incidents such as the boycott of the Moscow Olympics, it seems that the Government is more willing to become politically involved with sport at a local level than in the international sporting affairs of national representatives.

If the Government were to take an authoritative stance and prohibit a national team from competing in an event due to concerns over human rights, corruption or illegitimate wars, for instance, the team should assent to their government's wishes. It should be emphasised that this is an obligation for a national team and not a bunch of like-minded athletes. In a country such as Britain, where the governing party is democratically elected, we can maintain that this provides the Government with the authority to make decisions that affect the society which it governs, including making resolutions regarding our behaviour and attitude towards the governments of other countries. This was the situation faced by the British athletes in the Moscow Olympics (in which the British athletes competed under the Olympic flag and not the British one) and Mike Gatting's select XI who toured South Africa under apartheid in the 1980s. Such a position enables a government to take a strong moral stance, using sport as a political tool, but still allows individual athletes to reach their own conclusions and decide what action they as individuals wish to take.

CAN SPORT POSITIVELY AFFECT POLITICAL EVENTS?

A counter-argument to this conclusion, held by those who believe that sport should be kept free from political interference, maintains that doing so can have beneficial political effects. For instance, it can play a part in encouraging hostile nations to restart diplomatic talks as was indicated in the tale of 'ping-pong diplomacy' that was recounted in Chapter 26. Sport, therefore, can provide a means for positive political change.

So the question may not be *whether* sport should be used as a political tool but *how* it should be used. On the one hand, there are those who argue that sport enables and continues a form of communication between countries and as such should be left alone. Sport in this respect, provides a shared locus of attention from which other dialogue may emerge. On the other hand, there is the belief that in today's global economy, where sport is not only a source of national pride but also a source of revenue, restricting a country's access to this revenue is a form of sanctioning. There are those who argue that the sporting sanctions against South Africa during apartheid were significantly more effective than the half-hearted trade sanctions that had also been imposed.

The notion that sport and politics should not mix; that sport should be kept free from political interference is a commonly cited one. Such positions may stem from the low regard and cynicism many have for political decisions, which to these minds are not determined from consistently applied moral values. Perhaps the problem is that we like to retain the view that sport is better than politics, that it has a higher moral standing than politics because it is an area where humans can cooperate yet at the same time compete with one another in a consensual paradigm. Things often seem relatively simple in sport because the rules are clearly set out; the ball was either in or it was out, it is either a goal or it is not a goal. And if there is a difficult decision to make, there is an adjudicator whose decision is final. Naturally, things are not always so straightforward, as is discussed in Chapter 6, but the fundamental difference is that decisions taken on sport's constitutive rules are not considered moral ones. Nevertheless, sport as a part of human life must reside in an environment in which moral and ethical decisions have to be made. It is therefore necessary to determine with whom the duty and responsibility for these moral decisions lies.

INDEPENDENT STUDY QUESTIONS:

- *To what extent is it possible to keep sport free from politics?*
- *In what ways have the Olympics been used as a political tool?*
- *Whose responsibility should it be to make decisions on participation in politically sensitive sporting events?*
- *Are sporting boycotts morally justified?*

30 DOES COMMERCIALISM RUIN SPORT?

Sport changed markedly during the 20th century. It was transformed from a leisure activity, where even at the elite end amateurism was the predominant ideal, to a multi-national entertainment business within which athletes can earn up to seven-figure salaries. Broadcasting rights and advertising space at sporting events are highly lucrative and the most popular sports franchises make more from their merchandise off the pitch than they do from the ticket sales for their games. The principal value of modern professional sport seems to be as an entertainment business. Critics argue that this commercialism has a corrosive effect upon sport and sport's intrinsic values, which have been replaced by extrinsic ones that create an environment ripe for corruption and cheating. Others maintain that commercialism enables a greater level of athletic excellence and opportunities to succeed. This chapter will consider the effects of commercialisation and recommendations to ensure that the core values of sport remain.

WHAT IS THE COMMODIFICATION OF SPORT?

Commodities refer to goods and resources that can be bought and sold. The typical understanding of a free market is that is an arena in which the price of commodities rises or falls depending on demand and supply. A commodity in low supply and for which there is a high demand will be expensive, while a commodity in high supply and for which there is a low demand will be cheap. Advocates of free markets argue that they lead to efficiency, technological advancements in the drive for efficiency, and more choice for the consumer as the greater the demand, the greater the competition to service that demand. Commodities are commercialised when they are made available to be sold on a mass market and are specifically targeted and advertised to an audience in order to increase its demand, and thus its value.

The notion of a commodity stems from distinguishing between two ways of valuing a particular item. An item can have a use-value and/or an exchange-value. The use-value refers to an item's intrinsic worth while the exchange-value refers to an item's price within a market. Commodification occurs when the value of an item changes from having a use-value only to having both a use-value and an exchange-value. More recent understandings of commodification maintain that there does not necessarily have to be a physical exchange of goods for it to be commodification; it also includes an attitude or way of viewing an item. When an item is regarded as having a monetary value, even if it is never sold, it can be said to have been commodified.[1]

The commodification of sport refers to the way in which it is viewed as a resource to be sold to a consumer. This may relate to sporting competition itself, in terms of selling tickets for live events or television rights for coverage of particular games, or related merchandise such as team shirts, scarves, mugs and a variety of other paraphernalia. It also includes the players and athletes whose services are bought and sold within a market.

Walsh and Giulianotti distinguish between two types of commodification: dirty commodification and quasi-commodification.[2] Dirty commodification is when money is illegally used to subvert the outcome of games. There have been many incidents of match fixing in professional sport, such as deliberately allowing goals to be scored in football, runs to be scored in cricket, or bouts to be won in boxing. Match fixing ultimately undermines the internal good of fair competition. Good sport can only occur if all competitors try their best to win within the constraints dictated by the rules. Match fixing undermines this principle because it requires participants to fail to do their best.

Quasi-commodification refers to the way in which money is directly used to influence the outcome of sporting competition, albeit not illegally; for example, if a rich benefactor enables a team to acquire the best players by attracting them with the highest wages. In this instance, there is a direct correlation between finance and sporting victory. This means that victory will be monopolised by those with the most money and leads to much of the criticism of the free market in sport.

IS THE COMMERCIALISATION OF SPORT A RECENT PHENOMENON?

A popular conception of sport is that, until the late 20th century, it was dominated by an ethos of amateurism whereby the sole reason for competition was for its intrinsic value. Yet in many respects this is a myth. For instance, victorious athletes in the ancient Greek Olympics were not simply rewarded with an olive wreath, but also with goods in kind and a free meal a day for the rest of their lives. In many ancient Greek games victors were also rewarded with cash prizes and goods of great value. As a consequence, the most successful athletes in the ancient games would be the equivalent of millionaires today.[3] Such was the commercialisation of sport in this period that it raised concern among Greek intellectuals that the excess of money had led many athletes to lose balance and moderation in their lives by pursuing physical excellence at any cost.[4] As Heather Reid notes, the ancient Greek games were not a golden age of amateurism since, 'there's little doubt that professionalism, entertainment concerns, and even cheating were present in ancient sport.'[5] Equally, while the common perception of sport in the 19th and early 20th century was that participants were motivated solely by internal goods, many sports, such as boxing, wrestling and dog and horse racing, were highly commercialised. Similarly, the spirit that led to the different codes of rugby in the early 20th century, stemmed from disagreements about the commercialisation of the sport.

Nevertheless, as Walsh and Giulianotti point out, the recent commodification of sport has led to an increasing commercialisation that bears no resemblance to any previous sporting periods:

> 'A time-travelling English visitor to the Lords Cricket Ground from the 19th century would certainly not fail to notice the changes to the way that cricket is now played in response to commercial pressures, from the advertising hoardings that hug the boundary fences to the commercial language of many of the administrators to the entertainment-driven type of game that is played to attract new markets.'

The rate and pace of commercialisation of sport over the past few decades has accelerated at an almost exponential level. For instance, the rights to broadcast English Premiership football matches rose from 191 million pounds in 1992 to 5.136 billion pounds in 2016.[6] Walsh and Giulianotti refer to this substantive increase in the commercialisation of sport as 'hyper-commercialisation' and outline four determinants that define it:

- the transformation of sports clubs into corporations;
- a rise in the number of professional athletes;
- an excessive propagation of advertising and merchandising;
- the 'venalisation' of the sport ethos (i.e. a predominance of financial profit as a motive for success).

WHAT ARE THE CRITICISMS OF THE COMMERCIALISATION OF SPORT?

The central criticism of the commercialisation of sport is that it shifts the value of sport from intrinsic ones such as the joy of participation and the development of athletic excellence, to the extrinsic one as a means to make financial profit. By instilling market values, commercialism changes the way sport is viewed and valued.[7]

One of the effects of this marketisation is a change to the nature of the sport. Robert Simon points to the way in which sports are increasingly designed to be marketable to the non-specialist fan who may not appreciate the subtle nuances of the game. Rule changes are brought in to increase the entertainment value through faster and higher-scoring games, but at the detriment of other skills.[8] While Simon cites changes to baseball and basketball, this criticism extends to sports such as cricket, which has recently moved towards promoting the faster and shorter 20/20 version that is played over the course of an evening, and away from the longer five-day test match. Critics argue that many of the skills required for the five-day game are now being lost.

Another effect of commercialisation is that it places greater demands on participants and spectators. For Walsh and Giulianotti, sport is one of the basic goods that enables us to lead a good life: commercialisation effectively prices the poorest out of the market. Even for those with greater means, the commercialisation of sport leads to more fixtures, longer seasons, and frequent changes to team shirts, which places increasing financial demands on genuine fans who wish to support their team. It also has a negative effect on the players and athletes who suffer more injuries and 'burn-out' due to the demands and expectations that a longer season imposes.

Rampant commercialisation engenders unfairness as success is bought rather than achieved through fair means. Walsh and Giulianotti maintain that the hyper-commercialisation of sport has a negative influence on the notion of justice, particularly desert goods (that is, those goods that are deserved by merit). The purpose of sport is to rank competitors according to their athletic skill so that the most athletically skilful (which is determined by the rules of the particular sport) are ranked the highest and receive the greatest reward. This principle of desert is undermined if a competitor can gain higher ranking and reward through financial means rather than talent and hard work. Although there will always be financial inequalities in sport, hyper-commercialisation accentuates this.

Walsh and Giulianotti warn of four moral pathologies that are made more likely by the commercialisation of sport:

- A *motivational pathology* that disposes athletes to an extrinsic motivation for participating in sport and can lead to cheating, such as doping and match fixing.
- An *instrumentalist pathology* whereby all aspects of sport are seen as a means to the end of creating financial profit. One element of this is in the way that human athletes themselves are treated as commodities to be bought and sold.
- A *distributive pathology* that reduces justice, such as the way in which genuine sports fans are priced out of watching live sport due to high ticket prices.
- A *pragmatic pathology* whereby all the other pathologies end up undermining a sport's existence, for instance, when a lack of investment in the 'grass roots' reduces the number and quality of players available to sustain the game.

Most criticism of the commodification of sport does not advocate a return to the myth of amateurism where cheating rarely occurred and everyone participated for the love of it. Indeed, there are arguably many benefits to commercialisation, including greater opportunities to play sport at a professional level, which leads to an increase in athletic skill, which provides more entertainment for spectators.[9] Rather, it is more of a measured criticism that draws attention to the negative effects of commercialisation such as the instrumental focus upon external rewards and the dehumanisation of the athletes. The charge against commercialisation is that a change in motivation from an autotelic one (carried out for its own sake) to an instrumental one (carried out as a means for the sake of something else, e.g. increasing monetary profit) erodes sport's value. Walsh and Giulianotti take an Aristotelian perspective and argue that hyper-commercialisation adversely affects the possibility of human flourishing. The 'gravitational pull' that the influence of money has upon sport tends towards vice rather than virtue and, as such, its effects should be moderated.

HOW CAN THE COMMERCIALISATION OF SPORT BE TEMPERED?

Walsh and Giulianotti maintain that markets are not necessarily bad, but they must be well regulated. They also argue that there are some aspects of sport that ought to remain outside market control and propose several recommendations to reduce the adverse effects of commercialisation.

First, regulation is needed to avoid corruption. Corruption is problematic in that it leads to decisions based upon favours and bribes rather than fair and transparent processes. If these decisions are made for financial interests then they are likely to adversely affect the nature of the sport and the enjoyment of spectators and participants. Tight regulation of the rules within which sports businesses operate reduces the possibility of corruption and allows for the punishment of offenders.

Second, regulation should reduce inequalities. Good sport is founded upon 'the sweet tension of uncertainty of outcome'[10] but this may be undermined by hyper-commercialism. For instance, a criticism of the English football premiership is that it is dominated by a handful of super-rich teams and that although there may be rare occasions when a smaller team will win against a larger one, the league is only ever likely to be won by one of a few very rich clubs. This is also seen in highly technological sports such as Formula 1 motor racing, which tends to be dominated by the teams with the deepest pockets. When Ferrari dominated in the early part of the 21st century, although they had a highly skilful driver in the form of Michael Schumacher, their success was predominantly down to the amount of money they were able to invest in the technology. In response, Robert Simon argues that sports should ensure a standardisation of equipment so that more wealthy participants do not have an unfair technological advantage.[11] This was one of the reasons that A1 racing was devised, which gave all drivers the same car, although it never reached the popularity of F1 and eventually went into liquidation. Another option is to regulate the amount that clubs and teams are able to spend, for instance, 'capping' wages or transfer fees. However, it requires the mutual agreement of all parties and that governing bodies are able to resist lobbying by those who wish such caps to be lifted. Alternatively, a draft system such as the one operated by the NFL aims to make sporting competition more equal by allowing the poorest performing teams to have first 'pick' of the best newcomers.

Third, sports' governing bodies should ensure that there is opportunity for genuine fans to have access to the sport. One of the criticisms of the commercialisation of sport is that at big sporting occasions a large number of seats are bought by corporate businesses, which then fail to utilise them, while genuine fans are priced out of events. However, there is some indication that governing bodies are taking this problem seriously. At the London 2012 Olympics and 2015 Rugby World Cup, tickets were released by means of a lottery at various price levels in order to allow those without large financial means to bid for lower-price tickets.

Fourth, national governments should ensure that there are free-to-air sporting events. This was the case in the UK following the 1996 Broadcasting Act, which protected the status of several sporting events as free-to-air. These included the FIFA World Cup, the FA Cup final, the Grand National horse race, the Olympic and Paralympic Games and the Wimbledon tennis championships. However, this list is frequently under review and faces competition from lobbyists who wish to make more revenue from airing events via subscription or paid-for channels.

Fifth, elite clubs must be compelled to invest in grass-roots sports. This is pragmatically sensible on the basis that without such investment elite clubs would fail to survive, but it also has a moral element in that it ensures that there is greater access to the basic good of sport. Furthermore, Walsh and Giulianotti recommend that elite sports clubs should be owned by community groups rather than multi-national corporations whose sole interest is profit. Community ownership does not preclude commercial activity but does reduce the dominance of the instrumental motivation since communities are interested in more than profit.

Finally, Walsh and Giulianotti maintain that athletes and those involved in sport should receive formal moral education and training. Forcing athletes and administrators to think critically and reflectively about the intrinsic values of sport is more likely to lead to morally good decision-making and governance.

Ultimately, the commodification of sport has a tendency to skew its value to an extrinsic one. Even those that enter sport for intrinsic reasons, when given the time and opportunity, become corrupted, as can be seen by the recent scandals attached to the largest and richest governing bodies such as FIFA, the IAAF, and previously the IOC. Measures therefore need to be put in place to maintain the intrinsic values that are outlined in Chapter 16, such as the pursuit of excellence, the virtues of courage, justice and wisdom and the notion of play. This is the true value of sport; as part of a life worth living, and without it, it is worthless.

INDEPENDENT STUDY QUESTIONS:

- *What are the adverse effects of commercialisation in sport?*
- *What is meant by 'hyper-commercialisation'?*
- *What are the benefits of commercialising sport?*
- *How can good sport continue to exist in a market-driven world?*

INTERVIEW WITH A PHILOSOPHER

SIGMUND LOLAND

Sigmund Loland is a Professor and former Rector at the Norwegian School of Sport Sciences. He is a former President of the International Association of the Philosophy of Sport and the European College of Sport Science. He also serves on the World Anti-Doping Agency ethics council. As an alpine skier and coach, he continues to take part in winter sports activities.

- *Can you give me a little bit on your background and what got you interested in the philosophy of sport?*

  o I have been an athlete and have taken part in and coached many sports, in particular alpine skiing, which is a passion of mine. Being a sport student in the 1980s made me reflect upon not just the scientific facts of sport but even more its values and meanings. In the Scandinavian countries there has always been a close link between philosophy and ethics and sport and outdoor education. We have a strong outdoor education and adventure tradition with pioneers who linked their activities to philosophical ideals. There has always been a keen interest in the value of sport to the individual and society. Sport philosophy is not looked upon as something exotic and marginal but as a key issue in practice and education in sport. At the time I was studying, Gunnar Breivik lectured on the philosophy of sport, and I was immediately attracted to the field. I combined philosophy studies at the University of Oslo with a Master's degree on doping and utilitarianism. In 1986 I got a scholarship to the US and studied with Scott Kretchmar at Penn State for a year. Scott made up a reading list and gave me a systematic introduction to the field of sport philosophy. It was invaluable for my later work. I went back to Oslo and wrote a PhD on the ideal of fair play in sport based on contractualist ethics. Here I am, almost 30 years later, still being mainly engaged in sport philosophy. And I love it.

- *What do you think is the most interesting problem in the philosophy of sport?*

  o My main interests have been ethical and epistemological perspectives on sport and movement. I remember well working on my Masters thesis in the mid-1980s with a hypothesis that the ban on doping in sport could not be justified. Philosophical reflection however led me in other directions. I felt somehow that entering philosophy was like opening doors to new and sometimes unexpected insights. It was deeply fascinating. Being a skier and semi-professional coach I also reflected upon the knowing and execution of advanced technical movement skills. I read some phenomenology of the body, in particular Merleau-Ponty. I wrote a piece on a methods exam where I compared biomechanical and phenomenological perspectives on movement, which later became a *JPS* article. I guess I have stayed with ethical and epistemological perspectives throughout my career although eco-philosophy and in particular the ideal of sustainable development have entered the picture.

- *What book or paper has influenced you the most and why?*
  - That's easy. Within philosophy, John Rawls' *A Theory of Justice* has made the strongest impression on me. An extremely thoughtful and well-structured book and a modern classic. Rawls combines the big picture and launches a fascination theory of justice as fairness while at the same time exploring it in detail with examples from many spheres of society and human practice. Rawls' methodology of reflective equilibrium in which considered judgements in concrete cases are to reflect general principles and vice versa, has also made a strong impact. I find most philosophical questions relevant and concrete. General questions such as 'what is true?', and 'what is good and right?' beg for distinctions and practical examples. Applied and practical questions 'How can we better understand intentional, complex human movement?' or 'How should I act in sport competitions?' beg for general insights into epistemology and ethics. Warren Fraleigh's *Right Actions in Sport: Ethics for Contestants* was also impressive to me as a student with its rigorous, systematic dealing with the norms and values of competition.

Key Readings

Loland S., 'Against Genetic Tests for Sport Talent: The Primacy of the Phenotype', *Sports Medicine*, 45 (9) (2015), pp. 1229–1233.

Loland, S., *Fair Play in Sport. A Moral Norm System* (London: Routledge, 2002).

Loland, S., 'Olympic Sport and the Ideal of Sustainable Development', *Journal of the Philosophy of Sport*, 33 (2006), pp. 144–156.

INTERVIEW WITH A PHILOSOPHER
ANGELA SCHNEIDER

An Olympic silver medallist for Canada in rowing's coxless fours in the 1984 Olympics, Professor Angela Schneider currently teaches sports ethics at the University of Western Ontario, Canada. She is former President of the International Association of the Philosophy of Sport and has written on doping and genetic technology in sport; gender; and the concept of play and its relation to sport.

- *Can you give me a little bit on your background and what got you interested in the philosophy of sport?*

  - I came to university primarily to play sport. I was enrolled in Physical Education when I took my first introductory Philosophy course in summer school. I fell in love with philosophy but because there were no combined degrees for Physical Education and Philosophy, I ended up taking separate degrees while training for the Olympics in rowing.

- *What do you think is the most interesting problem in the philosophy of sport?*

  - Genetic doping because it takes the whole concept of doping on a quantum leap. Genetic doping is transformative in the sense that it changes everything. In a different area, the concept of pre-lusory goals in sport is also interesting. I wrote a paper criticising Suits' ideas on it but never had any response from him. I don't know if that was because he had to concede the argument.

- *What book or paper has influenced you the most and why?*

  - I took a course called 'the metaphysics of witchcraft', which highlighted the condemnation of women's bodies. One of the texts was *Malleus Maleficarum* by Kramer and Sprenger. It made me so angry about the way that women were treated and how women's bodies bear the load of evil everywhere. It was from this that I became interested in the way that women were seen in sport.

Key Readings

Schneider, A. and Friedman, T. (Eds.), *Gene Doping in Sports: The Science and Ethics of Genetically Modified Athletes* (Oxford: Elsevier, 2006).

Schneider, A., 'Pre-Lusory Goals: A Gambit Declined', Journal of the Philosophy of Sport, 24 (1997), pp. 38–46.

Schneider, A., 'On the definition of 'woman' in the sport context', in Tännsjö, T. and Tamburrini, C. (Eds.), *Values in Sport* (London: Routledge, 2000), pp. 123–138.

NOTES

CHAPTER 1

1   Huizinga, J., *Homo Ludens: A Study of the Play-Element in Culture* (London: Routledge and Kegan Paul, 1949).
2   Caillois, R., *Man, Play and Games* (trans. Barash, M.) (New York: Free Press of Glencoe, 1961).
3   Slusher, H.S., *Man, Sport and Existence: A Critical Analysis* (Philadelphia: Lea & Febiger, 1967).
4   Weiss, P., *Sport. A Philosophic Inquiry* (Carbondale: Southern Illinois University Press, 1969).
5   Metheny, E., *Connotations of Movement in Sport and Dance* (Dubuque, IA: W.C. Brown, 1965) and Metheny, E., *Movement and Meaning* (New York: McGraw Hill, 1968).
6   Davis, E.C. and Miller, D.M., *The Philosophic Process in Physical Education* (2nd ed) (Dubuque, IA: W.C. Brown, 1961).
7   Webster, R.W., *Philosophy of Physical Education* (Dubuque, IA: W.C. Brown, 1965).
8   Zeigler, E.F., *Problems in the History and Philosophy of Physical Education and Sport* (Englewood Cliffs, NJ: Prentice-Hall, 1968).
9   Kretchmar, R.S., 'Philosophy of Sport', in Messengale, J.D. and Swanson, R.A. (Eds.), *The History of Exercise and Sports Science* (Leeds: Human Kinetics, 1997).
10 McFee, G., 'Are There Philosophical Issues with Respect to Sport (Other than Ethical Ones)?', in McNamee, M.J. and Parry, S.J. (Eds.), *Ethics and Sport* (London: Taylor and Francis, 1998).
11 Best, D., *Philosophy and Human Movement* (London: George Allen and Unwin, 1978), p. 122.
12 Suits, B., *The Grasshopper: Games, Life and Utopia*, (introduction by Hurka, T.) (Toronto: Broadview, 2005).
13 Since Socrates never wrote anything down, it is not clear whether he actually said this but it stems from a passage in Plato's *Apology*.
14 This definition is outlined in more detail in Chapter 2.

CHAPTER 2

1   The Analytic/Continental distinction is a generalisation but it is normally used to highlight contrasting methods of analysis.
2   Suits, B., 'What is a Game?', *Philosophy of Science*, 34 (1967), pp. 148–156.
3   The reason why Suits used the term 'lusory' in many of his elements was to refer to its game-playing nature. 'Lusory' comes from the Latin meaning 'belonging to a player' and relates to the term 'ludere' – 'to play'.
4   There are other types of rules that are outlined in Chapter 3.

5   This argument is called the logical incompatibility thesis. It is also is a cornerstone of the theory of formalism. This theory is discussed further in Chapters 3 and 20 as it relates to discussion about the spirit of the game, spoiling and gamesmanship.

6   Suits, B., 'The elements of sport', in Morgan, W.P. and Meier, K.V. (Eds.), *Philosophic Inquiry in Sport* (Leeds: Human Kinetics, 1995), p. 11.

7   Suits originally maintained that all sports were games but later conceded that there may be activities that are sport but not games. Suits, B., 'Tricky Triad: Games, Play and Sport', *Journal of the Philosophy of Sport*, 15(1) (1988), pp. 1–9.

8   Roberts, K., *The Leisure Industries* (Basingstoke: Palgrave MacMillan, 2004).

9   Coakley, J., *Sport in Society: Issues and Controversies* (New York: McGraw-Hill, 2003), p. 21.

10   McBride, F., 'Towards a non-definition of Sport', *Journal of the Philosophy of Sport*, 2(1) (1975), pp. 4–11.

11   McFee, G., *Sport, Rules and Values: Philosophical Investigations into the Nature of Sport* (Routledge, 2004).

12   Connor, S., *A Philosophy of Sport* (London: Reaktion Books, 2011).

CHAPTER 3

1   Lehman, C.K., 'Can Cheaters Play the Game?', *Journal of the Philosophy of Sport*, 8 (1981): pp. 41–46.

2   A syllogism is a form of argument that uses logical deduction to reach conclusions based upon premises. More information on syllogisms can be found in Ryall, E., *Critical Thinking for Sports Students* (Exeter: Learning Matters, 2010).

3   Morgan, W., 'The Logical Incompatibility Thesis and Rules: A Reconsideration of Formalism as an Account of Games', *Journal of the Philosophy of Sport*, 14 (1987), p. 1.

4   Lehman, C.K., 'Can Cheaters Play the Game?', *Journal of the Philosophy of Sport*, 8 (1981), pp. 41–46.

5   D'Agostino, F., 'The Ethos of Games', *Journal of the Philosophy of Sport*, 8 (1981), pp. 7–18.

6   Kreider, A.J., 'Game Playing without Rule-following', *Journal of the Philosophy of Sport*, 38 (2011), pp. 55–73.

7   McFee, G., *Sport, Rules and Values: Philosophical Investigations into the Nature of Sport* (Routledge, 2004).

8   Torres, C., 'What counts as part of a game? A look at skills', *Journal of the Philosophy of Sport*, XXVII (2000), pp. 81–92.

9   UCI Cycling Regulations: 14.10.294 www.uci.ch/Modules/BUILTIN/getObject. asp?MenuId=&ObjTypeCode=FILE&type=FILE&id=NDc3MDk&LangId=1 Accessed July 2014.

10   IRB Laws: 13.1b www.irblaws.com/index.php?section=7 Accessed July 2014.

11   Lehman, C.K., 'Can Cheaters Play the Game?', *Journal of the Philosophy of Sport*, 8 (1981): pp. 41–46.

12   Simon, R. L., 'Internalism and Internal Values in Sport', *Journal of the Philosophy of Sport*. 27 (2000), pp. 1–16.

CHAPTER 4

1   For *A* substitute a name, e.g. 'Alice'. For *P* substitute a proposition, e.g. 'Nicola Adams became the first woman to win Olympic Gold in boxing'. 'Iff' stands for 'if and only if'.

2   Dancy, J., *Introduction to Contemporary Epistemology* (Oxford: Blackwell, 1985).
3   Bonjour, L., *Epistemology: Classic Problems and Contemporary Responses* (Plymouth: Rowman and Littlefield, 2010).
4   Ryle, G., *The Concept of Mind* (London: Penguin, 2000).
5   Polanyi, M. *Personal Knowledge.* (Routledge, 2012).
6   Ramachandran, V.S. and Blakeslee, S., *Phantoms in the Brain* (London: Fourth Estate, 1998).
7   Phenomenology is the study of phenomena, although as has been demonstrated by the recent argument between Martinkova and Eichberg in the journal *Sport, Ethics and Philosophy*, there is scope for disagreement about how this is manifested in practice. To have a phenomenal experience is to experience it subjectively; it cannot be put into words, for instance, what it is like to see the colour blue.
8   Breivik, G., 'Sporting Knowledge', in Torres, C. (Ed.), *The Bloomsbury Companion to the Philosophy of Sport* (London: Bloomsbury, 2014), p. 204.

CHAPTER 5

1   That is: methods that collect primary data from the external world, such as experiments, questionnaires and interviews.
2   Its methods also generally reflect the fact that there are ontological and ethical differences with studying humans. At the very least, it is the only time whereby the object of study (i.e. a human participant) is the same as the subject doing the study (i.e. a human researcher). Ryall, E., 'The notion of a science of sport: some conceptual considerations', in Schulz, H., Wright, P.R. and Hauser T. (Eds.), *Exercise, Sports and Health* (Chemnitz: Chemnitz University of Technology, 2011).
3   Hempel, C.G., 'Valuation and Objectivity in Science', in Cohen, R.S. and Laudan, L. (Eds.) *Physics, Philosophy and Psychoanalysis: Essays in Honor of Adolf Grünbaum* (Dordrecht: Reidel, 1983), pp. 73–100.
4   Chalmers, A.F., *What is this Thing Called Science?* (3rd ed) (London: Open University Press, 1999), p. 46.
5   Cited in Chalmers, A.F., *What is this Thing Called Science?* (3rd ed) (London: Open University Press, 1999).
6   Popper, K., *Conjectures and Refutations: The Growth of Scientific Knowledge* (London: Routledge, 2002).
7   Kuhn, T., *The Structure of Scientific Revolutions* (London: University of Chicago Press, 1996).
8   The development and ascendancy of research ethics has rightly ensured that human (and some animal) participants are treated in an appropriate way (although this wasn't always the case – there are past examples of deeply disconcerting experiments on humans). However, one of the drawbacks is that variables cannot be tightly controlled due to the necessity of adhering to principles such as ensuring voluntary informed consent is obtained and risk of harm is mitigated.
9   Kuhn, a trained physicist, always rejected interpretations of his work that read him as advocating a form of relativism in that science is whatever a group of people define it as being. He insisted that he always wanted to defend science as a practice and that he wasn't making a relativistic argument.
10 Taleb, N., *The Black Swan: The Impact of the Highly Improbable* (London: Penguin, 2010), p. 184.
11 There are admittedly problems with this notion in quantum theory, which demonstrates that at a sub-atomic level the future is not predictable in the same way that Newtonian theory describes.

12   Winch, P., *The Idea of a Social Science and its Relation to Philosophy* (3rd ed, introduction by Gaita, R.) (London: Routledge, 2007).
13   Wittgenstein, L., *The Blue & Brown Books* (Oxford: Basil Blackwell, 1969), p. 18.

CHAPTER 6

1   IRB, 2015, 6.A.4a.
2   Collins, H., 'The Philosophy of Umpiring and the Introduction of Decision-Aid Technology', *Journal of the Philosophy of Sport*, 37 (2010), pp. 135–146.
3   BBC SPORT ONLINE, 'World Cup 2010: Fifa evades technology questions', 28 June 2010. Available at http://news.bbc.co.uk/sport1/hi/football/world_cup_2010/8766423.stm.
4   Ryall, E., 'Are there any Good Arguments Against Goal-Line Technology?', *Sport, Ethics and Philosophy*, 6(4) (2012), pp. 439–450.
5   Rivlin, J., 'Rugby at Twickenham: Thanks to video technology, referees are too scared to do their job.' *The Telegraph* (2013). Available at: http://blogs.telegraph.co.uk/technology/jackrivlin/100011361/rugby-at-twickenham-thanks-to-video-technology-referees-are-too-scared-to-do-their-job/
6   Bordner, S., 'Call 'Em as they are: What's Wrong with Blown Calls and What to do about them', *Journal of the Philosophy of Sport*, 42(1) (2015), pp. 101–120.
7   See Chapter 3, 'Can cheaters play the game?'
8   Bordner, S., 'Call 'Em as they are: What's Wrong with Blown Calls and What to do about them', *Journal of the Philosophy of Sport*, 42(1) (2015), p. 104.
9   Ryall, E., 'Are there any Good Arguments Against Goal-Line Technology?', *Sport, Ethics and Philosophy*, 6(4) (2012), pp. 439–450.
10   Hawkins, P., 'Open Letter to Sepp Blatter from Hawk-Eye', *Hawk-Eye Innovations*, 22 September 2009. Available at: www.Hawk-Eyeinnovations.co.uk/files/FifaOpenLetter.pdf.
11   Collins, H. and Evans. R., 'You cannot be serious! Public understanding of technology with special reference to 'Hawk-Eye'', *Public Understanding of Science*. 17 (2008), pp. 283–308.

CHAPTER 7

1   'technology', Stevenson, A. (Ed.), *Oxford Dictionary of English* (Oxford University Press, 2010). *Oxford Reference Online*. Oxford University Press. University of Gloucestershire. 10 July 2012 http://www.oxfordreference.com/views/ENTRY.html?subview=Main&entry=t140.e0848700
2   'technology', Calhoun, C. (Ed.), *Dictionary of the Social Sciences* (Oxford University Press 2002). *Oxford Reference Online*. Oxford University Press. University of Gloucestershire. 5 October 2010 http://www.oxfordreference.com/views/ENTRY.html?subview=Main&entry=t104.e1667
3   Dunne, J., *Back to the Rough Ground: 'Phronesis' and 'Techne' in Modern Philosophy and in Aristotle* (University of Notre Dame Press: Notre Dame, 1993).
4   Butryn, T., 'Cyborg Horizons: Sport and the Ethics of Self-Technologization', in Miah, A. and Eassom, S. (Eds.), *Sport Technology: History, Philosophy and Policy. Research in Philosophy and Technology*, Vol. 21 (2002), Series Ed: Mitcham, C. (Oxford: Elsevier Science Ltd).
5   Tenner, E. and Segal, H.P., 'Why things bite back: new technology and the revenge effect', *Nature*, 382(6591) (1996), p. 504.

6   Sailors, P.R., 'More than a pair of shoes: Running and technology', *Journal of the Philosophy of Sport*, 36(2) (2009), pp. 207–216.

7   This issue is covered in more detail in chapter 24.

8   FINA, 'Report from the FINA swimwear approval commission', 13 December 2010. http://www.fina.org/H2O/docs/misc/Dubai-FINA-Bureau-SAC_1210_v13d_s-2%20 in1.pdf Accessed July 2014.

9   Ryall, E., 'Are there any Good Arguments Against Goal-Line Technology?', *Sport, Ethics and Philosophy*, 6(4) (2012), pp. 439–450.

10 Loland, S., 'The Ethics of Performance-Enhancing Technology in Sport', *Journal of the Philosophy of Sport*, 36(2) (2009), pp. 152–161.

CHAPTER 8

1   Van Dalen, D.B. and Bennett, B.L., *A World History of Physical Education: Cultural, Philosophical, Comparative* (Englewood Cliffs, New Jersey, Prentice-Hall, 1971).

2   The modern incarnation of this was seen in the film *The Matrix*, in which the lead character Neo discovers that he wasn't an office clerk at all, but was merely being used as a support system for an alien life.

3   Ryle, G., *The Concept of Mind* (London: Penguin, 2000).

4   Saltman, K., 'Men With Breasts', in Davis, P. and Weaving, C. (Eds.), *Philosophical Perspectives on Gender in Sport and Physical Activity* (London: Routledge, 2010), p. 103.

5   Loland, S., 'The Logic of Progress and the Art of Moderation in Competitive Sports', in Tännsjö, T. and Tamburrini, C. (Eds.), *Values in Sport* (London: Routledge, 2000).

6   Leon Culbertson provides an excellent analysis of this in his paper 'The Paradox of Bad Faith and Elite Competitive Sport', *Journal of the Philosophy of Sport*, 32 (2005), pp. 65–86.

7   See Chapter 27 for an outline of Kant's theory.

8   Reid, H., *Introduction to the Philosophy of Sport* (Plymouth: Rowman and Littlefield, 2012).

CHAPTER 9

1   Some of this chapter has been adapted from Caddick, N. and Ryall, E., 'The Social Construction of 'Mental Toughness' – a Fascistoid Ideology?', *Journal of the Philosophy of Sport*, 39(1) (2012), pp. 137–154.

2   Jones, G., Hanton, S., and Connaughton, D., 'What is this thing called mental toughness? An investigation of elite sports performers', *Journal of Applied Sports Psychology*, 14(3) (2002), p. 209.

3   Gucciardi, D.F. and Gordon, S., *Mental Toughness in Sport: Developments in Theory and Research* (London: Routledge, 2012), p. 238.

4   Crosson, S., *Sport and Film* (London: Routledge, 2013), p. 65.

5   Barry, R., 'Question T-Mac's knee, not his toughness', *Sporting News*, 5 January 2009. http://www.britannica.com/bps/additionalcontent/18/36370029/Question-TMacsknee-not-his-toughness

6   Jones, G., Hanton, S., and Connaughton, D., 'A framework of mental toughness in the world's best performers', *The Sport Psychologist*, 21(2) (2007), pp. 243–264.

7   Reid, H., 'Aristotle's Pentathlete', *Sport, Ethics and Philosophy*, 4(2) (2010), pp. 183–194.

8   Hundley, J., 'The Overemphasis on Winning: A philosophical look', in Holowchak, M.A. (Ed.), *Philosophy of Sport: Critical Readings, Crucial Issues* (Upper Saddle River, NJ: Prentice Hall, 2002), pp. 206–219.
9   Harwood, C.G., Spray, C.M., and Keegan, R., 'Achievement goal theories in sport', in Horn, T.S. (Ed.), *Advances in Sport Psychology* (2nd ed) (Champaign, IL: Human Kinetics, 2008), pp. 157–185.
10 This is explored further in Chapters 8 and 16.

CHAPTER 10

1   This has been explored further in Crincoli, S.M., 'You Can Only Race if You Can't Win? The Curious Cases of Oscar Pistorius & Caster Semenya', *Texas Review of Entertainment & Sports Law*, 12(2) (2011), pp. 133–187.
2   Tännsjö, T., 'Against sexual discrimination in sports', in Tännsjö, T. and Tamburrini, C. (Eds.), *Values in Sport* (London: Routledge, 2000).
3   Coggon, J., Hammond, N., and Holm, S., 'Transsexuals in Sport – Fairness and Freedom, Regulation and Law', *Sport, Ethics and Philosophy*, 2(1) (2008), pp. 4–17.
4   Tännsjö, T., 'Against sexual discrimination in sports', in Tännsjö, T. and Tamburrini, C. (Eds.), *Values in Sport* (London: Routledge, 2000), p. 110.
5   Tännsjö, T., 'Against sexual discrimination in sports', in Tännsjö, T. and Tamburrini, C. (Eds.), *Values in Sport* (London: Routledge, 2000), p. 107.
6   This record set by Florence Griffith-Joyner in 1988 is itself subject to doubts over accuracy due to defective measuring equipment.

CHAPTER 11

1   The term 'trans*' encompasses a number of related terms such as 'transgender', 'transsexual', 'transvestite', 'gender-queer', 'agender' and so on. It follows Sam Killerman's use, who states: 'Trans* is one word for a variety of identities that are incredibly diverse, but share one simple, common denominator: a trans* person is not your traditional cisgender wo/man.' (Killerman, S. http://itspronouncedmetrosexual. com/2012/05/what-does-the-asterisk-in-trans-stand-for/)
2   Sailors, P.R., 'Gender roles roll', *Sport, Ethics and Philosophy*, 7(2) (2013), pp. 245–258.
3   Sailors, P.R., 'Gender roles roll', *Sport, Ethics and Philosophy*, 7(2) (2013), pp. 253–254.
4   Department for Culture, Media and Sport, 'Transsexual People and Sport: Guidance for Sporting Bodies', PP771 May 2005.
5   Coggon, J., Hammond, N., and Holm, S., 'Transsexuals in Sport – Fairness and Freedom, Regulation and Law', *Sport, Ethics and Philosophy*, 2(1) (2008), pp. 4–17.
6   Ljungqvist, A., 'Statement on the Stockholm Consensus on the Status of Sex Reassignment in Sport', 2004. http://www.olympic.org/content/news/media-resources/manual-news/1999-2009/2004/05/18/ioc-approves-consensus-with-regard-to-athletes-who-have-changed-sex/ [Accessed June 2013]
7   Tännsjö, T., 'Against sexual discrimination in sports', in Tännsjö, T. and Tamburrini, C. (Eds.), *Values in Sport* (London: Routledge, 2000).

CHAPTER 12

1   Jones, C. and Howe, P.D., 'The Conceptual Boundaries of Sport for the Disabled: Classification and Athletic Performance', *Journal of the Philosophy of Sport*, 32 (2005), pp. 133–146.

2   Jones, C., 'Disability and Sport', in Torres, C. (Ed.), *The Bloomsbury Companion to the Philosophy of Sport* (London: Bloomsbury, 2014).

3   Edwards, S.D., *Disability: Definitions, Value and Identity* (Oxford: Radcliffe Publishing, 2005.

4   Nordenfelt, L., 'Action, Theory, Disability and ICF', *Disability and Rehabilitation*, 25(18) (2003), pp. 1075–1079.

5   International Paralympic Committee, *A Layman's Guide to Classification in Paralympic Winter Sports*, 2012, http://m.paralympic.org/sites/default/files/document/121203164523073_wintersportlaymens.pdf [Accessed August 2014]

6   Ibid. p. 10.

7   IPC Statement on USA Swimmer Victoria Arlen, 2013, http://www.paralympic.org/news/ipc-statement-usa-swimmer-victoria-arlen [Accessed August 2014]

8   Jones, C. and Howe, P.D., 'The Conceptual Boundaries of Sport for the Disabled: Classification and Athletic Performance', *Journal of the Philosophy of Sport*, 32 (2005), p. 134.

9   Jones, C. and Howe, P.D., 'The Conceptual Boundaries of Sport for the Disabled: Classification and Athletic Performance', *Journal of the Philosophy of Sport*, 32 (2005), pp. 133–146.

10   Arbitration CAS 2008/A/1480 Pistorius v/IAAF, award of 16 May 2008, 7, www.jurisprudence.tas-cas.org/sites/CaseLaw/.../1480.pdf [Accessed August 2014]

11   http://www.bbc.co.uk/sport/0/disability-sport/28893804

CHAPTER 13

1   McFee, G., 'Are There Philosophical Issues with Respect to Sport (Other than Ethical Ones)?', in McNamee, M.J. and Parry, S.J. (Eds.), *Ethics and Sport* (London: Taylor and Francis, 1998).

2   Kretchmar, R.S., *Practical Philosophy of Sport and Physical Activity* (2nd ed), (Leeds: Human Kinetics, 2005).

3   Hurka, T., and Tasioulas, J., 'Games and the Good', *Proceedings of the Aristotelian Society, Supplementary Volumes* (2006), pp. 217–264.

4   Baier, K., *Moral Point of View: A Rational Basis of Ethics* (New York: Cornell University Press, 1958).

5   Nozick, R., *Anarchy, State, and Utopia* (New York: Basic Books, 1974).

6   Kretchmar, R.S., *Practical Philosophy of Sport and Physical Activity* (2nd ed), (Leeds: Human Kinetics, 2005).

CHAPTER 14

1   Suits, B., *The Grasshopper: Games, Life and Utopia* (introduction by Hurka, T.), (Toronto: Broadview, 2005), p. 9.

2   Suits, B., *The Grasshopper: Games, Life and Utopia* (introduction by Hurka, T.), (Toronto: Broadview, 2005), p. 156.

3   Suits, B., *The Grasshopper: Games, Life and Utopia* (introduction by Hurka, T.), (Toronto: Broadview, 2005), p. 41.

4   Hurka, T., in Suits, B., *The Grasshopper: Games, Life and Utopia* (Toronto: Broadview, 2005), p. 17.

5   See Chapter 3, 'Can cheaters ever win?'

6 The similar form that these two worlds share forms the basis of Andrew Edgar's (2013) argument in his paper, 'Sport and Art: An Essay in the Hermeneutics of Sport', *Sports, Ethics and Philosophy*, 7(1) (2013), pp. 1–171.
7 Suits, B., *The Grasshopper: Games, Life and Utopia* (introduction by Hurka, T.), (Toronto: Broadview, 2005), pp. 171–172.
8 Suits, B., *The Grasshopper: Games, Life and Utopia* (introduction by Hurka, T.), (Toronto: Broadview, 2005), p. 178.
9 Skillen, T., 'Sport is for Losers', in McNamee, M.J. and Parry, S.J. (Eds.), *Ethics and Sport* (London: Routledge, 1998), pp. 169–181.
10 Edgar, A., 'Sportworld', *Sport, Ethics and Philosophy*, 7(1) (2013), pp. 30–54.
11 Thompson, K., 'Sport and Utopia', *Journal of the Philosophy of Sport*, 31(1) (2004), pp. 60–63.

CHAPTER 15

1 These are qualified rights to an extent, which can be affected by specific factors, e.g. the age at which one can vote or get married, and circumstances whereby rights are taken away, e.g. prison sentences, or maturation of embryos.
2 Mill, J.S., *Utilitarianism. Liberty. Representative Government* (London: J.M. Dent & Sons Ltd, 1962), p. 73.
3 Ryall, E. and Olivier, S., 'Ethical Issues in Coaching Dangerous Sports', in Jones, C. and Hardman, A. (Eds.), *The Ethics of Sports Coaching* (London: Routledge, 2010).
4 Brown, W.M., 'Paternalism, Drugs, and the Nature of Sports', *Journal of the Philosophy of Sport*, 11(1) (1985), p. 21.
5 Anderson, L., 'Doctoring Risk: Responding to Risk Taking in Athletes', *Sport, Ethics and Philosophy*, 1(2) (2007), pp. 119–134.
6 Such as Russell (2005), Breivik (2007; 2011), Krein (2007), Ilundáin-Agurruza (2007), Moller (2007) and Howe (2008).
7 Burke, E., *A Philosophical Enquiry into the Sublime and Beautiful* (London: Penguin, 1998).
8 Thomen, C., 'Sublime Kinetic Melody: Kelly Slater and the Extreme Spectator', *Sport, Ethics and Philosophy*, 4(3) (2010), pp. 319–331.
9 Ilundáin-Agurruza, J., 'Kant goes skydiving: understanding the extreme by way of the sublime', in McNamee, M.J. (Ed.), *The Ethics of Sports: A Reader* (Oxford: Routledge, 2010), pp. 467–480.
10 Howe, L., 'Remote sport: risk and self-knowledge in wilder places', *Journal of the Philosophy of Sport*, 35(1) (2008), p.13.
11 Breivik, G., 'The Quest for Excitement and the Safe Society', in McNamee, M.J. (Ed.), *Philosophy, Risk and Adventure Sports* (London: Routledge, 2007).

CHAPTER 16

1 Reid, H., 'Plato's Gymnasium', *Sport, Ethics and Philosophy*, 4 (2010), pp. 170–182.
2 Finley, M.I. and Pleket, H.W., *The Olympic Games: The First Thousand Years* (London: Book Club Associates, 1976).
3 International Olympic Committee, Olympic Charter, Lausanne: International Olympic Committee, 2010, 11.

4 Parry, J., 'Ethical Aspects of the Olympic Idea', *International Olympic Academy: Report on the IOAs Special Sessions and Seminars 1997* (Greece: International Olympic Academy, 1998).

5 This is explored further in Chapter 8.

6 Silva, C.F. and Howe, P.D., 'The (In)validity of *Supercrip* Representation of Paralympic Athletes', *Journal of Sport and Social Issues*, 36(2) (2012), pp. 174–194.

7 Aristotle, *The Nichomachean Ethics* (London: Penguin, 2004).

8 Dombrowski, D.A., *Contemporary Athletics and Ancient Greek Ideals* (London: University of Chicago Press, 2009).

9 Reid, H., 'The Soul of an Olympian: Olympism and the Ancient Philosophical Ideal of Areté', in Austin, M. and Reid, H. (Eds.), *The Olympics and Philosophy* (Kentucky: University of Kentucky Press, 2012).

10 Reid, H., 'Wrestling with Socrates', *Sport, Ethics and Philosophy*, 4(2) (2010), pp. 157–169.

11 Reid, H., 'The Soul of an Olympian: Olympism and the Ancient Philosophical Ideal of Areté', in Austin, M. and Reid, H. (Eds.), *The Olympics and Philosophy* (Kentucky: University of Kentucky Press, 2012), p. 94.

12 See Chapter 22 for more discussion on the nature of competition.

13 Reid, H., 'The Soul of an Olympian: Olympism and the Ancient Philosophical Ideal of Areté', in Austin, M. and Reid, H. (Eds.), *The Olympics and Philosophy* (Kentucky: University of Kentucky Press, 2012).

14 Dombrowski, D.A., *Contemporary Athletics and Ancient Greek Ideals* (London: University of Chicago Press, 2009), p. 132.

15 Reid, H., 'The Soul of an Olympian: Olympism and the Ancient Philosophical Ideal of Areté', in Austin, M. and Reid, H. (Eds.), *The Olympics and Philosophy* (Kentucky: University of Kentucky Press, 2012).

16 Reid, H., 'The Soul of an Olympian: Olympism and the Ancient Philosophical Ideal of Areté', in Austin, M. and Reid, H. (Eds.), *The Olympics and Philosophy* (Kentucky: University of Kentucky Press, 2012.

17 Cantor, P.A. and Hufnagel, P., 'The Olympics of the Mind: Philosophy and Athletics in the Ancient Greek World', in Austin, M. and Reid, H. (Eds.), *The Olympics and Philosophy* (Kentucky: University of Kentucky Press, 2012), pp. 59–60.

18 Suits, B., *The Grasshopper: Games, Life and Utopia* (introduction by Hurka, T.), (Toronto: Broadview, 2005).

19 Reid, H., 'Plato's Gymnasium', *Sport, Ethics and Philosophy*, 4 (2010), pp. 170–182.

CHAPTER 17

1 Mumford, S., *Watching Sport* (London: Routledge, 2013).

2 Edgar, A., 'Sport and Art: An Essay in the Hermeneutics of Sport', *Sports, Ethics and Philosophy*, 7(1) (2013), pp. 1–171.

3 Best, D., *Philosophy and Human Movement* (London: George Allen and Unwin, 1978).

4 Cordner, C., 'Differences between Sport and Art', *Journal of the Philosophy of Sport*, 15 (1988), pp. 31–47.

5 Mumford, S., *Watching Sport* (London: Routledge, 2013).

6 Boxill, J., 'Beauty, Sport, Gender', *Journal of the Philosophy of Sport*, 11 (1984), pp. 36–47.

7 Edgar, A., 'Sport and Art: An Essay in the Hermeneutics of Sport', *Sports, Ethics and Philosophy*, 7(1) (2013), pp. 1–171.

8   Reid, L., 'Sport, the Aesthetic and Art', *British Journal of Educational Studies* (Oxford: Basil Blackwell and Mott, 1970), pp. 245–258.

9   Ziff, P., 'A Fine Forehand', *Journal of the Philosophy of Sport*, 1 (1974), pp. 92–109.

10 Ibid. p. 93.

11 Kuntz, P., 'Aesthetics Applies to Sports as Well as to the Arts', *Journal of the Philosophy of Sport*, 1 (1974), pp. 6–35.

12 Kuntz, P., 'Aesthetics Applies to Sports as Well as to the Arts', *Journal of the Philosophy of Sport*, 1 (1974), p. 20.

13 Bannister, R., *The Four-Minute Mile* (New York: Dodd, Mead & Co, 1956), pp. 11–12.

14 This is direct opposition to Suits' conception, which argues that the ends and means in games and sports are indistinguishable.

15 Best, D., *Philosophy and Human Movement* (London: George Allen and Unwin, 1978), p. 122.

16 Gleadell, C., 'How Damien Hirst tried to transform the art market' *The Telegraph*, 21 March 2012. http://www.telegraph.co.uk/culture/art/art-features/9157252/How-Damien-Hirst-tried-to-transform-the-art-market.html

17 Boxill, J., 'Beauty, Sport, Gender', *Journal of the Philosophy of Sport*, 11 (1984), p. 36.

18 Bredemeier, B.J. and Shields, D.L., 'Values and Violence in Sports Today: The Moral Reasoning Athletes Use in their Games and in their Lives', *Psychology Today*, 19 (1985), pp. 22–32.

19 Edgar, A., 'Sport and Art: An Essay in the Hermeneutics of Sport', *Sports, Ethics and Philosophy*, 7(1) (2013), pp. 1–171.

20 Cordner, C., 'Differences between Sport and Art', *Journal of the Philosophy of Sport*, 15 (1988), p. 43.

CHAPTER 18

1   Best, D., *Philosophy and Human Movement* (London: George Allen and Unwin, 1978).

2   The *Fédération Internationale de Gymnastique* provides very detailed guidance about how to award and when to deduct points. See for instance: http://www.fig-gymnastics.com/publicdir/rules/files/mag/MAG%20CoP%202013-2016%20(FRA%20ENG%20ESP)%20Feb%202013.pdf

3   'Zatopek, 78, Ungainly Running Star, Dies', *New York Times*, 23 November 2000, http://www.nytimes.com/2000/11/23/sports/23ZATO.html [Accessed June 2013]

4   Ziff, P., 'A Fine Forehand', *Journal of the Philosophy of Sport*, 1 (1974), pp. 92–109.

5   Best, D., *Philosophy and Human Movement* (London: George Allen and Unwin, 1978), p. 105.

6   Lacerda, T. and Mumford, S., 'The Genius in Art and in Sport: A contribution to the investigation of aesthetics of sport', *Journal of the Philosophy of Sport*, 37(2) (2010), pp. 182–193.

7   Lacerda, T. and Mumford, S., 'The Genius in Art and in Sport: A contribution to the investigation of aesthetics of sport', *Journal of the Philosophy of Sport*, 37(2) (2010), p. 184.

8   Lacerda, T. and Mumford, S., 'The Genius in Art and in Sport: A contribution to the investigation of aesthetics of sport', *Journal of the Philosophy of Sport*, 37(2) (2010), p. 192.

CHAPTER 19

1   Dixon, N., 'The Ethics of Supporting Sports Teams', *Journal of Applied Philosophy*, in Morgan, W.J. (Ed.), *Ethics in Sport* (2nd ed) (Leeds: Human Kinetics, 2007), p. 441.
2   Mumford, S., *Watching Sport* (London: Routledge, 2013), p. 16.
3   Mumford, S., *Watching Sport* (London: Routledge, 2013), p. 443.
4   Wann, D., Melnick, M., Russell, G. and Pease, D., *Sports Fans: The Psychology and Social Impact of Spectators* (New York: Routledge, 2001).
5   Tännsjö, T., 'Is Our Admiration for Sports Heroes Fascistoid?', *Journal of the Philosophy of Sport*, 25(1) (1998), pp. 23–34.
6   See Chapter 25.
7   Mumford includes other forms of sensory experience in the use of the term 'watching' that go beyond the visual, such as auditory and olfactory. Spectating at a live game is a much deeper experience than merely watching a match visually.
8   Gumbrecht, H.U., *In Praise of Athletic Beauty* (London: Harvard University Press, 2006), p. 16.
9   This is considered by Stephen Mumford in his paper, 'Emotions and aesthetics: an inevitable trade-off?', *Journal of the Philosophy of Sport*, 39(2) (2012).
10 Mumford, S., 'Moderate Partisanship as Oscillation', *Sport, Ethics and Philosophy*, 6(3) (2015), pp. 369–375.
11 Culbertson, L., 'Perception, Aspects and Explanation: Some Remarks on Moderate Partisanship', *Sport, Ethics and Philosophy* (2015).

CHAPTER 20

1   International Council of Sport and Physical Education (1976) Declaration on Fair Play. *FIEP Bulletin*, 46(2), pp. 10–20.
2   Sheridan, H., 'Conceptualizing 'fair play': A review of the literature', *European Physical Education Review*, 9(2) (2003), pp. 163–184.
3   The issue of gamesmanship is considered further in Chapter 23.
4   Butcher, R. and Schneider, A., 'Fair Play as Respect for the Game', *Journal of the Philosophy of Sport*, 25 (1998), pp. 1–22.
5   These are actions that ought to be done for reasons of rationality regardless of preferences, motivations or consequences.
6   The exact translations are: 'Act only according to that maxim whereby you can at the same time will that it should become a universal law without contradiction' and 'Act in such a way that you treat humanity, whether in your own person or in the person of any other, never merely as a means to an end, but always at the same time as an end.' Kant, I., *Groundwork of the Metaphysics of Morals* (Cambridge: Cambridge University Press, 2012).
7   The Kantian notion of 'respect' is discussed further in Chapter 27.
8   Butcher, R. and Schneider, A., 'Fair Play as Respect for the Game', *Journal of the Philosophy of Sport*, 25 (1998), p. 9.
9   Butcher, R. and Schneider, A., 'Fair Play as Respect for the Game', *Journal of the Philosophy of Sport*, 25 (1998), p. 11.
10 Sheridan, H., 'Conceptualizing 'fair play': A review of the literature', *European Physical Education Review*, 9(2) (2003), pp. 163–184.
11 Rawls, J., *A Theory of Justice* (Oxford: Oxford University Press, 1971).
12 Loland, S., *Fair Play in Sport: A Moral Norm System* (London: Routledge, 2002).

13 Sheridan, H., 'Conceptualizing 'fair play': A review of the literature', *European Physical Education Review*, 9(2) (2003), p. 172.
14 Loland, S. and McNamee, M., 'Fair Play and the Ethos of Sports: An Eclectic Theoretical Framework', *Journal of the Philosophy of Sport*, 27(1) (2000), p. 63.
15 See Chapter 6 for more discussion on this.

CHAPTER 21

1   McIntosh, P., *Fair Play: Ethics in Sport and Education* (London: Heinemann, 1979).
2   Shields, D.L. and Bredemeier, B.J., *Character Development and Physical Activity* (Leeds: Human Kinetics, 1995), p. 198.
3   Russell, J., 'The Moral Ambiguity of Coaching Youth Sport', in Hardman, A. and Jones, C. (Eds.), *The Ethics of Sports Coaching* (London: Routledge, 2011), pp. 92–93.
4   Morgan, W.J., *Why Sports Morally Matter* (London: Routledge, 2006).
5   Bredemeier, B.J. and Shields, D.L., 'Values and Violence in Sports Today: The Moral Reasoning Athletes Use in their Games and in their Lives', *Psychology Today*, 19 (1985), pp. 22–32.
6   Howe, L.A., 'Self and Pretence: Playing with Identity', *Journal of Social Philosophy*, 39(4) (2008), pp. 564–582.
7   Joulwan, M., '*Rollergirl: Totally True Tales from the Track*' (New York: Touchstone, 2007), p. 253.
8   For example, the mid-range sanction in rugby for illegal and dangerous conduct is a 6–12-week playing ban. This includes behaviour such as punching, head butting and biting. The maximum ban for this kind of behaviour is 52 weeks. In English law, even common assault can carry a prison sentence and Actual Bodily Harm can lead to a five-year sentence. (http://www.englandrugby.com/mm//Document/Governance/Regulations/01/30/35/21/RFU_Regulation_19_appendix_2_Neutral.pdf   [Accessed February 2015])
9   McFee, G., *Sport, Rules and Values: Philosophical Investigations into the Nature of Sport* (Routledge, 2004).
10 McFee, G., 'Olympism and Sport's Intrinsic Value', *Sport, Ethics and Philosophy*, 6(2) (2012), pp. 211–231.
11 Reid, H., *Introduction to the Philosophy of Sport* (Plymouth: Rowman and Littlefield, 2012), p. 150.

CHAPTER 22

1   Ogilvie, B.D. and Tutko, T., 'Sports: If You Want to Build Character, Try Something Else', *Psychology Today* (Oct 1971), pp. 61–62.
2   The morally educational value of sport is explored further in Chapter 21.
3   Nietzsche, F., *The Will to Power* (trans. Kaufmann, W. (Ed.) and Hollingdale, R.J.) (New York: Random House, 1967).
4   Orwell, G., 'The Sporting Spirit', *Tribune* (London, December 1945). Retrieved from: http://orwell.ru/library/articles/spirit/english/e_spirit
5   Simon, R., *Fair Play: The Ethics of Sport* (2nd ed.) (Oxford: Westview, 2004).
6   See Bernard Suits' definition of game playing in Chapter 2.
7   Delattre, E.J., 'Some Reflections on Success and Failure in Sport', *Journal of the Philosophy of Sport*, 2(1) (1975), p. 134.

8   Simon, R., *Fair Play: The Ethics of Sport* (2nd ed.) (Oxford: Westview, 2004), p. 27.
9   This forms Chapter 2 in Simon's (2002) *Fair Play*.
10 Dombrowski, D.A., *Contemporary Athletics and Ancient Greek Ideals* (London: University of Chicago Press, 2009), p. 97.
11 Hyland, D.A., 'Competition and friendship', in Morgan, W.J. and Meier, K.V. (Eds.), *Philosophic Enquiry in Sport* (Champaign, Illinois, Human Kinetics, 1988), p. 236.
12 Russell, J., 'Competitive Sport, Moral Development and Peace', in Torres, C. (Ed.), *The Bloomsbury Companion to the Philosophy of Sport* (London: Bloomsbury, 2014), p. 237.
13 Attributed to Fraleigh by Kretchmar in: Kretchmar, R.S., 'From Test to Contest: An Analysis of Two Kinds of Counterpoint in Sport', *Journal of the Philosophy of Sport*, 2 (1975), pp. 23–30.

CHAPTER 23

1   McFee, G., 'Spoiling: A direct reflection of sport's moral imperative?', in Tännsjö, T. and Tamburrini, C. (Eds.), *Values in Sport* (London: Routledge, 2000), p. 180.
2   See Chapters 13, 14 and 15.
3   Howe, L.A., 'Gamesmanship', *Journal of the Philosophy of Sport*, 31(2) (2004), p. 214.
4   Russell, J., 'The Moral Ambiguity of Coaching Youth Sport', in Hardman, A. and Jones, C. (Eds.), *The Ethics of Sports Coaching* (London: Routledge, 2011), p. 91.

CHAPTER 24

1   According to a WADA document published in 2011, the sport with the highest percentage for positive test results was, rather surprisingly, the winter Olympic sport of curling: http://web.archive.org/web/20140710050756/http://www.wada-ama.org/Documents/Resources/Testing-Figures/WADA-2011-Laboratory-Testing-Figures.pdf
2   WADA (2009) *World Anti-Doping Code*. Retrieved from http://www.wada-ama.org/Documents/World_Anti-Doping_Program/WADP-The-Code/WADA_Anti-Doping_CODE_2009_EN.pdf, Article 2.
3   Ibid. Article 2.1.1.
4   The Royal Society for Chemistry (N.D.), *Nandrolone Controversy*. Retrieved from http://www.rsc.org/get-involved/hot-topics/drugs-in-sport/nandrolone-controversy.asp
5   Millar, D., *Racing Through the Dark: The Fall and Rise of David Millar* (London: Orion Books, 2012), p. 84.
6   Asch, S.E., 'Effects of group pressure on the modification and distortion of judgements', in Swanson, G.E., Newcomb, T.M. and Hartley E.L. (Eds.), *Readings in social psychology*, (2nd ed., 1952), pp. 2–11 (New York: NY Holt).
7   Zimbardo, P., *The Lucifer Effect: How Good People Turn Evil* (Reading: Random House, 2007).
8   Milgram, S., 'Behavioral Study of Obedience', *Journal of Abnormal and Social Psychology* 67 (4) (1963), pp. 371–378.
9   Glover, J., *Humanity: A Moral History of the Twentieth Century* (London: Yale University Press, 2001).

CHAPTER 25

1 As a matter of fact, it can be noted that most athletes are not seen as role models, since the majority of athletes participate in low-key sports and are unknown to the general population. (Petersen, T.S., 'Good Athlete–Bad Athlete? On the Role-Model Argument for Banning Performance-Enhancing Drugs', *Sport, Ethics and Philosophy*, 4(3) (2010), pp. 332–340.)

2 Hume, D., *Treatise of Human Nature* (1739). Available at http://www.davidhume.org/texts/thn.html [Accessed August 2015]

3 Charles Barkley interview (Cited in Petersen, T.S., 'Good Athlete–Bad Athlete? On the Role-Model Argument for Banning Performance-Enhancing Drugs', *Sport, Ethics and Philosophy*, 4(3) (2010), pp. 332–340)

4 Jones, C., 'Drunken Role Models: Rescuing Our Sporting Exemplars', *Sport, Ethics and Philosophy*, 5(4) (2011), pp. 414–432.

5 MacIntyre, A., *After Virtue – A Study in Moral Theory* (London: Duckworth, 1985).

6 Tännsjö, T., 'Is it fascistoid to admire sports heroes?', in Tännsjö, T. and Tamburrini, C. (Eds.), *Values in Sport* (London: Routledge, 2000), p. 10.

7 Ibid. p. 13.

8 Tamburrini, C., 'Sports, Fascism and the Market', in Tännsjö, T. and Tamburrini, C. (Eds.), *Values in Sport* (London: Routledge, 2000).

9 See Chapter 19 for more details on a moral defence of partisanship in sport.

CHAPTER 26

1 Dixon, N., 'Moderate Patriotism in Sport', in Tännsjö, T. and Tamburrini, C. (Eds.), *Values in Sport* (London: Routledge, 2000), p. 76.

2 Keller, S., 'Patriotism as Bad Faith', *Ethics*, 115 (2005), pp. 563–592.

3 Keller, S., 'Patriotism as Bad Faith', *Ethics*, 115 (2005), p. 577.

4 Keller, S., 'Patriotism as Bad Faith', *Ethics*, 115 (2005), pp. 563–592.

5 Gomberg, P., 'Patriotism is Like Racism', *Ethics*, 101 (1990), pp. 144–150.

6 MacIntyre, A., *Is Patriotism a Virtue?*, The Lindley Lecture (University of Kansas, 1984). Can be accessed at https://kuscholarworks.ku.edu/bitstream/handle/1808/12398/Is%20Patriotism%20a%20Virtue-1984.pdf;jsessionid=F755645491DBE37B2F8F7A348AA4B195?sequence=1

7 Baron, M., 'Patriotism and 'Liberal' Morality', *Mind, Value and Culture: Essays in Honor of E.M. Adams*, 1989 (cited in Keller, 2005).

8 Nussbaum, M., 'Patriotism and Cosmopolitianism', in Nussbaum, M. (Ed.), *For the Love of Country* (Boston: Beacon Press, 2002).

9 Nathanson, S., 'In Defense of Moderate Patriotism', *Ethics*, 99 (1989), pp. 535–552.

10 Keller, S., 'Patriotism as Bad Faith', *Ethics*, 115 (2005), p. 580.

11 Morgan, W.J., 'Sports and the Moral Discourse of Nations', in Tännsjö, T. and Tamburrini, C. (Eds.), *Values in Sport* (London: Routledge, 2000).

12 Dixon, N., 'Moderate Patriotism in Sport', in Tännsjö, T. and Tamburrini, C. (Eds.), *Values in Sport* (London: Routledge, 2000).

13 Morgan, W.J., 'Sports and the Moral Discourse of Nations', in Tännsjö, T. and Tamburrini, C. (Eds.), *Values in Sport* (London: Routledge, 2000).

14 Morgan, W.J., 'Sports and the Moral Discourse of Nations', in Tännsjö, T. and Tamburrini, C. (Eds.), *Values in Sport* (London: Routledge, 2000), p. 62.

15 For example, Kerri Strug, the US gymnast, was coerced to complete a vault in the 1996 Olympics despite being injured, in an attempt to beat the Russian team.
16 Jones, C., and Fleming, S., 'I'd Rather Wear a Turban than a Rose: A Case Study of the Ethics of Chanting', in McNamee, M.J. (Ed.), *The Ethics of Sports: A Reader* (London: Routledge, 2010).
17 Dixon, N., 'Moderate Patriotism in Sport', in Tännsjö, T. and Tamburrini, C. (Eds.), *Values in Sport* (London: Routledge, 2000).
18 Nathanson, S., 'In Defense of Moderate Patriotism', *Ethics*, 99 (1989), pp. 535–552.
19 The use of 'non-serious' here does not imply that those who are taking part do not take it seriously in the normal sense but rather it is 'outside' the bounds of 'normal life'. See Chapters 13 and 14 for more discussion on this.
20 There are arguably other ideological, religious or political reasons for going to war which are not directly related to access to limited resources, although an argument could be made that it is (lack of) access to these resources that is at the foundation of particular ideological beliefs.

CHAPTER 27

1 Kant, I., *Groundwork of the Metaphysics of Morals* (Cambridge: Cambridge University Press, 2012.
2 Tuxill, C. and Wigmore, S., "Merely Meat?' Respect for Persons in Sport and Games', in McNamee, M.J., and Parry, S.J. (Eds.), *Ethics and Sport* (London: E & FN Spon, 1998), pp. 104–115
3 Downie, R. and Telfer, E., *Respect for Persons* (Allen and Unwin, 1969).
4 Feezell, R., 'Sport and the view from nowhere', *Journal of the Philosophy of Sport*, 28 (2001), pp. 1–17.
5 Dixon, N., 'On Sportsmanship and 'Running Up the Score'', *Journal of the Philosophy of Sport*, 19(1) (1992), p. 11.
6 Tuxill, C. and Wigmore, S., "Merely Meat?' Respect for Persons in Sport and Games', in McNamee, M.J., and Parry, S.J. (Eds.), *Ethics and Sport* (London: E & FN Spon, 1998), pp. 104–115.
7 Bredemeier, B.J. and Shields, D.L., 'Values and Violence in Sports Today: The Moral Reasoning Athletes Use in their Games and in their Lives', *Psychology Today*, 19 (1985), pp. 22–32.
8 Simon, R., *Fair Play: The Ethics of Sport* (2nd ed.) (Oxford: Westview, 2004).

CHAPTER 28

1 Gotesky, R., 'Social force, social power, and social violence', in Stanage, S.M. (Ed.), *Reason and Violence* (Totowa, New Jersey: Littlefield, Adams, 1974). (Cited in Smith, M., 'What is Sports Violence?', in Boxill J. (Ed.), *Sport Ethics: An Anthology* (Oxford: Blackwell, 2003).)
2 Levinas, E., *Totality and Infinity: An Essay on Exteriority* (trans. Lingis, A.) (Pittsburgh: Duquesne University Press, 1969).
3 Miller, R.B., 'Violence, force and coercion', in Shaffer J.A. (Ed.), *Violence* (New York: David McKay, 1971). (Cited in Boxill, 2003.)
4 Parry, S.J., 'Violence and Aggression in Contemporary Sport', in McNamee, M.J. and Parry, S.J. (Eds.), *Ethics and Sport* (London: Taylor and Francis, 1998).

5 Smith, M.D., *Violence and Sport* (Toronto: Butterworth & Co Ltd, 1983).

6 Smith, M., 'What is Sports Violence', in Boxill, J. (Ed.), *Sport Ethics: An Anthology* (Oxford: Blackwell, 2003), p. 207.

7 As designated by Law 42.6 in the ICC Laws.

8 Duff, R.A., *Intention, Agency and Criminal Liability: Philosophy of Action and the Criminal Law* (London: John Wiley & Sons, 1990). (Cited in Parry, 1998.)

CHAPTER 29

1 Ryall, E., 'Cricket, Politics, and Moral Responsibility: Where Do the Boundaries Lie?', in Sheridan, H., Howe, L. and Thompson, K. (Eds.), *Sporting Reflections: Some Philosophical Perspectives* (Meyer & Meyer, 2007).

2 Durant, J., *Highlights of the Olympics: From Ancient Times to the Present* (New York: Hastings House Publishers, 1973), p. 185.

3 Turner, M. and Kurylo, E., 'Group Protests Gender Bias in Games', *The Atlanta Journal*, 26 January 1995.

4 BBC Radio 4 Today programme, 10 March 2004.

5 Russell, B., "Cricket Must Show Some Moral Backbone', says Hain.', *The Independent*, News section, p. 2, 6 January 2003.

6 Lawton, J., 'Cricket: Coe Insists Cricketers Should Avoid the Trap of Empty Gesture', *The Independent*, Sport section, p. 24, 9 January 2003.

CHAPTER 30

1 Anderson, E., *Value in Ethics and Economics* (Cambridge, MA: Harvard University Press, 1993). (Cited in Walsh and Giulianotti.)

2 Walsh, A. and Giulianotti, R., *Ethics, Money and Sport: This Sporting Mammon* (London: Routledge, 2007), p. 14.

3 Miller, S., *Ancient Greek Athletics* (New Haven: Yale University Press, 2004).

4 Ibid.

5 Reid, H., *Introduction to the Philosophy of Sport* (Plymouth: Rowman and Littlefield, 2012), p. 87.

6 BBC SPORT. 'Premier League TV Rights: Sky and BT pay £5.1bn for live games', 10 February 2015. http://www.bbc.co.uk/sport/0/football/31357409 [Accessed September 2015].

7 Morgan, W.J., *Leftist Theories of Sport: A Critique and Reconstruction* (Chicago: University of Illinois Press, 1994).

8 Simon, R., *Fair Play: The Ethics of Sport* (2nd ed.) (Oxford: Westview, 2004).

9 Ciomaga, B. and Kent, C., 'Rethinking the consequences of commercializing sport', *Sport, Ethics and Philosophy*, 9(1) (2015), pp. 18–31.

10 See Chapter 22 for a further discussion regarding the value of fair competition within sport.

11 Simon, R., *Fair Play: The Ethics of Sport* (2nd ed.) (Oxford: Westview, 2004).

ACKNOWLEDGEMENTS

When I was first approached by Kirsty Schaper to undertake this project, I had no idea how difficult it would be to complete. Even a relatively new field such as the philosophy of sport has uncovered such a wealth of issues, topics and ideas that it is impossible to do justice to all of them in a short volume such as this. It took me over a year of reading to realise that condensing all the ideas and arguments that have been posited since the 1970s was unfeasible if the book was ever going to be published within a reasonable amount of time. As such, I have had to be fairly pragmatic about what I have chosen to cover, and what I have unfortunately had to leave out. There are many discussions and debates that I haven't included, particularly around the relationship between play and sport, a greater focus on the nature of games and game playing, and more detailed discussions on technology. And I'm sure there will be some who read this and think that I have omitted some of the most important debates in the philosophy of sport. To those, I can only apologise.

Most of this book is taken from material that I have used in my teaching and I have to thank my students for their engagement and thought-provoking comments, which have helped to develop my own thinking on these questions. What I have attempted to do in this book is to present some of the central questions in the philosophy of sport and provide some answers to them. But I acknowledge that there is a lot more that could have been said. I hope I have represented the key ideas of others fairly but any mistakes are of course my own.

A huge degree of gratitude goes to all those working in the field who have been so willing to answer questions about who they are and what they consider to be important and influential: thank you Warren Fraleigh, Scott Kretchmar, Jim Parry, Mike McNamee, Pam Sailors, Takayuki Hata, Randolf Feezell, Heather Reid, Stephen Mumford, Graham McFee, Sigmund Loland and Angela Schneider. For students, recognising that the authors whose work they read are just 'normal' people is important. It also highlights the variety of backgrounds that scholars come from and the many different ways in which they have unearthed questions in the philosophy of sport.

In particular I wish to thank my friends in the British Philosophy of Sport Association, notably, Lisa Edwards, Carwyn Jones, Alun Hardman, Paul Davis, Andrew Edgar, Cathy Devine, Mike McNamee, Jim Parry, Stephen Mumford, Leon Culbertson and Steve Olivier; and in the International Association for the Philosophy of Sport, notably, Charlene Weaving, Leslie Howe, Pam Sailors, Sarah Teetzel, Jesús Ilundáin-Agurruza, Heather Reid, John Russell, Jeff Fry, Cesar Torres and Tim Elcombe. The friendship found in the philosophy of sport is rarely found elsewhere in philosophy circles.

I also wish to thank my colleagues and former colleagues at the University of Gloucestershire who have supported me and my attempts to keep the philosophy of sport as an integral part of the sports courses, notably, Wendy Russell, Malcolm MacLean, David Webster, Will Large, Roy Jackson, Claire Mills, John Parker, Steve Draper, Jim Clough, Simon Padley, Jo Hardman, Denise Hill, Jon Cryer, Abbe Brady, Debbie Cox, Steve How, Mark Jeffreys, Phil Shirfield, Steve Piper, Andrew Parker, Nic Matthews, Kate Mori and Chris Potter.

Finally, I wish to thank Bloomsbury for asking me to write this book and Kirsty Schaper and Vicki Allen for all their help and enduring patience while I asked for extension after extension. It goes without saying that any mistakes or misrepresentations are my responsibility.

BIBLIOGRAPHY

Anderson, E., *Value in Ethics and Economics* (Cambridge, MA: Harvard University Press, 1993). (Cited in Walsh and Giulianotti.)

Anderson, L., 'Doctoring Risk: Responding to Risk Taking in Athletes', *Sport, Ethics and Philosophy*, 1(2) (2007), pp. 119–134.

Aristotle, *The Nichomachean Ethics* (London: Penguin, 2004).

Asch, S.E., 'Effects of group pressure on the modification and distortion of judgements', in Swanson, G.E., Newcomb, T.M. and Hartley, E.L. (Eds.), *Readings in social psychology* (2nd ed., 1952), pp. 2–11 (New York: NY Holt).

Baier, K., *Moral Point of View: A Rational Basis of Ethics* (New York: Cornell University Press, 1958).

Bannister, R., *The Four Minute Mile* (New York: Dodd, Mead & Co, 1956).

Baron, M., 'Patriotism and 'Liberal' Morality', *Mind, Value and Culture: Essays in Honor of E.M. Adams*, 1989 (cited in Keller, 2005).

Best, D., *Philosophy and Human Movement* (London: George Allen and Unwin, 1978).

Bonjour, L., *Epistemology: Classic Problems and Contemporary Responses* (Plymouth: Rowman and Littlefield, 2010).

Bordner, S., 'Call 'Em as they are: What's Wrong with Blown Calls and What to do about them', *Journal of the Philosophy of Sport*, 42(1) (2015), pp. 101–120.

Boxill, J., 'Beauty, Sport, Gender', *Journal of the Philosophy of Sport*, 11 (1984), pp. 36–47.

Bredemeier, B.J. and Shields, D.L., 'Values and Violence in Sports Today: The Moral Reasoning Athletes Use in their Games and in their Lives', *Psychology Today*, 19 (1985), pp. 22–32.

Breivik, G., 'Sporting Knowledge', in Torres, C. (Ed.), *The Bloomsbury Companion to the Philosophy of Sport* (London: Bloomsbury, 2014).

Breivik, G., 'The Quest for Excitement and the Safe Society', in McNamee, M.J. (Ed.), *Philosophy, Risk and Adventure Sports* (London: Routledge, 2007).

Brown, W.M., 'Paternalism, Drugs, and the Nature of Sports', *Journal of the Philosophy of Sport*, 11(1) (1985), pp. 14–22.

Burke, E., *A Philosophical Enquiry into the Sublime and Beautiful* (London: Penguin, 1998).

Butcher, R. and Schneider, A., 'Fair Play as Respect for the Game', *Journal of the Philosophy of Sport*, 25 (1998), pp. 1–22.

Butryn, T., 'Cyborg Horizons: Sport and the Ethics of Self-Technologization', in Miah, A. and Eassom, S. (Eds.), *Sport Technology: History, Philosophy and Policy. Research in Philosophy and Technology*, Vol. 21 (2002), Series Ed: Mitcham, C. (Oxford: Elsevier Science Ltd).

Caddick, N. and Ryall, E., 'The Social Construction of 'Mental Toughness' – a Fascistoid Ideology?', *Journal of the Philosophy of Sport*, 39(1) (2012), pp. 137–154.

Caillois, R., *Man, Play and Games* (trans. Barash, M.) (New York: Free Press of Glencoe, 1961).

Cantor, P.A. and Hufnagel, P., 'The Olympics of the Mind: Philosophy and Athletics in the Ancient Greek World', in Austin, M. and Reid, H. (Eds.), *The Olympics and Philosophy* (Kentucky: University of Kentucky Press, 2012).

Chalmers, A.F., *What is this Thing Called Science?* (3rd ed) (London: Open University Press, 1999).

Ciomaga, B. and Kent, C., 'Rethinking the consequences of commercializing sport', *Sport, Ethics and Philosophy*, 9(1) (2015), pp. 18–31.

Coakley, J., *Sport in Society: Issues and Controversies* (New York: McGraw-Hill, 2003).

Coggon, J., Hammond, N., and Holm, S., 'Transsexuals in Sport – Fairness and Freedom, Regulation and Law', *Sport, Ethics and Philosophy*, 2(1) (2008), pp. 4–17.

Collins, H., 'The Philosophy of Umpiring and the Introduction of Decision-Aid Technology', *Journal of the Philosophy of Sport*, 37 (2010), pp. 135–146.

Collins, H. and Evans. R., 'You cannot be serious! Public understanding of technology with special reference to 'Hawk-Eye'', *Public Understanding of Science*, 17 (2008), pp. 283–308.

Connor, S., *A Philosophy of Sport* (London: Reaktion Books, 2011).

Cordner, C., 'Differences between Sport and Art', *Journal of the Philosophy of Sport*, 15 (1988), pp. 31–47.

Crincoli, S.M., 'You Can Only Race if You Can't Win? The Curious Cases of Oscar Pistorius & Caster Semenya', *Texas Review of Entertainment & Sports Law*, 12(2) (2011), pp. 133–187.

Crosson, S., *Sport and Film* (London: Routledge, 2013).

Culbertson, L., 'Perception, Aspects and Explanation: Some Remarks on Moderate Partisanship', *Sport, Ethics and Philosophy*, 9 (2015), pp. 182–204.

Culbertson, L., 'The Paradox of Bad Faith and Elite Competitive Sport', *Journal of the Philosophy of Sport*, 32 (2005), pp. 65–86.

D'Agostino, F., 'The Ethos of Games', *Journal of the Philosophy of Sport*, 8 (1981), pp. 7–18.

Dancy, J., *Introduction to Contemporary Epistemology* (Oxford: Blackwell, 1985).

Davis, E.C. and Miller, D.M., *The Philosophic Process in Physical Education* (2nd ed) (Dubuque, IA: W.C. Brown, 1961).

Delattre, E.J., 'Some Reflections on Success and Failure in Sport', *Journal of the Philosophy of Sport*, 2(1) (1975), pp. 133–139.

Dixon, N., 'Moderate Patriotism in Sport', in Tännsjö, T. and Tamburrini, C. (Eds.), *Values in Sport* (London: Routledge, 2000).

Dixon, N., 'On Sportsmanship and 'Running Up the Score'', *Journal of the Philosophy of Sport*, 19(1) (1992), pp. 1–13.

Dixon, N., 'The Ethics of Supporting Sports Teams', *Journal of Applied Philosophy*, in Morgan, W.J. (Ed.), *Ethics in Sport* (2nd ed) (Leeds: Human Kinetics, 2007).

Dombrowski, D.A., *Contemporary Athletics and Ancient Greek Ideals* (London: University of Chicago Press, 2009).

Downie, R. and Telfer, E., *Respect for Persons* (Allen and Unwin, 1969).

Duff, R.A., *Intention, Agency and Criminal Liability: Philosophy of Action and the Criminal Law* (London: John Wiley & Sons, 1990). (Cited in Parry, 1998.)

Dunne, J., *Back to the Rough Ground: 'Phronesis' and 'Techne' in Modern Philosophy and in Aristotle* (University of Notre Dame Press: Notre Dame, 1993).

Durant, J., *Highlights of the Olympics: From Ancient Times to the Present* (New York: Hastings House Publishers, 1973).

Edgar, A., 'Sport and Art: An Essay in the Hermeneutics of Sport', *Sports, Ethics and Philosophy*, 7(1) (2013), pp. 1–171.

Edgar, A., 'Sportworld', *Sport, Ethics and Philosophy*, 7(1) (2013), pp. 30–54.

Edwards, S.D., *Disability: Definitions, Value and Identity* (Oxford: Radcliffe Publishing, 2005).

Feezell, R., 'Sport and the view from nowhere', *Journal of the Philosophy of Sport*, 28 (2001), pp. 1–17.

Finley, M.I. and Pleket, H.W., *The Olympic Games: The First Thousand Years* (London: Book Club Associates, 1976).

Glover, J., *Humanity: A Moral History of the Twentieth Century* (London: Yale University Press, 2001).

Gomberg, P., 'Patriotism is Like Racism', *Ethics*, 101 (1990), pp. 144–150.

Gotesky, R., 'Social force, social power, and social violence', in Stanage, S.M. (Ed.), *Reason and Violence* (Totowa, New Jersey: Littlefield, Adams, 1974). (Cited in Smith, M., 'What is Sports Violence', in Boxill J. (Ed.), *Sport Ethics: An Anthology* (Oxford: Blackwell, 2003).)

Gucciardi, D.F. and Gordon, S., *Mental Toughness in Sport: Developments in Theory and Research* (London: Routledge, 2012).

Gumbrecht, H.U., *In Praise of Athletic Beauty* (London: Harvard University Press, 2006).

Harwood, C.G., Spray, C.M., and Keegan, R., 'Achievement goal theories in sport', in Horn, T.S. (Ed.), *Advances in sport psychology* (2nd ed) (Champaign, IL: Human Kinetics, 2008), pp. 157–185.

Hempel, C.G., 'Valuation and Objectivity in Science', in Cohen, R.S. and Laudan, L. (Eds.) *Physics, Philosophy and Psychoanalysis: Essays in Honor of Adolf Grünbaum* (Dordrecht: Reidel, 1983), pp. 73–100.

Howe, L.A., 'Gamesmanship', *Journal of the Philosophy of Sport*, 31(2) (2004), pp. 212–225.

Howe, L.A., 'Remote sport: risk and self-knowledge in wilder places', *Journal of the Philosophy of Sport*, 35(1) (2008), pp.1–16.

Howe, L.A., 'Self and Pretence: Playing with Identity', *Journal of Social Philosophy*, 39(4) (2008), pp. 564–582.

Huizinga, J., *Homo Ludens: A Study of the Play-Element in Culture* (London: Routledge and Kegan Paul, 1949).

Hume, D., *Treatise of Human Nature* (1739).

Hundley, J., 'The Overemphasis on Winning: A philosophical look', in Holowchak, M.A. (Ed.), *Philosophy of Sport: Critical readings, crucial issues* (Upper Saddle River, NJ: Prentice Hall, 2002), pp. 206–219.

Hurka, T., and Tasioulas, J., 'Games and the Good', *Proceedings of the Aristotelian Society, Supplementary Volumes* (2006), pp. 217–264.

Hyland, D.A., 'Competition and friendship', in Morgan, W.J. and Meier, K.V. (Eds.), *Philosophic Enquiry in Sport* (Champaign, Illinois, Human Kinetics, 1988).

Ilundáin-Agurruza, J., 'Kant goes skydiving: understanding the extreme by way of the sublime', in McNamee, M.J. (Ed.), *The Ethics of Sports: A Reader* (Oxford: Routledge, 2010), pp. 467–480.

Jones, C., 'Disability and Sport', in Torres, C. (Ed.), *The Bloomsbury Companion to the Philosophy of Sport* (London: Bloomsbury, 2014).

Jones, C., 'Drunken Role Models: Rescuing Our Sporting Exemplars', *Sport, Ethics and Philosophy*, 5(4) (2011), pp. 414–432.

Jones, C., and Fleming, S., 'I'd Rather Wear a Turban than a Rose: A Case Study of the Ethics of Chanting', in McNamee, M.J. (Ed.), *The Ethics of Sports: A Reader* (London: Routledge, 2010).

Jones, C. and Howe, P.D., 'The Conceptual Boundaries of Sport for the Disabled: Classification and Athletic Performance', *Journal of the Philosophy of Sport*, 32 (2005), pp. 133–146.

Jones, G., Hanton, S., and Connaughton, D., 'A framework of mental toughness in the world's best performers', *The Sport Psychologist*, 21(2) (2007), pp. 243–264.

Jones, G., Hanton, S., and Connaughton, D., 'What is this thing called mental toughness? An investigation of elite sports performers', *Journal of Applied Sports Psychology*, 14(3) (2002), pp. 205–208.

Joulwan, M., '*Rollergirl: Totally true tales from the track*' (New York: Touchstone, 2007).

Kant, I., *Groundwork of the Metaphysics of Morals* (Cambridge: Cambridge University Press, 2012).

Keller, S., 'Patriotism as Bad Faith', *Ethics*, 115 (2005), pp. 563–592.

Kreider, A.J., 'Game Playing without Rule-following', *Journal of the Philosophy of Sport*, 38 (2011), pp. 55–73.

Kretchmar, R.S., 'From Test to Contest: An Analysis of Two Kinds of Counterpoint in Sport', *Journal of the Philosophy of Sport*, 2 (1975), pp. 23–30.

Kretchmar, R.S., 'Philosophy of Sport', in Messengale, J.D. and Swanson, R.A. (Eds.), *The History of Exercise and Sports Science* (Leeds: Human Kinetics, 1997).

Kretchmar, R.S., *Practical Philosophy of Sport and Physical Activity* (2nd ed), (Leeds: Human Kinetics, 2005).

Kuhn, T., *The Structure of Scientific Revolutions* (London: University of Chicago Press, 1996).

Kuntz, P., 'Aesthetics Applies to Sports as Well as to the Arts', *Journal of the Philosophy of Sport*, 1 (1974), pp. 6–35.

Lacerda, T. and Mumford, S., 'The Genius in Art and in Sport: A contribution to the investigation of aesthetics of sport', *Journal of the Philosophy of Sport*, 37(2) (2010), pp. 182–193.

Lehman, C.K., 'Can Cheaters Play the Game?', *Journal of the Philosophy of Sport*, 8 (1981), pp. 41–46.

Levinas, E., *Totality and Infinity: An Essay on Exteriority* (trans. Lingis, A.) (Pittsburgh: Duquesne University Press, 1969).

Loland, S., *Fair Play in Sport: A Moral Norm System* (London: Routledge, 2002).

Loland, S., 'The Ethics of Performance-Enhancing Technology in Sport', *Journal of the Philosophy of Sport*, 36(2) (2009), pp. 152–161.

Loland, S., 'The Logic of Progress and the Art of Moderation in Competitive Sports', in Tännsjö, T. and Tamburrini, C. (Eds.), *Values in Sport* (London: Routledge, 2000).

Loland, S. and McNamee, M., 'Fair Play and the Ethos of Sports: An Eclectic Theoretical Framework', *Journal of the Philosophy of Sport*, 27(1) (2000), pp. 63–80.

MacIntyre, A., *After Virtue – A Study in Moral Theory* (London: Duckworth, 1985).

MacIntyre, A., *Is Patriotism a Virtue?*, The Lindley Lecture (University of Kansas, 1984).

McBride, F., 'Towards a non-definition of Sport', *Journal of the Philosophy of Sport*, 2(1) (1975), pp. 4–11.

McFee, G., 'Are There Philosophical Issues with Respect to Sport (Other than Ethical Ones)?', in McNamee, M.J. and Parry, S.J. (Eds.), *Ethics and Sport* (London: Taylor and Francis, 1998).

McFee, G., 'Olympism and Sport's Intrinsic Value', *Sport, Ethics and Philosophy*, 6(2) (2012), pp. 211–231.

McFee, G., 'Spoiling: A direct reflection of sport's moral imperative?', in Tännsjö, T. and Tamburrini, C. (Eds.), *Values in Sport* (London: Routledge, 2000).

McFee, G., *Sport, Rules and Values: Philosophical investigations into the Nature of Sport* (Routledge, 2004).

McIntosh, P., *Fair Play: Ethics in Sport and Education* (London: Heinemann, 1979).

Metheny, E., *Connotations of Movement in Sport and Dance* (Dubuque, IA: W.C. Brown, 1965).

Metheny, E., *Movement and Meaning* (New York: McGraw Hill, 1968).

Milgram, S., 'Behavioral Study of Obedience', *Journal of Abnormal and Social Psychology* 67 (4) (1963), pp. 371–378.

Mill, J.S., *Utilitarianism. Liberty. Representative Government* (London: J.M. Dent & Sons Ltd, 1962), p. 73.

Millar, D., *Racing Through the Dark: The Fall and Rise of David Millar* (London: Orion Books, 2012).

Miller, R.B., 'Violence, force and coercion', in Shaffer J.A. (Ed.), *Violence* (New York: David McKay, 1971). (Cited in Boxill, 2003.)

Miller, S., *Ancient Greek Athletics* (New Haven: Yale University Press, 2004).

Morgan, W.J., *Leftist Theories of Sport: A Critique and Reconstruction* (Chicago: University of Illinois Press, 1994).

Morgan, W.J., 'Sports and the Moral Discourse of Nations', in Tännsjö, T. and Tamburrini, C. (Eds.), *Values in Sport* (London: Routledge, 2000).

Morgan, W., 'The Logical Incompatibility Thesis and Rules: A Reconsideration of Formalism as an Account of Games', *Journal of the Philosophy of Sport*, 14 (1987), pp. 1–20.

Morgan, W.J., *Why Sports Morally Matter* (London: Routledge, 2006).

Mumford, S., 'Emotions and aesthetics: an inevitable trade-off?', *Journal of the Philosophy of Sport*, 39(2) (2012), pp. 267–279.

Mumford, S., 'Moderate Partisanship as Oscillation', *Sport, Ethics and Philosophy*, 6(3) (2015), pp. 369–375.

Mumford, S., *Watching Sport* (London: Routledge, 2013).

Nathanson, S., 'In Defense of Moderate Patriotism', *Ethics*, 99 (1989), pp. 535–552.

Nietzsche, F., *The Will to Power* (trans. Kaufmann, W. (Ed.) and Hollingdale, R.J.) (New York: Random House, 1967).

Nordenfelt, L., 'Action, Theory, Disability and ICF', *Disability and Rehabilitation*, 25(18) (2003), pp. 1075–1079.

Nozick, R., *Anarchy, State, and Utopia* (New York: Basic Books, 1974).

Nussbaum, M., 'Patriotism and Cosmopolitanism', in Nussbaum, M. (Ed.), *For the Love of Country* (Boston: Beacon Press, 2002).

Ogilvie, B.D. and Tutko, T., 'Sports: If You Want to Build Character, Try Something Else', *Psychology Today* (Oct 1971), pp. 61–62.

Orwell, G., 'The Sporting Spirit', *Tribune* (London, December 1945).

Parry, J., 'Ethical Aspects of the Olympic Idea', *International Olympic Academy: Report on the IOA's Special Sessions and Seminars 1997* (Greece: International Olympic Academy, 1998).

Parry, S.J., 'Violence and Aggression in Contemporary Sport', in McNamee, M.J. and Parry, S.J. (Eds.), *Ethics and Sport* (London: Taylor and Francis, 1998).

Petersen, T.S., 'Good Athlete–Bad Athlete? On the Role-Model Argument for Banning Performance-Enhancing Drugs', *Sport, Ethics and Philosophy*, 4(3) (2010), pp. 332–340.

Popper, K., *Conjectures and Refutations: The Growth of Scientific Knowledge* (London: Routledge, 2002).

Ramachandran, V.S. and Blakeslee, S., *Phantoms in the Brain* (London: Fourth Estate, 1998).

Rawls, J., *A Theory of Justice* (Oxford: Oxford University Press, 1971).

Reid, H., 'Aristotle's Pentathlete', *Sport, Ethics and Philosophy*, 4(2) (2010), pp. 183–194.

Reid, H., *Introduction to the Philosophy of Sport* (Plymouth: Rowman and Littlefield, 2012).

Reid, H., 'Plato's Gymnasium', *Sport, Ethics and Philosophy*, 4 (2010), pp. 170–182.

Reid, L., 'Sport, the Aesthetic and Art', *British Journal of Educational Studies* (Oxford: Basil Blackwell and Mott, 1970), pp. 245–258.

Reid, H., 'The Soul of an Olympian: Olympism and the Ancient Philosophical Ideal of Aretē', in Austin, M. and Reid, H. (Eds.), *The Olympics and Philosophy* (Kentucky: University of Kentucky Press, 2012).

Reid, H., 'Wrestling with Socrates', *Sport, Ethics and Philosophy*, 4(2) (2010), pp. 157–169.

Roberts, K., *The Leisure Industries* (Basingstoke: Palgrave MacMillan, 2004).

Russell, B., *The Problems of Philosophy* (Oxford: Oxford University Press, 1912).

Russell, J., 'Competitive Sport, Moral Development and Peace', in Torres, C. (Ed.), *The Bloomsbury Companion to the Philosophy of Sport* (London: Bloomsbury, 2014).

Russell, J., 'The Moral Ambiguity of Coaching Youth Sport', in Hardman, A. and Jones, C. (Eds.), *The Ethics of Sports Coaching* (London: Routledge, 2011).

Ryall, E., 'Are there any Good Arguments Against Goal-Line Technology?', *Sport, Ethics and Philosophy*, 6(4) (2012), pp. 439–450.

Ryall, E., 'Cricket, Politics, and Moral Responsibility: Where Do the Boundaries Lie?', in Sheridan, H., Howe, L. and Thompson, K. (Eds.), *Sporting Reflections: Some Philosophical Perspectives* (Meyer & Meyer, 2007).

Ryall, E., *Critical Thinking for Sports Students* (Exeter: Learning Matters, 2010).

Ryall, E., 'The notion of a science of sport: some conceptual considerations', in Schulz, H., Wright, P.R. and Hauser T. (Eds.), *Exercise, Sports and Health* (Chemnitz: Chemnitz University of Technology, 2011).

Ryall, E. and Olivier, S., 'Ethical Issues in Coaching Dangerous Sports', in Jones, C. and Hardman, A. (Eds.), *The Ethics of Sports Coaching* (London: Routledge, 2010).

Ryle, G., *The Concept of Mind* (London: Penguin, 2000).

Sailors, P.R., 'Gender roles roll', *Sport, Ethics and Philosophy*, 7(2) (2013), pp. 245–258.

Sailors, P.R., 'More than a pair of shoes: Running and technology', *Journal of the Philosophy of Sport*, 36(2) (2009), pp. 207–216.

Saltman, K., 'Men With Breasts', in Davis, P. and Weaving, C. (Eds.), *Philosophical Perspectives on Gender in Sport and Physical Activity* (London: Routledge, 2010), pp. 97–111.

Sheridan, H., 'Conceptualizing 'fair play': A review of the literature', *European Physical Education Review*, 9(2) (2003), pp. 163–184.

Shields, D.L. and Bredemeier, B.J., *Character Development and Physical Activity* (Leeds: Human Kinetics, 1995).

Silva, C.F. and Howe, P.D., 'The (In)validity of *Supercrip* Representation of Paralympic Athletes', *Journal of Sport and Social Issues*, 36(2) (2012), pp. 174–194.

Simon, R. L., *Fair Play: The Ethics of Sport* (2nd ed.) (Oxford: Westview, 2004).

Simon, R. L., 'Internalism and Internal Values in Sport', *Journal of the Philosophy of Sport*. 27 (2000), pp. 1–16.

Skillen, T., 'Sport is for Losers', in McNamee, M.J. and Parry, S.J. (Eds.), *Ethics and Sport* (London: Routledge, 1998), pp. 169–181.

Slusher, H.S., *Man, Sport and Existence: A Critical Analysis* (Philadelphia: Lea & Febiger, 1967).

Smith, M.D., *Violence and Sport* (Toronto: Butterworth & Co Ltd, 1983).

Smith, M., 'What is Sports Violence?', in Boxill, J. (Ed.), *Sport Ethics: An Anthology* (Oxford: Blackwell, 2003).

Suits, B., 'The elements of sport', in Morgan, W.P. and Meier, K.V. (Eds.), *Philosophic Inquiry in Sport* (Leeds: Human Kinetics, 1995).

Suits, B., *The Grasshopper: Games, Life and Utopia* (introduction by Hurka, T.), (Toronto: Broadview, 2005).

Suits, B., 'Tricky Triad: Games, Play and Sport', *Journal of the Philosophy of Sport*, 15(1) (1988), pp. 1–9.

Suits, B., 'What is a Game?', *Philosophy of Science*, 34 (1967), pp. 148–156.

Taleb, N., *The Black Swan: The Impact of the Highly Improbable* (London: Penguin, 2010).

Tamburrini, C., 'Sports, Fascism and the Market', in Tännsjö, T. and Tamburrini, C. (Eds.), *Values in Sport* (London: Routledge, 2000).

Tännsjö, T., 'Against sexual discrimination in sports', in Tännsjö, T. and Tamburrini, C. (Eds.), *Values in Sport* (London: Routledge, 2000).

Tännsjö, T., 'Is it fascistoid to admire sports heroes?', in Tännsjö, T. and Tamburrini, C. (Eds.), *Values in Sport* (London: Routledge, 2000).

Tännsjö, T., 'Is Our Admiration for Sports Heroes Fascistoid?', *Journal of the Philosophy of Sport*, 25(1) (1998), pp. 23–34.

Tenner, E. and Segal, H.P., 'Why things bite back: new technology and the revenge effect', *Nature*, 382(6591) (1996), pp. 504.

Thomen, C., 'Sublime Kinetic Melody: Kelly Slater and the Extreme Spectator', *Sport, Ethics and Philosophy*, 4(3) (2010), pp. 319–331.

Thompson, K., 'Sport and Utopia', *Journal of the Philosophy of Sport*, 31(1) (2004), pp. 60–63.

Torres, C., 'What counts as part of a game? A look at skills', *Journal of the Philosophy of Sport*, XXVII (2000), pp. 81–92.

Turner, M. and Kurylo, E., 'Group Protests Gender Bias in Games', *The Atlanta Journal*, 26 January 1995.

Tuxill, C. and Wigmore, S., "Merely Meat?' Respect for Persons in Sport and Games', in McNamee, M.J., and Parry, S.J. (Eds.), *Ethics and Sport* (London: E & FN Spon, 1998), pp. 104–115.

Van Dalen, D.B. and Bennett, B.L., *A World History of Physical Education: Cultural, Philosophical, Comparative* (Englewood Cliffs, New Jersey, Prentice-Hall, 1971).

Walsh, A. and Giulianotti, R., *Ethics, Money and Sport: This Sporting Mammon* (London: Routledge, 2007).

Wann, D., Melnick, M., Russell, G. and Pease, D., *Sports Fans: The Psychology and Social Impact of Spectators* (New York: Routledge, 2001).

Webster, R.W., *Philosophy of Physical Education* (Dubuque, IA: W.C. Brown, 1965).

Weiss, P., *Sport. A Philosophic Inquiry* (Carbondale: Southern Illinois University Press, 1969).

Winch, P., *The Idea of a Social Science and its Relation to Philosophy* (3rd ed, introduction by Gaita, R.) (London: Routledge, 2007).

Wittgenstein, L., *The Blue & Brown Books* (Oxford: Basil Blackwell, 1969).

Zeigler, E.F., *Problems in the History and Philosophy of Physical Education and Sport* (Englewood Cliffs, NJ: Prentice-Hall, 1968).

Ziff, P., 'A Fine Forehand', *Journal of the Philosophy of Sport*, 1 (1974), pp. 92–109.

Zimbardo, P., *The Lucifer Effect: How Good People Turn Evil* (Reading: Random House, 2007).

www.bbc.co.uk/sport/0/disability-sport/28893804

www.bbc.co.uk/sport/0/football/31357409

www.britannica.com/bps/additionalcontent/18/36370029/Question-TMacsknee-not-his-toughness

www.davidhume.org/texts/thn.html

www.englandrugby.com/mm//Document/Governance/Regulations/01/30/35/21/RFU_Regulation_19_appendix_2_Neutral.pdf

www.fig-gymnastics.com/publicdir/rules/files/mag/MAG%20CoP%202013-2016%20(FRA%20ENG%20ESP)%20Feb%202013.pdf

www.fina.org/H2O/docs/misc/Dubai-FINA-Bureau-SAC_1210_v13d_s-2%20in1.pdf

www.Hawk-Eyeinnovations.co.uk/files/FifaOpenLetter.pdf

www.irblaws.com/index.php?section=7

www.jurisprudence.tas-cas.org/sites/CaseLaw/.../1480.pdf

www.nytimes.com/2000/11/23/sports/23ZATO.html

www.olympic.org/content/news/media-resources/manual-news/1999-2009/2004/05/18/ioc-approves-consensus-with-regard-to-athletes-who-have-changed-sex/

www.oxfordreference.com/views/ENTRY.html?subview=Main&entry=t140.e0848700

www.oxfordreference.com/views/ENTRY.html?subview=Main&entry=t104.e1667

www.paralympic.org/news/ipc-statement-usa-swimmer-victoria-arlen

www.rsc.org/get-involved/hot-topics/drugs-in-sport/nandrolone-controversy.asp

www.telegraph.co.uk/culture/art/art-features/9157252/How-Damien-Hirst-tried-to-transform-the-art-market.html

www.uci.ch/Modules/BUILTIN/getObject.asp?MenuId=&ObjTypeCode=FILE&type=FILE&id=NDc3MDk&LangId=1

www.wada-ama.org/Documents/World_Anti-Doping_Program/WADP-The-Code/WADA_Anti-Doping_CODE_2009_EN.pdf

http://itspronouncedmetrosexual.com/2012/05/what-does-the-asterisk-in-trans-stand-for/

https://kuscholarworks.ku.edu/bitstream/handle/1808/12398/Is%20Patriotism%20a%20Virtue-1984.pdf;jsessionid=F755645491DBE37B2F8F7A348AA4B195?sequence=1

http://m.paralympic.org/sites/default/files/document/121203164523073_wintersportlaymens.pdf

http://news.bbc.co.uk/sport1/hi/football/world_cup_2010/8766423.stm

http://orwell.ru/library/articles/spirit/english/e_spirit

http://web.archive.org/web/20140710050756/http://www.wada-ama.org/Documents/Resources/Testing-Figures/WADA-2011-Laboratory-Testing-Figures.pdf

INDEX

Note: page numbers in *italic* refer to illustrations